A blessed Christmas
to you, Mother

    Affectionately,

        Evelyn

1960

CAPTIVES OF THE MIGHTY

CAPTIVES OF THE MIGHTY

Christ and the Japanese Enigma

By
DOROTHY PAPE

LONDON
CHINA INLAND MISSION
Overseas Missionary Fellowship
AGENTS : LUTTERWORTH PRESS

First published 1959

© CHINA INLAND MISSION

MADE AND PRINTED IN GREAT BRITAIN FOR
THE CHINA INLAND MISSION, NEWINGTON GREEN,
LONDON, N.16, BY THE CAMELOT PRESS LTD.,
LONDON AND SOUTHAMPTON
TRADE AGENTS: THE LUTTERWORTH PRESS,
4 BOUVERIE STREET, LONDON, E.C.4

CONTENTS

LIST OF ILLUSTRATIONS

PREFACE

WHEN I was first asked to consider writing this book nearly four years ago, the suggestion was that it should be "something modest and tentative as would become a mission which had just begun to get its roots in a new field". Now we as a group have been at work for over five years in Japan, and I am sure none of us feel we could yet speak authoritatively on Japan from our own limited experience. Most of our work has been in either Hokkaido or northern Aomori prefecture, two areas of the country which are not typical. The few of us who have been in Tokyo have mostly been using English, and cannot claim to be really at home with the Japanese language; and Tokyo again is not typical Japan. However, we do meet there most of the leaders of other work, both Japanese and missionary, and so hear a good deal of what is going on. This, together with some training in sociology and a residence of several years in four different countries—which should enable one to look more objectively and understandingly at national customs—are the only qualifications I have for writing this book.

The fact which has really made this writing possible, however, is that there is such a rich field of literature about Japan, written both by foreigners and by Japanese with the ability to write excellent English. So wherever possible I have used the opinions of Japanese to illustrate my points.

The three books by foreign writers which I believe to be most valuable for gaining an understanding of Japan are Ruth Benedict's *The Chrysanthemum and the Sword*, F. J. Horner's *A Case History of Japan*, and in rather lighter reading *Five Gentlemen of Japan*, by Frank Gibney. Several Japanese have told us that Mrs. Benedict's description of their race is true. Another missionary related that his Japanese teacher had told him emphatically that no Westerner would ever be able to understand the Japanese, but when a Japanese version of the book was published and he was given a copy he grudgingly admitted that ninety-five per cent of it was true. In spite of all the books which have been written, however, I have not seen one which dealt in any detail with the relation of their peculiar national culture to the difficulties of establishing a strong evangelical Christianity in Japan.

Some may have wondered how the China Inland Mission came to have work in Japan. It was the result of clear guidance at a conference of Mission leaders at the time we had to pull out of China. Though all of us who came to Japan were new to it, it was good to find that Hudson Taylor was already known, both by name, and from his own spiritual ministry in this land. A letter written in 1893 by a Japanese Christian to Mr. Barclay Buxton's mother in England states:

"I must thank God and you for sending Mr. Buxton here. Perhaps you will be interested if I tell you what was the beginning of the great movement here. It seems to date from Mr. Buxton's first convention in Kobe, when Mr. Hudson Taylor joined him: for it was about that time that the Lord began to pour out His Spirit abundantly."

Kanzo Uchimura has had more influence than perhaps any other Japanese Christian, and often had some very bitter criticisms of missionaries and Western Christianity, and yet he sent an annual subscription to the C.I.M. towards the support of a Chinese doctor, and it was one of his followers in the Non-Church Movement who translated the first life of Hudson Taylor into Japanese.

Sociologists sometimes give a warning in their books that a knowledge of other oriental countries, such as China, may be no help, and even a real hindrance to understanding the Japanese. When one of our former missionaries came out to Japan under his own Church Board he was warned on arrival that this was Japan, and few people would want to know how they had done things in China. So we realize we cannot presume on our experience of work in China for success in Japan. We do have evidence however that the life and message of Hudson Taylor brought real blessing in this land, and so our aim is to carry on in his faith and spirit in the small areas where work has begun.

Our grateful thanks are due to The Evangelical Alliance Mission who helped us in many ways when we first entered Japan, especially in getting premises and teachers, and also giving us the use of their Tokyo facilities; to the Central Japan Pioneer Mission and Japan Evangelistic Band who invited our earliest workers to visit some of their stations and see some Japanese work at first hand; to the Japanese Presbyterian Church in Hokkaido who made openings for a number of our workers to gain experience in three of their churches; and to Mr. and Mrs. Roy Hasegawa who gave much help in the early days in opening our centre at Anegasaki, and providing accommodation for our family at the Seminary, as well as giving us other helpful contacts and information about Japan.

Part One

THE ENVIRONMENT—CULTURAL BACKGROUND

Chapter I

A PEOPLE UNEXCELLED

WHEN the first Roman Catholic missionary, Francis Xavier, entered Japan in 1549, he sent home a report in which he stated: "These are the best people so far discovered, and it seems to me that among the unbelievers no people can be found to excel them." As if to confirm this view, 1,500 had accepted his teaching when he left the country two years later, and other priests came to carry on his work.

These men were welcomed by Nobunaga the *Shogun* (ruling war-lord) who thought their coming would encourage foreign trade. A number of the great feudal lords accepted the new religion, as well as many of lower social rank. Japan had experienced several centuries of devastating civil war when the central authority of the Emperor and Shogun was reduced to a mere name. Buddhism had degenerated into militant political intrigue, priests often wearing armour beneath their robes. Native Shinto was an extremely primitive religion without ethical foundation. Men had no source of true inner peace, or hope for the future, so the new religion met a great need in the unsatisfied hearts of those men and women who received it. After about thirty years there were 200 churches and 150,000 converts. The Western teachers taught there was only one true God, so their new followers zealously tore down the stone idols and lacquered ancestor tablets which stood in their homes and temple courtyards. Later when persecutions came, thousands met death heroically for their faith.

This picture of zeal and fidelity is apt to make the modern missionary experience a twinge of envy; for it is said that today, even among the homes of professing Christians, the number without Buddhist and Shinto shrines is very small. The compromise of the majority of Christians and pastors with State Shinto during the Second World War has been felt to be one of the darkest pages in the history of Christianity. Since the war too, the phenomenon known as "the rear exit"—by which the numbers of new baptisms each year only, or barely, replace former members who just seem to fade out of the picture—has brought much disappointment to the missionary. Moreover, the number of non-returning missionaries is said to be the highest in the world.

Why is it that the sixteenth-century Christians appear outstanding while the twentieth-century Christians seem so weak? It is certainly not that the earlier ones suffered less persecution, for little more than thirty years after the coming of Xavier, official opposition to the new religion began without warning. It continued with gradually increasing intensity during the next half-century until almost all the Christians were martyred or exiled, and the few remaining could worship only in secret.

Nobunaga, the ruling war-lord who had been friendly to the early Christians mainly for political reasons, was assassinated by one of his followers. The man who succeeded him, Hideyoshi —one of the greatest military and administrative geniuses of Japanese history—one summer evening in 1587 held a banquet to celebrate one of his victories. During the feast the subject of Christianity came up. Some said it was only a ruse of the foreigners to invade Japan, while others claimed the missionaries were teaching the people insubordination to their rulers. That very night Hideyoshi issued an order for the arrest of all missionaries, and gave them twenty days to leave the country. This period was later extended, and it was some time before real persecution began. When it did it was of "remarkable ingenuity", as one Japanese has expressed it, but was met by the most dauntless faith and heroism on the part of many of the early Christians.

I have heard the opinion expressed that these early Christian martyrs had no choice in the matter, that they belonged to a political group who would have been liquidated whether they renounced their faith or not. This is probably true in the case of two of the biggest mass executions. The last of these entailed the killing of 37,000 people in a besieged area where Christians had joined with the local people in rebelling against their

particularly evil and unjust feudal lord, and was called by the
Japanese "The Christian Rebellion". However there are
numerous stories which give us another side of the picture. The
first official executions were of six missionaries and twenty
Japanese Christians who were crucified on 5th February, 1597.
But there had been other cases of individual martyrdoms by
anti-Christian feudal lords earlier than this. Another report
tells of fifty-two Christians being burned to death in Kyoto.
Eleven carts conveyed these people to the place of execution
and a herald preceded them calling out that they were to die
because they were Christians. From time to time the Christians
answered, "It is true; we die for Jesus, blessed be Jesus." As
nine of the eleven carts were filled with women and children,
it seems likely that they were taken more for their faith than
their political party. Again, one of the forms of torture invented
was that of suspending a victim head downwards over a pit,
bound in such a way as to retard the circulation of the blood in
the head. It was two or three days at the earliest before death
could release them from this agony. The victim generally had
one arm left free, however, with which to make the required
sign of his recantation of the Christian faith.

A Japanese Christian friend, a professor at one of the Tokyo
universities, has recently written a short biography of one of
these early Christians. It is such an inspiring story I think it is
worth giving in some detail as illustrating the typical ideal
Japanese wife who always puts her husband's wishes first, with
the one exception of her Christian convictions.

This lady's name was Tama, who had married a feudal lord
named Hosokawa. It was her father who, shortly after his
daughter's wedding, had assassinated the military ruler
Nobunaga, whom we have mentioned already. No one is
certain why he did this. Some say it was revenge for Nobunaga
spreading a story that he had killed his own mother. Others
say it was because Nobunaga had insulted him by tapping a
tune on his head at a feast with a fan. At any rate Nobunaga,
in spite of being one of Japan's most honoured heroes, was
known to be very selfish and brutal, thinking nothing of insulting his closest followers.

Tama's father in turn was killed by Hideyoshi, who succeeded Nobunaga as ruler of the country, always, of course, in the name of the Emperor, who was kept very much in the background. Her father's act naturally brought disgrace on his whole family and also upon Tama's husband and his father. So for a time she had to part from him, and went into retreat in a lonely temple.

Soon after Hideyoshi killed Tama's father it was rumoured that all his relatives were to be killed too. Hearing this, one of her husband's *samurai* (warrior retainer) who was guarding Tama at the temple, suggested that rather than wait until she was killed she should commit suicide, and so preserve her honour. Tama quietly answered that she belonged to her husband and until he gave her leave, she had no right to kill herself. "If I were to commit suicide, it would be an act of filial piety to the memory of my father, but until permission is given by my husband I must wait." The Japanese biographer continues in praise of her: "Thus Tama showed that whatever happened she never forgot that as a wife her first duty was towards her husband's wishes." It is necessary to make this point clear in view of what happened later.

In this deserted temple Tama began to study various religions, Buddhism, Shinto, and Christianity, trying to find out which was the best. She sought for one which would console her troubled spirit and give her fresh hope. It happened that her maid, Mary Kiyohara, was a Christian, who taught her mistress all that she knew. Gradually Tama began to comprehend the teaching, and to long for further knowledge of Christianity.

At last, after two years, the time came when Hideyoshi's rule was firmly established. Her father's deed now forgotten, Tama was able to resume life with her husband in Osaka, though it was still thought best for her not to leave the house. This was a matter of great regret to her as she longed to go to a church and hear more about the Christian faith. Some of her husband's friends had become Christians and tried to influence him but he would not respond. One evening the Hosokawas had a musical recital when an old flautist who was a strong Catholic, baptized by Xavier himself, played with great feeling. Afterwards he told them much about Xavier and the power of the Gospel. A certain merchant who came to the house also was a Christian, and tried to help Tama know more of Christ.

Although her husband forbade her to become a Christian Tama's soul cried out for the peace she knew this would give and prayed for a chance to go to church and be baptized. On 1st March, 1587, her husband went to Kyoto with Hideyoshi, leaving strict instructions that his wife was not to leave the house. Ordering the servants never to let her out of their sight, he locked the main gates taking the keys with him.

Five weeks later there was a big Buddhist festival when many people went to the temples. Finding the back gates open Tama slipped out and for the first time in her life entered a church. She begged the priest to baptize her at once, but he said he could not do so until she had taken a course of instruction. She was still pleading with him when members of her household, having discovered her absence, came and took her home by force. After this the house was doubly guarded, and it was impossible for her to leave again. However, she started learning Portuguese and was soon able to read advanced theology in that language.

It was about two months after Tama's visit to the church that Hideyoshi issued his proclamation against Christianity. Her husband's Christian friend, Ukon, was one of those affected. He was urged by his friends to pretend to Hideyoshi that he had given up his faith. He would not listen to these suggestions, however, but sent word to Hideyoshi that as his faithful follower he would willingly lay down his life for his lord. But now he had a supreme Lord whom he must obey; he could never give up his religion. He and his old father then left all their earthly possessions and went into exile on a small island, after a painful farewell to his followers whom he urged never to forget their faith.

Meanwhile Tama was more anxious than ever to be baptized. She even thought of having a coffin made, and being carried in this to the church. But the priest would not consent to this idea, and advised Tama to wait for God's will. At last the Christian maid came home with the news that the priest had authorized her to baptize her mistress, and the ceremony took place immediately. Tama was twenty-five years of age at this time, and took the Christian name of Gracia.

Soon after this her husband returned from the military expedition in Kyushu. He was very angry to hear his wife had done something which Hideyoshi had forbidden, and upbraided her for listening to the false teaching of the foreigners. But nothing he said could make her recant. Her husband's younger brother was so impressed by her strong faith he too believed and was baptized. Then his mother also became a Christian. The husband himself confessed later that only the wishes of his overlord kept him from being baptized too.

Once again he was obliged to leave home on a military expedition. Tama's beauty was now so striking he had reason to fear Hideyoshi would take her to his harem. Honesty and purity were not among the virtues of Japan's greatest hero. The latter indeed sent for her, but when he saw the dagger in her bosom decided to let her return unmolested.

Later another civil war broke out, and while her husband was away the opposing faction decided to take all the wives of the leaders of the other side, beginning with Tama. They sent orders for her to go, otherwise an army would come and capture her. Her husband's samurai then told her he had left orders that they were to kill her, and commit suicide themselves, rather than let her be defiled by the enemy. So she calmly met her death as the traditional ideal Japanese wife. At the same time she proved that there was one area in which the husband was not sovereign—that one must on occasion obey God rather than man.

I think it is obvious therefore that the turning to Christianity of the sixteenth century was not entirely a political matter, true though this may have been in some areas, but that many of these people did have a real faith which they were glad to pass on to others, and for which they were prepared to lose their lives. Why then was there not a similar experience in the twentieth-century period of persecution of Christianity?

It may be that the authority behind the Roman Church had a certain amount of appeal to the hierarchy-loving Japanese people which made them more loyal. But present day Roman priests seem to have the same experience as Protestants over the "rear exit", judging by the remarks made by a priest to one of our missionaries on a train journey. He said that after years of experience here he only baptizes enquiriers after they have been regularly attending at least two services a week for a year. Statistics in their schools also do not show a great number becoming Roman Catholics. So I do not think it was primarily the authority of the Church which kept them loyal to the point of death, but a real appreciation of the fact of Christ's love and death for them. When the persecution reached its height the test invented against those suspected of being Christians was to make them trample on a picture of Christ crucified, or one in which He was bound for scourging. Many refused to do this at the cost of their lives. The custom was continued long after all known Christianity had been stamped out. In certain areas every person in a community had to do this act of trampling on a picture of Christ every year until the nineteenth century.

There seems no doubt that the main cause for the closing of the door to Christianity by Hideyoshi and Ieyasu Tokugawa was the political connections and aspirations of the Roman Catholic Church. One incensed Spanish pilot who was captured when his ship was wrecked off the coast, warned the Japanese of the power of Spain, and claimed that his country first sent missionaries to prepare the way for their territorial conquests. And the bitter rivalry between the Portuguese Jesuits and Franciscan and Dominican orders from Spain and the Philippines—in spite of an order from the Pope that only Jesuits were to work in Japan—seems to give some substance to this claim. This constant bitter struggle between the Roman Catholic orders also brought dishonour to the name of Christ. Although the Jesuits are said to have translated the New Testament into Japanese they did not place it in the hands of their converts, and furthermore they allowed few Japanese into the priesthood, so that when the missionaries were removed the Christians had only their own personal experience or traditions to pass on to their followers.

These considerations would suggest that the sixteenth-century Christians had far more reason to have a weak faith and so forsake Christianity than their descendants of the twentieth century. The fact that they did not do so convinces me that the people themselves were different. Japanese history and sociological study give us a very clear picture of the way in which the country and the minds of the people have developed since Hideyoshi's day and the beginning of the famous Tokugawa period.

Everyone with any knowledge of Japan is familiar with the expression the "web society",[1] describing the close and inescapable way in which every Japanese is connected horizontally and vertically with his fellow countrymen, with the Emperor at the centre of the web. No book I have read has ever mentioned who the spider is however. Certainly it is not the Emperor, who more than anyone is held in the web.

Historically it was Ieyasu Tokugawa who established the pattern of the web, as we shall see in the next chapter. Other Japanese in more modern times have continued to tighten or repair it, rather than escape from it. I believe that Satan, the great enemy of souls, as he saw with Xavier the great potentialities of this island nation both for the receiving of the Gospel and transmitting it to others, deliberately used Tokugawa and his successors as his tools in frustrating one of the most strategic advances of the Gospel in the world.

For the past 300 years the victory has been almost entirely on his side. But as I was thinking of these things during the quiet of a holiday after we had been two years in Japan, and had time to recognize the difficulties of Christian work there, a verse in Isaiah impressed itself upon me, "Shall the prey be taken from the mighty, or the lawful captive delivered? But thus saith the Lord, Even the captives of the mighty shall be taken away, and the prey of the terrible shall be delivered: for I will contend with him that contended with thee. And all flesh shall know that I the Lord am thy Saviour. . . ." Could

[1] See especially *Five Gentlemen of Japan*, Frank Gibney.

these words apply to Japan, or were they only for the Jews, I wondered. Then I looked at the beginning of that chapter and read "Listen, O isles, unto me, and hearken, ye people, from far." Yes, surely that was meant for Japan, too.

As I have lived and worked and watched in this land for three more years it has become increasingly clear that the minds of these people have for centuries been blinded by a great delusion. They live unconsciously in bondage to a most rigid social system which leaves no room for the sovereignty of God. Here and there, however, there are those whose eyes have been opened, who have entered into spiritual life and are giving their lives now in the service of God, proving beyond a shadow of doubt that God *is* able to deliver even the captives of the mighty. As they and we work for the spread of the kingdom we have constantly to remember that the weapons of our warfare are not carnal, for nothing less than spiritual force can avail.

Chapter II

THE IMPRISONING WEB

AFTER the great war-lord Hideyoshi died, his former friend and chief assistant, Ieyasu Tokugawa, killed his heir and seized the government. It was his family which strengthened the web society to an incredible extent—a strength which enabled it to endure through two and a half centuries of their rule, and even through the dynamic days of the Meiji Restoration. Then when it seemed in danger of being shattered by the fresh winds of liberalism, democracy and the coming of Christianity, the militarists found means of strengthening it again so that it remained throughout the Pacific War and even through the occupation of the country by Western powers.

Hideyoshi had been prepared to develop foreign trade with the Portuguese and Spaniards, but Ieyasu, fearing with reason the predatory intentions of some of the foreigners, and realizing that the teaching of the sovereignty of God would undermine his own authority, determined to shut Japan off from all contact with the rest of the world. He deported or killed all the missionaries, forbade any foreign ships to come to Japanese ports, and destroyed all their own ocean-going vessels. When a final attempt was made by the Portuguese to send an embassy, most of the envoys and crew were executed. A ludicrous but tragic notice was posted up which stated, "So long as the sun warms the earth let no Christian be so bold as to come to Japan; and let all know that if the king of Spain, or the Christian's god, or the great god of all, violate this command, he shall pay for it with his head."

Thus the most serious effect of the Roman Catholic policy was the forbidding of any teaching about Christ, and the making of His Name even an object of scorn and loathing in the minds of the Japanese.

A trickle of foreign trade was still allowed with the Dutch

who, however, were confined to a stockade on a very small island near Nagasaki. There they were searched for any objects of religion, made to trample on the picture of Christ, forbidden to keep the sabbath, and when it was found that they had labelled a new warehouse with the Christian date A.D. 1640, they were compelled to demolish the whole building at once. The Dutch found the trade so lucrative, however, that they were apparently willing to put up with these and many other indignities.

Since the country had been through generations of anarchy with constant civil wars, and had just experienced more than a decade of increasing peace and prosperity under the strong hand of Hideyoshi, it seems the people were willing to accept any conditions now which ensured them the opportunity to live in peace and gain a livelihood. The plan of Ieyasu, Hideyoshi's successor, was to freeze his country rigidly into the prevailing social pattern for the purpose of keeping the ruling power in his own family. Accordingly laws were made which forbade anyone to move from one district to another without permission, or to change his occupation. The most detailed laws decreed the size of house and the kind of clothes different classes of people might have; the food they might eat and the presents they could give, and so on.

It has been said, "The Japanese more than any other sovereign nation have been conditioned to a world where the smallest details of conduct are mapped, and status is assigned. One trusted the map and was safe only when one followed it. One showed one's courage and integrity in conforming to it, not in modifying it or revolting against it."[1] Its rules were not absolute ethical principles like the Ten Commandments, but "tiny specifications of what was due in this situation or that". It was "unexpected" behaviour which was regarded as sin, and a samurai was at liberty to kill anyone for rudeness or "unexpectedness". These laws were designed to stamp out initiative and prevent progress. To enforce them, every member of a family was asked to "watch carefully the conduct of his fellow members and report thereon".

[1] *The Chrysanthemum and the Sword*, Ruth Benedict.

There seemed to be a familiar ring about this as I read it, reminiscent of conditions in China today. But it was only recently that I saw in Dr. Nitobe's famous book *Bushido*, published in 1904, that Karl Marx in his *Capital* "called the attention of his readers to the peculiar advantage of studying the social and political institutions of feudalism as then to be seen in living form only in Japan". I have little doubt that Marx was inspired by this study, that the "iron curtain" is but a copy of the "sea curtain" the Tokugawas maintained around the Japanese islands.

Let us examine in more detail the structure of this web society. It was arranged in hierarchical order, the Emperor nominally at the head but with no political power, below him the Shogun who for the next two centuries was from the house of Tokugawa. Beneath the Shogun were the feudal clan leaders (*daimyo*) with their warrior retainers known as *samurai*. These were all nobility who had the right to carry swords and use them freely on those beneath them.

Below these were the farmers upon whose labour and produce the whole upper classes depended. At least forty per cent and sometimes eighty per cent of the harvest was demanded by the landowners. Beneath the farmers were the merchants and tradespeople, lowest of whom were the *eta*, a pariah caste whose work was confined to butchering and tanning, and executions and torturing when the need arose.

Although the lot of the lower classes was extremely hard there were certain guarantees given to each class for which the people appear to have been thankful after the previous years of anarchy. If some of the feudal lords were particularly bad and did not observe these guarantees, the peasants could complain to the Shogun, and in about half the cases, judgment was given in favour of the peasants. In making the complaints the peasant leaders had, however, overstepped the strict law of hierarchy and consequently had to be crucified, boiled in oil, or beheaded. They went ahead with their petitions knowing quite well what the consequences would be for themselves. Their strong feeling of group responsibility made them undertake these tragic tasks. But we can readily see how this custom made the Japanese very unwilling to seek positions of responsibility if they were not born into them.

Confucian teaching had had a strong influence in Japan for many centuries, finding an easy growth in the soil prepared already by primitive Shinto ancestor worship. To the vertical duties and obligations to superiors and parents above, and children and employees below, a Japanese also has obligations and duties horizontally to immediate neighbours. The closest ring consists of the houses to left and right of one's own and the three in front. Then there is another wider ring of the village group, or Neighbourhood Association in the cities. The "in-laws", too, provided another irksome series of obligations. Each person was very consciously merely a part of a family or community, and later of the nation. He has ever to be at the service of each of these groups according to the prescribed pattern. A "good" person is one who fulfils all these obligations at whatever cost to himself. A Japanese writer, Dr. Anesaki, speaking of this cult of communal responsibility says, "The individual is almost nothing in the face of the community, and unreasoning submission to social sanction is the essential condition of individual life." There was, and still is in the country, no such thing as privacy. The whole house stands open through the day, except in cold areas. Everyone knows everything that is going on. The community and household reinforce each other's authority with a watchfulness that was no doubt inculcated by the Tokugawa laws.

Mrs. Sugimoto in her charming book *Daughter of the Samurai* gives us some idea of the effect of this web society upon the mind of an ordinary Japanese. She tells us her experience on being sent to a mission school where the girls each had their own little plot of garden, and were told they could plant what they liked. "No one knows the sense of reckless freedom which this act gave me, nor the consequences to which it led. I, with no violation of tradition, no stain on the family name, no shock to parent, teacher, or townspeople, no harm to anything in the world, was free to act."

Stifling as this system may seem to the Western mind, there is nothing basically unethical in such a uniform pattern of life provided it is not exploited for evil ends. In fact it has produced a nation among whom there is less serious crime than in any other major non-communist country.

The Japanese system of child training is probably the most effective in the world for producing the desired end, in their case to fit them for the web society. In some ways it resembles the culture of their world-famous dwarf trees. The pine trees in the gardens are trained in the most picturesque patterns of branches, the small stems and needles all pruned by hand to get the exact effect the gardener artist has in mind. Much training within confining bounds is needed to produce this effect, months when each branch is held within a web or frame of bamboos and rope, unable to follow its natural bent.

Although many people prefer natural growth, there is a real beauty and fascination in these trees produced at such cost. So too with the web society—some of its results are undoubtedly beneficial to the country, and its outward culture is sometimes a thing of beauty. Yet it is produced at great cost to those who are held within it. In a newspaper article on a certain Students' Residence in Tokyo it speaks of its "notable record" of not one suicide among the students in a decade! The reason given for this is that the students in the dormitory "are free from the mental pressure of disturbing family relationships and communal discipline". Again in a report on a Ministry of Welfare paper claiming 1,300,000 Japanese are psychotic, a Dr. Takeyama declared that "most Japanese children are subject to terrific pressures almost from birth", and "the expectations of the family, the worry of passing examinations and the maintenance of 'face', often cause young Japanese to suffer a nervous breakdown".

These however are the modern manifestations of the web society and we must return to its historical beginnings. For two centuries the Tokugawas managed to maintain their rigid system. But gradually the merchants became prosperous by providing the luxuries demanded by the highest nobles and through becoming money-lenders to the impoverished samurai. Much intermarriage finally took place between the merchants and the samurai. These people were largely responsible for the tremendous change which became known as the Meiji Restoration. It was in fact one of the greatest transformations which has ever taken place in a nation in so short a time.

The precipitating spark for this was the arrival in 1859 of Commodore Perry with American warships demanding in a politely worded threat that Japan should open her ports to foreign trade again.

The Shogunate which had become degenerate and pleasure-loving was realistic enough to see it could not stand against this modern armed might. Also that it could not depend on the loyalty of the majority of the people who were growing weary of their hard way of life. Many farmers had died of starvation in recent years and uprisings were occurring occasionally. Two million armed samurai with little fighting to do were growing tired of their idle lives. Some were already secretly studying all they could about the West. Others had begun to look back into forgotten history and resurrected the ancient records of the seventh century purporting to give details of the divine origin of the Emperor. When the Shogun finally signed a treaty with Perry these two very dissimilar groups touched off a public demand for the resignation of the Shogun and the restoration of the Emperor to real power. The Emperor at this time was a boy of fifteen, later to become the most famous of them all, the Emperor Meiji. He was brought in state from the centuries-old seclusion of the monarchs in Kyoto to the Shogun's palace in Tokyo.

With the Meiji Restoration the samurai class was liquidated, and the country changed almost overnight from a feudal agricultural economy to one that was industrial. While before it had been a crime punishable by death to leave the shores of Japan, now men were hastily sent by the government to study every form of Western civilization. Industry, transportation, education, and military training were adapted almost wholesale from the countries which seemed to suit their needs best. Thus industry was based on American lines: transportation and the Navy followed British models; and the Army adopted the German pattern. Most significantly education was based on the highly centralized French system.

We have already seen that the edict making the teaching or following of Roman Catholicism an act of treason, punishable by death, had also made the very name of Christ vile and hateful to the people for generations. Also sealing the country from all outside contact meant that it had no knowledge of any other form of Christianity for nearly two and a half centuries, as well as producing a change of character in the people which made it extremely difficult for them to be effective Christians when the opportunity finally came. As one Japanese Christian wrote, though there were many outward changes in life under the Meiji Restoration "The contents of the heads of the people remained largely unchanged".

Under the new treaty certain ports were opened to foreign trade. Both Roman Catholic and Protestant missionaries went to Japan as soon as possible to live in these ports. But the public notices condemning Christianity were still up. In the first twelve years of Protestant missionary work only ten converts were won. These had to be baptized in secret. It was found that there were still 50,000 Roman Catholics in Kyushu who had secretly maintained their faith, passing it on from generation to generation. Persecution broke out again and many were deported or tortured.

At last, due unfortunately to political pressure from abroad, missionaries were allowed to preach freely throughout Japan. Eventually for a short period from 1883-88 Christianity became quite popular and the number of Protestant converts rose from 4,000 to 25,000. There is evidence, however, that many at this time regarded Christian ethics as a necessary accessory to Western dress and civilization, a means to material improvement and favourable treatment abroad. There was even a suggestion that the Emperor should be baptized, so that Japan would be recognized as an equal by the West.

In 1890 a much publicized religious freedom was granted to the Japanese people in their Constitution, though in a rather limited sense which few people at the time seemed to notice. The wording was "Japanese subjects shall, within limits not prejudicial to peace and order, and not antagonistic to their duties as subjects, enjoy freedom of religious belief". Yet, from that very year of the official granting of religious liberty, a new spirit of nationalism began. Modern schools had been well started mainly by missionaries and Christian teachers who had answered the government's appeal for help in this before they had been allowed to reside inland to preach the Gospel. Then the Japanese took over full control. In a most elaborate system of centralized education they ensured that every child entering school should realize that as well as being part of the family and the community, they were also a part of the nation and were thus involved in a series of supreme obligations to the Emperor and nation. While it seems true that the majority of the new leaders really wanted a liberal form of government based on Western methods, a small group of militarists with Satanic shrewdness seem to have learnt the secret of manipulating this web. They made the country the most unified instrument of despotic military power it is possible to imagine. Even the cataclysmic crises of the loss of the war and foreign occupation have not broken the strands of the web.

It is easy to see that a country in which individualism scarcely exists presents a particularly hard field for the Gospel. The message of the Cross is for "whosoever" will receive it—it is an individual matter which must be settled in the heart and mind of each person. Yet a well-known sociologist, Takegi Kawashima, writing as late as 1948 on the Japanese family system says that it is impossible for individual responsibility to exist in it. The member is not aware of himself as having any individual worth. "His actions will always be determined by another. Therefore there would never be any occasion for him to judge for himself or act by himself, nor would he have the ability to do so." Other sociologists, American, French and British are agreed in this view. We also constantly prove it to be true as we live in Japan.

Nearly everyone is afraid of the responsibility of making a decision on their own. They always want a *soodan* (discussion) on a matter. Japanese committees rarely put a question to the vote. There is a gradual process of talking till the general feeling is finally determined.

Not long ago my husband preached in a church which a

short time before had appointed a committee of management when the missionary who had begun the work handed over the leadership to the Christians. They were neatly solving the problem of having to make decisions by seeing that there was never a quorum present at the meeting of the committee. Some other missionaries have had the similar experience of finding that as soon as a church becomes organized everything seems to come to a standstill.

After a series of lectures at the Seminary on the various forms of church government, my husband asked the students which they thought the most suitable for Japan. They suggested episcopal to begin with, perhaps changing to presbyterian later! Though the majority came from baptist churches they did not feel that the Japanese were really ready for the con-gregational form of church government. My husband en-courages the students to think for themselves as much as possible. He uses examination questions such as "Of the Old Testament prophets you have studied this term which in your opinion would make the best preacher for Tokyo?" This really baffles some of the newer students and they may not even attempt an answer. Others sometimes ask anxiously afterwards what is the right answer, only to be told, "Your opinion."

Except for a few big city churches, Japanese churches rarely seem to have an attendance of more than about fifty. Even the latest *Kyodan*[1] statistics I have seen reveal an average of fifty members to one pastor. We have often wondered about this, and have asked a number of Japanese the reason, but no one seems to know. I am beginning to think the answer may be that pastors do not want the responsibility of any larger numbers, for feudalistic ideas seem to be carried over into the churches. Pastors sometimes have to bear some of the responsibilities of a superior or even a parent to the members of the congregation. Another factor may be that the church people themselves do not want the burden of any more brothers or sisters in Christ with whom they may be involved in obligations.

In spite of the centuries of training and pressure, however, the

[1] *Kyodan*—United Church of Japan.

fact remains that these people were created by God—they are human and have the same natural impulses as the rest of mankind. We therefore find that there is need for a police force and prisons for those whose behaviour does not come up to the standard, and that there have always been some in whom individuality has been strong. For these, after the Meiji Restoration, there was opportunity to escape some of the confinements of the web society by emigrating to Manchuria, Formosa, Hokkaido, or even the West. There have always been some, also, who have had a real desire to know the truth.

One of these was Murata Wakasa, a chief officer of the Daimyo of Saga. In 1855 he found a book floating in the water and discovered it was a Dutch New Testament. He later heard that there was a Chinese translation of the same book and sent to Shanghai for it. With his younger brother he began a careful study of it. Seven years later he visited a treaty port to see if there were any foreigners there who could explain some of the difficult passages. He met a Mr. Verbeck, and later used to send a trusted messenger the two days' journey from his home to the port, with lists of questions arising from his Bible study. Four years later both brothers were baptized and at once reported their conversion to their feudal lord who did not molest them, though some of their books were burned by government order.

Another was Joseph Niishima who founded Doshisha, the first Christian university. He came from a samurai family and was very strictly brought up. He was very curious, however, to know why the Japanese were so critical of the Western barbarians. At last, at the risk of his life, he got in touch with some English merchants and managed to hide on the ship and work his passage to Shanghai, taking with him his most precious possessions, his two samurai swords. In Shanghai he sold one sword to buy a Chinese New Testament. By selling the other and working as a cabin boy he managed to get passage to America. There he was befriended by an official of the shipping company. After years of study he returned to Japan where he had been promised a pardon and offered a job as interpreter for the government after Perry's arrival.

To me, however, the most wonderful story of all is that of one of the Tokugawas. That very family which was the means of bringing so much trouble to Japan also produced one of the country's greatest Christians. When he became a Christian, however, he was turned out of his family and had to adopt his wife's name of Mimaki. He was able to witness to some of the highest families in the land, and also have meetings in the homes of some of these people he had led to Christ.

In the biography of Barclay Buxton, his son Godfrey gives the moving account of how this man consecrated his life to the Lord. He wrote to say that during a conference he and two others went out under the trees to pray one evening. They waited before the Lord and He drew near. "Then after a while His voice spoke to me, O so tenderly: 'Receive the fire—just now.' I hesitated. I shrank back. But I could not resist that voice. I yielded, I received by faith. After a time we came back to the house and went to bed. But I could not sleep. I got up and went out again under the pine trees, and waited before the Lord. I was kneeling at the stump of a tree, and half fancying it was my altar I laid myself upon it, to be the Lord's absolutely and for ever. I came away from the place melted by the Lord's love, but in the deep immovable confidence of faith."

One of the things remarkable about him was the frequent reference in his preaching to the Old Testament—rather rare among many Japanese pastors. In 1915 for instance there is a reference to him speaking "with great freshness and skill and boldness" on Zechariah, chapter 3, the priest with filthy garments. In 1937 he arranged a convention in Tokyo and invited the elderly Mr. Buxton to come from England to attend it. As the time drew near it became doubtful whether large meetings would be allowed in Tokyo, especially as feeling towards Britain was growing very cool. Mr. Mimaki stood in faith on the promises of Isaiah 44: 3 and 1 Kings 18: 41 which he felt the Lord had given him, and 600 Christian workers came to the preliminary meeting, and he was able to write later, "The great hunger of the people was apparent from the first and we were filled with joy when 1,100 came the first night. It was a strength to our faith that the promise we had received, Isaiah 44: 3, was the text of Mr. Buxton's address. 1,500 people were there at the end, even members of the Cabinet being present. Speaker, interpreter, and audience alike were hidden by the glorious burning living Presence which no one will be able to forget."

So there have always been some who were willing to be different, and today we rejoice in every girl who quietly refuses a non-Christian marriage; in each young man who is willing to be repudiated by his family, to be disinherited in order to follow Christ. Or for the girl who was forced to make special delicacies by her mother who then offered the entire amount to the ancestors, knowing that the girl would not partake of food offered to idols. Now, praise God, after years of patient witness the mother only offers a slice to the ancestors and leaves the rest untainted. That is just a small instance of the constant pressure that is brought to bear by other members of the family if one becomes a Christian, and the same sort of thing is often repeated in other and bigger ways by the community. Toyohiko Kagawa, whose name is probably the most familiar Japanese one to Western churches, has said that the decision to become a Christian is like sentencing oneself to death, and one can read in his books of the tremendous struggle it was to get even such new things of material benefit as medical co-operatives accepted. How much greater therefore is the opposition to such drastic action as putting God and His commands and worship first in one's life, instead of the customs and dictates of the community and family. God has promised to release the captives, however, and we look in faith for the day of greater things while we rejoice in each one we see now whose greatest desire is for God's will in their lives.

Chapter III

THE SPIRIT OF JAPAN
(1) ITS ORIGIN

WE once asked a Chinese Christian who has lived many years in Japan, and has done some evangelistic work there, why the Japanese church was still comparatively small and weak. After a moment's thought he replied, "Because the Japanese people's god is Japan."

One of the best-known Japanese Christians, Kanzo Uchimura, gave some support to this view by beginning an English magazine article some years ago with the words "I love two Js and no third: one is Jesus and the other is Japan. I do not know which I love more, Jesus or Japan." Western Christians are always very shocked to hear this, of course. It is only fair to give enough quotation to understand what Uchimura was trying to say in this article. "Jesus and Japan: my faith is not a circle with one centre; it is an elipse with two centres. My heart and mind revolve around the two dear names . . . Jesus strengthens and purifies my love for Japan, and Japan clarifies and objectivizes my love for Jesus. Were it not for the two I would become a dreamer, a fanatic, an amorphous universal man. . . .

"O Jesus—Thou art the Sun of my soul, my Saviour dear,
    I have given my all to Thee!
O Japan—Land of lands for thee we give
    Our hearts, our prayers, our service free.
    For thee thy sons shall nobly live
    And at thy need shall die for thee."

Perhaps such a sentiment is not so rare among Western Christians, though few would consciously admit it. Of course the majority of people feel their country is the best in the world. But for the Japanese this feeling is more than ordinary patriotism. It is not easy for a foreigner to understand it fully. The best way to do so I believe, is to trace the development of *Yamato damashii*, the concept of the "soul of Japan" or ".Japan spirit".

The aboriginal inhabitants of the Japanese islands were the Ainu, a number of whom still live in the northern island of Hokkaido. Then another group, largely of Malayan strain it seems, migrated to the islands from Southeast Asia. Some of these came direct to Japan. Others went to Korea and inter-married with mongolian stock, many of these later coming to Japan. It was the amalgamation of these two groups which constitutes the present Japanese race; the two physical types are still distinguishable. The Ainu were gradually driven north and are quite distinct from the other two types of Japanese.

The clan which finally achieved the supremacy had settled in the area called Yamato on the main island. It was the rulers of this clan who had the first official records written in the eighth century, in two books named the *Nihongi* and *Kojiki*. F. J. Horner says of these, "They are a collection of stories in which myth and legend play a very large part, stories which show a childishness and an indecency quite incredible. There is evidence, too, of a callow conceit still so integral a part of the Japanese character, yet at the same time the records show a very real sense of the beauty and love of nature. . . . The deification of the Emperor is clearly implied in these early records, and it is most probable this idea was brought into the country by the Kumaso invaders (of Yamato), for in the *Kojiki* the ancestor of the Yamato ruler is represented as having descended from heaven and alighted at Osumi."[1]

This place was in the south, the most likely place for these early invaders to land. The whole purpose therefore of this legend of a pair of gods making Japan with drips from a spear, and the sun goddess producing offspring in various odd ways before appointing one to be the ruler of Japan, was probably to bolster the claim of the reigning chieftain to be the permanent

[1] *A Case History of Japan*, F. J. Horner.

ruling family of the whole country. Chinese culture and Buddhism had also begun to penetrate Japan, so it was probably felt to be necessary to state something of Japan's own religion and history in permanent form.

The main characteristics of this Yamato clan were the feeling of racial superiority, prowess in arms, and intense loyalty to their ruler. "The spirit and prowess of these early conquerors have left an indelible impress upon the language and mind of the nation in the phrase 'Yamato damashii'—the spirit of (divine and unconquerable) Japan."[1]

So strong an impression did these words make, that this phrase came to be used to describe the ideal Japanese person. Uchimura says of a certain teacher that in him "the spirit of Yamato had concentrated itself. . . . He was Japan etherialized into a soul . . . sharp in outline, the soul of sincerity, an intense lover of righteousness and an intense hater of Western barbarians."

The religion of the early clans was a primitive animism, usually connected with some natural phenomenon in each locality. When the leader of each isolated community died, his spirit too became an object of worship. This is the basis of the Shinto religion and of the Japanese love of their country which Dr. Nitobe describes so well. "Its (Shinto) nature worship endeared the country to our inmost souls, while its ancestor worship, tracing from lineage to lineage, made the Imperial family the fountain-head of the whole nation. To us the country is more than land and soil from which to mine gold or reap grain—it is the sacred abode of the gods, the spirits of our forefathers; to us the Emperor is the bodily representative of Heaven on earth, blending in his person its power and its mercy."[2] So he too seems to confirm the opinion of our Chinese friend that the god of the Japanese is Japan.

Another historian wrote in the fourteenth century, "Great Japan is the land of the gods. Here the deity of the Sun has handed on her eternal rule. This is true only of our country and there is nothing like it in any other land."

So we see that the human and divine are almost never clearly

---

[1] *Religions of Japan*, W. C. Griffis.   [2] *Bushido*, I. Nitobe.

separate in the minds of these early Japanese. Everything has "essence" or spirit, a common feature of all animism. But there was also something approaching the Jewish idea of theocracy. The earliest word used for government was *matsurigoto*, "matters of worship".

The ruler of the Yamato clan remained supreme for some time after the compiling of the *Nihongi* records. But gradually the Yamato military strength must have waned, for we find strong feudal lords emerging, and constant civil wars, while the Emperor becomes merely the secluded religious head of the country.

Although the idea of the divinity of the Emperor became rather faint in the following centuries, the special feeling for the land and ancestors continued to be nurtured in ordinary Shinto worship. Even this, though, became fainter with the increasing spread of Buddhism.

Since "Yamato" was no longer a popular word among the jealous feudal lords, the need for some other form of inspiration or code of living was acutely felt by the samurai warriors. At that time the Confucian classics were their only literature, so naturally the unwritten code of conduct they evolved was considerably influenced by it. This has now become known as "Bushido" (the Retainers' Code of Honour, or the Way of the Warrior). But this name was actually not used until Dr. Nitobe wrote a book of that title in English for the benefit of foreigners in 1904. This book proved very popular, and was not only translated into a number of European languages but also into Japanese. It became "the most loved expression of the unwritten code" with which they were all familiar either by hearsay or early home training.

The main points Dr. Nitobe gives as the essence of Bushido are first, Rectitude or Righteousness, in the limited sense of the opposite of underhandedness.

There is none of the Biblical idea of holiness which the West has incorporated into the word.

Then come Courage and Fortitude, in particular the courage to live when it is right to live, and die when it is right to die.

Third is Benevolence—mindful of responsibility to ancestors and to Heaven, and therefore of obligation to vassals—in fact Paternalism.

Other qualities mentioned are Politeness, meaning discipline of the spirit more than mere etiquette; Veracity, lying being regarded as a sign of weakness rather than a sin; and Honour implying a vivid consciousness of one's personal dignity and worth, and therefore an acute awareness of "slights" offered by others.

Perhaps the most outstanding characteristic was that of Loyalty to one's overlord, at whatever personal cost to oneself, and also to the family head. The interests of the family and the individual members were inseparable.

With regard to the training of the samurai, Dr. Nitobe tells us it was primarily an education for the formation of character and power to make decisions. This I found very interesting in view of the marked absence of that quality today. Money was disdained, and luxury regarded as a menace to manhood. Self-control was the great aim. He who remained "level-minded" in all circumstances, showing no sign of joy or anger, was regarded as a strong character. The practice of *hara-kiri*—the cutting open of one's own abdomen (regarded as enshrining the soul) was a conspicuous example of self-control since "none could perform it without the utmost coolness of temper and composure of demeanour". It was in fact a legal ceremonial institution with strict rules of procedure, not at all a suicide committed during a time of disturbed emotions.

The hardening effect of such Spartan training was apt to outweigh the teaching of benevolence; and courtesy was usually confined to one's own social circle and superiors. Even fellow samurai who spent too much time on learning as an end in itself were called "book-smelling sots".

Historians are largely agreed that few lived up to these un-written laws. In practice the most obvious and general charac-teristics of the samurai families, and many of lower rank who also adopted this code for themselves, were fortitude in the face of pain and danger, complete loyalty to the feudal lord, a disdain of money, and a rather distorted sense of honour. In many cases this latter led to an excessive pride and exaggerated offence at trifling or imaginary insults.

Some feel that Dr. Nitobe may have unconsciously idealized feudal conditions, much as we may the times of chivalry in Europe. Or it may be that with an American wife and long contact with Christianity he may have read a Christian connotation into some of this feudal code which in reality was absent. According to Gurney Binford,[1] a missionary of the Society of Friends, Dr. Nitobe himself, however, was one of those rare souls whose life revealed the very best results of this training. We are told of his poised and relaxed manner when-ever the missionary met him—a thing rarely seen in modern Japanese—and the constant sense of calmness in his house although it was in fact guarded continually by secret police since he was in danger of assassination because of his liberal and pacifist views.

About that time Dr. Nitobe was asked if he would accept the appointment of Minister of Education, but he remarked to some of his Quaker friends, "I shall not be appointed because the country is not yet ready to accept the only condition upon which I am willing to accept the appointment. Our government educational policy is based upon the idea of creating sub-jects. . . . I think the object should be widened to the idea of making citizens."

How different the history of the country might have been had Dr. Nitobe been appointed Minister of Education! But again the devil scored a victory, and instead of being able to guide the schools into his own enlightened outlook it was Dr. Nitobe's early work *Bushido*, and the spirit it fostered, which was to become a useful tool in the hands of the militarists.

He was a little concerned at the effect his book was having on the younger generation after its publication in Japanese, because they admired its military ideals but failed to appreciate the character training implied in it. Accordingly he wrote a second book called *Discipline* (or Training), but still he was not satisfied with the result, and later said that both books had received an acclaim beyond their real value. As time went on

[1] *Forty Years in Japan*, Gurney Binford.

he became convinced, he said, "that high ideals and training in the way of living . . . do not give strength to the individual to carry out his purposes". Only religion, he believed, could supply the strength necessary for sustained endurance, and for him "religion meant the indwelling personality of Jesus Christ". A third book he felt was needed, *The Way of Faith*, but this book unfortunately was never written, and he is known primarily for his defence and explanation of the samurai code or spirit.

The majority of the Japanese felt that with the dissolution of the samurai class at the Meiji Restoration, and the loss of the sword, the samurai spirit would die. J. Imai said, "The spirit is gone with the sword. Soldiers from every class become inspired with Bushido with their rifles and bayonets. When these are put away and they return home they are farmers again, traders and students. So Bushido in khaki is alive, but it sleeps in other dresses."

Obviously then, this was not an adequate code to live by, for life is not all fighting. Bushido's greatest weakness lay in the fact that God was not included. Its doctrine was self-culture, self-reliance. Its standards of right and wrong rested entirely on tradition or the individual's natural instincts. Though influenced by Buddhism, Shinto and Confucian philosophy, the samurai relegated religions to the priests, and concerned himself with them only in so far as they nourished his courage.

Uchimura stated, "Bushido is the finest product of Japan, but Bushido by itself cannot save Japan. Christianity grafted upon Bushido will be the finest product in the world. It will save not only Japan but the whole world." This was written in 1916 when he believed Christianity was dying in Europe and America. War and materialism seemed to the Eastern world to be far more our prominent characteristics than Christian living.

Christianity never was firmly grafted on to Bushido, however, and Imai proved correct in his view that for the majority the samurai spirit was gone with the sword. No moral code was introduced to take its place, and thus the way was wide open for a new emphasis on *Yamato damashii* which was to bring war

and destruction to a large part of southeast Asia. Perhaps the
very attempt to graft Christianity on the national culture was
the cause of its failure, for the Scriptural pattern is the opposite.
It is the "wild" branch, which has to be grafted on to the true
tree of Christianity. It is the roots which determine the growth
of the branches. The Japanese "branch" of Bushido would
doubtless have proved an excellent channel for the growth of
Christianity. And for this reason it seems the devil has striven
with especial purpose for the hearts of these people.

While writing this chapter I attended a conference of the
Far East Officers' Christian Union where the subject for study
was "Satan". As we considered the meeting of God with Satan
in the heavenlies, and saw enacted on earth that drama which
must have held the attention of all heaven as Satan tried to
prove that Job would only give allegiance to God for what he
got from Him, I felt I began to understand what Satan has
been looking for ever since. To every assault on his property,
and even children Job only said, "The Lord gave and the
Lord hath taken away, blessed be the name of the Lord."
Even when his own body was stricken in the most painful and
public way he could say, "Though He slay me, yet will I trust in
Him." Can it be that ever since that day of his defeat Satan has
been seeking to counterfeit the spirit of Job whose loyalty to
God was given because of what He was, rather than for what He
gave? If so, he certainly found the most fertile soil in the heart
of the Japanese samurai.

Although historians agree that in the majority of cases the
loyalty of the followers depended on the ability of the lord to
provide adequately for them, there were instances of the most
costly devotion even to a dead lord. It is necessary to know
some of these before we can understand what this highly
admired samurai spirit was really like.

The first is the famous story of the Forty-seven *Ronin* (masterless samurai), the best-loved story in all Japan. Its influence on
the Japanese has been compared to that of the Bible on the
Christian. The bare essence of the story is as follows. A feudal
lord visiting the Shogun's palace was insulted there by a high
official, Lord Kira. He therefore tried to kill him, but only

succeeded in inflicting wounds. Everyone considered his act justified, but because it showed a lack of propriety to do it within the Shogun's residence it was judged that he should not continue to live, but was allowed the privilege of committing hara-kiri.

Afterwards forty-seven of his most loyal retainers vowed to avenge their lord of the insult by killing Lord Kira and then committing hara-kiri themselves. To allay the suspicions of the official, they first disbanded and even broke up their families. Some even murdered members of their own families. The sister of one went as concubine into Lord's Kira's house in order to give information of his movements. Another divorced his wife and began living a thoroughly debauched life in the gay quarters. There a friend of their former lord found him in a drunken stupor and spat in his face for this apparent lack of concern to avenge his former master. Even this insult was received without resistance. Finally all suspicion was allayed, and at last came the day planned for revenge. The forty-seven *ronin* got their man, and carried his head to their master's grave. There they left a written address to their lord which said in part: "We have escorted my Lord Kira hither to your tomb. This sword which you entrusted to us we now bring back. We pray you take it and strike the head of your enemy a second time and dispel your hatred for ever. This is the respectful statement of forty-seven men." Then they all committed hara-kiri. The man who had formerly spat at them was filled with remorse for misjudging them, so also killed himself. There are now forty-eight graves in a much visited temple in Tokyo.

The epitaph of these men was that "for *giri* (loyalty) to their lord they forsook their wives, parted with their children, and lost (killed) their parents". For Japanese this was the highest form of praise, implying as it did the personal sacrifice of all they held most dear. While we cannot help admiring the loyalty of these men, the methods used to demonstrate it are enough to show us that it did not originate in the mind of God. There is, however, another story which comes a little nearer the Christian concept. A well-loved lord named Michizane fell the victim of jealousy and calumny and was exiled.

The aim of his unrelenting enemies was the extinction of his whole family. Searching for his young son they learned he had been hidden in a village school kept by a former vassal of Michizane. When orders were sent to the teacher to deliver the head of the lord's son on a certain day, he at once tried to find a suitable substitute. But none of the village children bore the least resemblance to his aristocratic pupil. "His despair is only momentary, however, for a new scholar is announced, a comely boy the same age as his master's son, escorted by his mother. No less conscious of the resemblance between infant lord and infant retainer were the mother and boy himself. In the privacy of the home both had laid themselves on the altar; the one his life, the other her heart, yet without sign to the outer world."

On the day appointed an officer arrived to identify and receive the head of the boy. Will he be deceived by the false head, wondered the teacher fearfully? The officer took up the gruesome object before him, calmly went over each feature, and in a deliberate, business-like tone pronounced it genuine. This officer was actually the father of the dead boy whose head he examined so carefully! He had been forced by circumstances to work for his former lord's enemy, and could not be untrue to his new master. But his father had received many kindnesses from Michizane, so his son could serve the cause of the grandfather's lord. Since it was known he had been acquainted with the exiled Michizane's family, his new master had given him the task of identifying the boy's head. So when he had finished his gruesome task he returned home and as he crossed the threshhold cried out to his wife, "Rejoice my wife, our darling son has proved of service to his lord!"

In concluding this story Dr. Nitobe points out, "This child was a conscious and willing victim: it is a story of vicarious death . . . as significant as, and not more revolting than the story of Abraham's intended sacrifice of Isaac. In both cases it was obedience to the call of duty, utter submission to the command of a higher voice."

To us, the difference in the case of Abraham was that God plainly forbade the actual killing of Isaac—in contrast to the heathen practice of the time which did include the sacrifice of children to the gods. No doubt even in those early days Satan was trying to counterfeit the devotion to God of men like Job. Certainly in the Japanese he has found a people capable of the most costly heights of devotion and loyalty. It is no wonder he has been at such pains through the centuries to keep their hearts and minds from recognizing Christ as the Lord of lords. So even after decades of gospel preaching in the early Meiji era, we find no real grafting of the branch of the spirit of Bushido on to Christianity. There was only a degeneration of that spirit which then required further diabolic indoctrination to make it function again in a way which would most hinder the progress of true Christianity.

Chapter IV

THE SPIRIT OF JAPAN
(2) ITS MODERN GUISE

EVEN before the coming of Commander Perry and his warships some of the samurai had become tired of their diet of Confucian Classics and epigrammatic Japanese poetry, and had set to work deciphering their own meagre ancient Japanese literature. There they discovered the Emperor's early prominent position in the country. Also the wider concept of *Yamato damashii* was brought to light again. This was something which could be demanded of every Japanese, not merely the personal retainers of a particular feudal lord. As the militarists clarified their aim this revived concept gradually became more and more impressed upon the people, especially through the schools where attendance was now compulsory.

One of the chief means to inculcate this spirit was the Imperial Rescript on Education, issued in 1900. This has been described as the Bible, or Mosaic law of the Japanese, and innumerable commentaries have been written on it. Each school had its own copy, kept in a very special place. So great was the reverence for it that if a school principal made a slip of the tongue in reading it he would usually resign from his position. G. H. Moule writing in 1913 to describe the reading of it in a school where he taught, says, "Teachers and pupils all stand at attention, and then at the word of command bow their heads reverentially, while the principal solemnly takes the Rescript out of its yellow silken wrappings and unrolling the scroll, declaims its contents in a sonorous monotone. The Emperor's picture, before whom this ceremony takes place, is often unveiled at the same time, and the whole school bows towards it."[1] Yoko Matsuoka in *Daughter of the Pacific* gives the added details that the principal had white gloves and all the men teachers

[1] *Spirit of Japan*, G. H. Moule.

morning coats and striped trousers. The children had to wear their best clothes for the reading of the Rescript four times a year, and had to bow at an angle of more than ninety degrees during the reading. The following is the official translation of the Rescript:

"Know ye our subjects: Our Imperial Ancestors have founded our Empire on a basis broad and everlasting and have deeply and firmly implanted virtue. Our subjects ever united in loyalty and filial piety have from generation to generation illustrated the beauty thereof. This is the glory of the fundamental character of our Empire, and herein also lies the source of our education. Ye, our subjects, be filial to your parents, affectionate to your brothers and sisters; as husbands and wives be harmonious, as friends true; bear yourselves in modesty and moderation; extend your benevolence to all, pursue learning and cultivate arts; thoroughly develop intellectual faculties and perfect moral powers, furthermore, advance public good and promote common interests; always respect the constitution and observe the laws; should emergency arise, offer yourself courageously to the State and thus guard and maintain the property of our Imperial Throne coeval with heaven and earth. So shall ye not only be our good and faithful subjects, but render illustrious the best traditions of your forefathers.

"The Way herein set forth is indeed the teaching bequeathed by our Imperial Ancestors to be observed alike by their descendants and their subjects, infallible in all ages and true in all places."

To us this may seem at first glance a very innocuous document, and it is not surprising that many Christians and missionaries saw no harm in having this read in mission schools. Since it was only read four times a year it may be wondered how it could have such a strong influence. To quote F. J. Horner again, the Imperial Rescript was however "so far as the Japanese schools were concerned, the basis on which the whole science of morals rested". Normally two hours a week were devoted to this subject in every grade of school and college and "its flavour permeated every subject. It must be understood that 'morals' to Japanese authority are entirely divorced from religion, the teaching of which is forbidden in all schools. But this regulation did not affect the teaching of State Shinto, which had officially been declared as being above all religion and thus exempt. In short, the teaching of morals was not concerned with . . . developing good men and women, but with developing *good Japanese*. This was done by inculcating the Japanese spirit, *Yamato damashii*. An examination of the text of the Rescript reveals that two virtues are essentially emphasized as having always been characteristic of the Japanese: namely Loyalty and Filial Piety, and that the rest of the document comprises a succession of pious platitudes, the vagueness of which lends itself to an infinitude of interpretations."[1]

Miss Matsuoka bears this out in her account of the ceremony of the Rescript which she merely says prescribed loyalty to the Emperor, filial piety, and conformity to the traditions of the past as the foundation of education. In the stories taught to lower grade children it was usually diligence, and perseverance under great difficulties, which were taught—qualities very useful in national subjects.

Though Dr. Nitobe tells us that loyalty to the feudal lord was not meant to be given at the cost of conscience, in general it had been customary to do any act, however immoral, which would further the cause of the lord. This loyalty, with its implication of unquestioning obedience to authority, was now transferred to the Emperor and—more important in practice —to his representatives in the government, down to the village head, and local policeman. "Along this path of utter obedience must the Japanese student tread. He must accept unquestioningly and with his whole being any dogma put before him by authority; his whole training was designed to make him accept it enthusiastically."

Increasing pressure in the schools was felt to be necessary because of a growing spirit of lawlessness among some of the adult population. A Socialist plot to take the Emperor's life had been discovered, and blame for this was placed at Christianity's door, since Christianity was "the egg from which

[1] *A Case History of Japan.*

Socialism hatched". The very presence of missionaries was said by some to constitute an insult to the Emperor.

The following is an example of the teaching of National History as put out in a Primary School Teachers' Manual. "We people who are under such an august royal family are mostly the descendants of the *Kami* (gods) . . . who came down (into Japan) in the train of the Imperial Grandson, or we are the descendants of those who were naturalized from China and Korea . . . and Kumaso, who lived in Japan from ancient times, but these were assimilated into our nation. . . . All these people have found their centre in the Imperial family and have manifested a united loyalty. Thus the antiquity of the establishment of our state is already seen as superior to that of any other country, and since then the passing of summers and winters have piled up to thousands of years . . . however the relation of trunk and branch which exists between Emperor and subjects has not been in the slightest disturbed and the eternal and changeless national organization has never felt even a little tremor."

In 1911 the Department of Education issued orders to the effect that a spirit of "reverence for the gods" should be more strictly inculcated in the minds of young Japan. Schools were directed to take all children to the local Shinto Shrines at festival times and teach them to make obeisance there before the spirits of the dead. Moule writing in comment on this situation states, "The Christian Church, which willingly accepted the Imperial Rescript on Education, and acquiesced in the custom of bowing towards the Emperor's picture, is not likely to leave unchallenged the orders of the Department of Education with regard to visits to the Shrines."[1] Though there was considerable controversy about this, some saying that Shinto was thus recognized as the State religion, many held the view that visits to the Shrines were not worship, but merely reverence for the memory of national heroes. The Church never seems to have taken a united stand on the issue.

The morals classes in the schools had done their work well, so well that in 1927 we find a Japanese bishop, when speaking

[1] *Spirit of Japan.*

of the government Institution of Shrines, states (the italics are mine), "While still a part of Shinto, the Institution of Shrines is *officially* declared to be without religious significance. Shinto is a religion of ancestor worship combined with the worship of nature, while the Institution of Shrines is an expression of affection and respect for Imperial ancestors and the great men of the past. *The Government* clearly defines the difference between the two. The fact that the Shrines were formerly the place of Shinto worship, and that the rites and ceremonies performed in Shrines today still retain many features of Shinto, leads some people to think that the shrines are still religious institutions. (*Not unnaturally!*) Shinto may die out with the development of a true religious consciousness on the part of the people, but the Shrines will not. . . . The attitude of the Japanese Christians towards the Shrines should be, I think, *to understand them as the government wants them to be understood.*"[1]

His idea that primitive Shinto beliefs would gradually die out is a plausible one. It is one which has proved true in English culture where we no longer associate the original pagan beliefs with our own Christmas tree, nor our days of the week with the pagan deities after whom they were named. In Japan, however, with few exceptions, it seems that the Christians failed to realize the purpose for which the State Shrines had been separated, or the general direction in which the country was headed. This same bishop writing of the international consciousness in Japan at that time (1927) says, "The old spirit of nationalism has been profoundly modified, and loyalty to international organization has been stimulated to such a degree, Japan finds herself today an ardent member and advocate of the League of Nations. . . . Among the Japanese the Christians are those most interested in international and racial problems. . . . It can almost be said," he adds with some pride, "that they take more interest in international politics than in Japan's own internal political affairs." How true, and how tragic, and how much this neglect on the home front was to cost them in the coming years! Yet again today we are seeing the same thing happen.

[1] *Japan Speaks For Herself*, SCM Press, London.

From the records I have been able to see, it would appear that most missionaries also failed to recognize the real sentiment behind the Shrines or the strength of the national religions which were actually experiencing revival rather than gradual decay. Since the help and advice of all kinds of Western educators and missionaries had been sought so enthusiastically in the early days of the Restoration, it was understandable that many of them should have the conviction it was they who were leading Japan into her new and wonderfully expanding national life. Dr. Nitobe, however, says, "The change was entirely self-generated. . . . Japan of herself chose to learn from Europe methods of organization, civil and military . . .", and the reason for this was not admiration of Western ways but the Spirit of Bushido—"the sense of honour which cannot bear being looked down upon as an inferior power".

Some of the Japanese intelligentsia had a clearer idea of the issues than the missionaries. Dr. Fukuzawa, the founder of Keio University, one of the most famous liberal reformers and advocates of Western ideas, nevertheless denounced Christianity in his newspaper because of its denationalizing tendencies. "Christianity is baneful to our national power . . . will destroy patriotism, filial duty and loyalty to the Mikado." However, he did later advocate the adoption of Christianity in order that Japan might be received into the comity of Western nations! Dr. Fukuzawa was a great exponent of the external and material aspects of Western culture but his conception of learning was strictly utilitarian. He was not concerned with either religion or morality. It was probably largely due to his influence that we find the present insatiable desire among students for book knowledge, but without the ability to form convictions or reach decisions which was a valuable part of samurai training.

Other scholars a decade later sought a revival of Shinto as the only means of counteracting the denationalizing effects of intercourse with the West, and propounded the following questions for consideration by Japanese Christians.

"1. Can the worship of His Sacred Majesty the Emperor,

which every loyal Japanese performs, be reconciled with the worship of God and Christ by Christians?

"2. Can the existence of authorities that are quite independent of the Japanese State, such as God, Christ, the Bible, the Pope, the Czar (head of the Greek Church) be regarded as harmless?

"3. Can a Japanese who is a faithful servant of Christ be regarded as at the same time a faithful servant of the Emperor, and a true friend of His Majesty's faithful subjects? Or to put the question in another way, is our Emperor to follow the wake of Western emperors and pray, 'Son of God, have mercy upon me?' Can the Christian convert answer the above questions in a manner that will satisfy our reason?"

The importance of these questions seems to have received little acknowledgement from the majority of missionaries, however. Probably many thought that they were the result of a faulty understanding of Christianity which would disappear as the knowledge of it became more widespread. They assumed that the Japanese government was becoming a democratic one after the pattern of their own. This misconception was as far from the reality as the view of some Japanese on Christianity. Others no doubt, remembering the centuries when Christianity had been completely excluded from Japan felt it would be wiser to go quietly and quickly on with their work of preaching the Gospel for the conversion of souls, rather than engage in an open battle with the extreme nationalists who were in any case thought to be a very small minority.

These questions therefore remained unanswered by the majority, but a decade later another revealing article appeared in a monthly magazine. "We can see how earnest the believers are in the spread of Christianity, and how strongly they desire to make Japan a Christian nation. . . . Supposing these movements should be successful, our Empire will be changed into a Christian country, our unique history extending over a period of 2,500 years will be trampled on, and the Spirit of Japan will be destroyed. Not only is the Christian spirit not sufficient to lead the new generation, but it will make the people weak and hypocritical, and will destroy their characters. . . . Long live the non-Christian spirit, long live the spirit of the world, of the flesh, of self-confidence, of determination, of patriotism."

Others criticized Christianity, along with other religions, for being an unscientific superstition; but found Christianity particularly obnoxious because "it demands that all shall recognize and serve the one God whom it proclaims. It places that God above the national rulers: but Japanese should never acknowledge that any being is higher than the Emperor. . . . The Rescript and Christianity are absolutely irreconcilable. . . . No educated Japanese should look with unconcern upon the spread of a religion whose acceptance would from an intellectual point of view be a step backwards, and from that of a patriot, would portend danger to the State."

The only religious observance these men favoured was reverence for the spirits of the dead, particularly those of the Imperial house. Yoko Matsuoka in her book[1] tells how even her father, a very modern, progressive and liberal newspaper editor, took her a fourteen-hour train journey south to the famous Ise Shrine, and a similar distance north from Tokyo to his old family home, to announce to both the Imperial ancestors and their own family ancestors her departure to America to study.

Early in the twentieth century those who were so violently imperialist and anti-Christian were probably a very small minority. With the wisdom of hindsight we can now see that had the Christians clearly defined their position from the beginning they might possibly have been able to avert some of their future difficulties, and would have encouraged others to stand against the militarists. The latter, however, kept a strict watch on every phase of life, particularly in the schools. At last in 1937 they felt confident enough to publish through the Ministry of Education the Basis of National Polity which contained the following statement of instruction for teachers and other public officials. "The Emperor is not merely a so-called sovereign, monarch, ruler or administrator, such as is seen among foreign nations, but reigns over this country as a deity incarnate, in keeping with the great

[1] *Daughter of the Pacific*, Yoko Matsuoka.

principle that has come down to us since the founding of the Empire."

To us these sound strange words to be written in the twentieth century in a country with fast developing heavy industry and modern communications, but the words "deity incarnate" do not at all mean the same to the average Japanese as they do to us. We are apt to think they attribute to the Emperor all the attributes of God. In fact their idea of divinity is very small and vague. They have never distinguished very clearly between the human and divine, and have no conception at all of omniscience, omnipotence or omnipresence as divine characteristics. The idea of divinity in the Emperor had its origin in the legend that the first Emperor was a descendant of the Sun Goddess, and that his line has continued unbroken—according to their very elastic methods of perpetuating families—ever since. As descendants of the first Emperor Jimmu, all partake of this strain of divinity.

Most of the intelligentsia did not believe in the deity of the Emperor even in their limited sense of the word. They thought of him as the "organ of state". The fundamental weakness of the Japanese culture, however, is the fact that there is no absolute ethical standard. The idea that one must be loyal to the ruling power made it impossible for the majority to stand against this principle.

There were some, however, who had the courage to disagree with the new policy. To quote F. J. Horner again: "In spite of their 1,000-year-old national tradition of absolute submission and obedience to authority as part of the very air they have breathed from birth, we are given the figure of 59,000 Japanese who overcame this tremendous incubus, who resisted it and were glad to fight against it, knowing well that torture and possible death might be the result. The majority of these were by no means Communist. They were urged on by the craving for intellectual and spiritual freedom, for which they were willing to give their lives, as indeed many did." That some of these were Christians I know; just how many there seems no means of finding out.

The *Japan Times* reports that from 1933-36, 59,013 persons

were arrested on charges of preaching, carrying into practice
or merely harbouring "dangerous thoughts". Reports that the
police tortured the majority into pleading guilty are only too
well authenticated. I have heard of at least one who protested
without even being imprisoned, however. A Miss T. Allen
tells how after much difficulty she and her Japanese co-workers,
a Mr. and Mrs. Y., bought some land for a rural Christian
centre. But no sooner had they signed the deed than the police
came and said they must give up the land as there was a Kobe
company coming to extract ore for the government. "At that
time to say the government wanted it was to say the Emperor
wanted it, but Mr. Y. said we were going to do a bigger work
than the government; that that was God's land and we couldn't
give it up. He talked to the policeman for three hours, telling
him the story of Jesus and the resurrection. Finally the police
said we could keep the land, they couldn't do anything with
people who had such faith." When the building was finished
the Japanese Army saw it and wanted it. Mr. Y. went to the
commanding officer and told him they could not have it. The
officer said they could confiscate the building, and Mr. Y.
replied, "Yes, you can take it, and I can also burn it down
tonight." Miss Allen continued, "You didn't talk to army
officers that way in 1941, and why he wasn't shot at dawn I
don't know; but he wasn't, and our building was saved."
Perhaps the secret of this man's courage was revealed in the
very beginning of his joining that work. He stated he would
never receive any salary from the mission because "I want to
know that I am giving my whole life to the Lord". He was one
of the few apparently who had recognized that Christ is Lord
of lords and had given his loyalty accordingly.

For the majority, however, the samurai tradition, enhanced
by every trick of modern psychology and propaganda, had
done its work. At last the militarists had a nation thoroughly
prepared, mentally and physically, for war. As one man who
was a university student at the time has since expressed it,
"By this time everyone was burning with the spirit that we were
the liberators of all Asia. Our pent-up abhorrence of Western
imperialism was suddenly unleashed. I firmly believed that this

war was thrown upon us, and that we had no alternative but to fight—fight to free all Asia or die in the attempt."[1]

The ancient classics had contained a passage in which the Sun Goddess's descendants were urged to put the "eight corners of the earth under one roof". The militarists were quick to grasp the potentiality of this utterance, and had the following new patriotic song written, and sung by the whole nation.

See, the sky opens over the Eastern Sea
The Rising Sun climbs higher, radiant in its flight.
The Spirit of Heaven and Earth is throbbing with vigour
And hope dances through the eight islands of Japan.
With an unbroken line of Emperors
We are blessed with light and eternity
We the people, all of us
Conforming to the Divine Mission of the Virtue of this
    Imperial Majesty.
Go forth to make the eight corners of the world our home.

When Pearl Harbour was attacked many Japanese were shocked and doubted a successful outcome of the war. But those at home dutifully did what was demanded of them; while most of those sent overseas sincerely expected the countries they invaded would be proud to have a place, however lowly, in the Japanese hierarchy.

The militarist clique in power, while fully aware that they were "hiding behind the sleeves of the Emperor"—the classic phrase for manipulating the Emperor for their own ends, as had the Shoguns before them—yet believed a good deal of their own propaganda, at least about the peculiar superiority of their own race. Japan in over 2,000 years of history had never experienced a conquering invasion. Many of these men knew little about the outside world. They had no realization of technical needs and believed that "spirit" was more important than material equipment. In their sight Americans were undisciplined, luxury-loving creatures who would be no match for *Yamato damashii*—the Japanese spirit.

[1] *Five Gentlemen of Japan.*

The loss of the war for the Japanese was more than a military defeat, but also that of the national philosophy and faith. As Frank Gibney says, "A political system which pretended to omnipotence, traded in the supernatural and confirmed its appeal by its historical success, had failed."[1]

This terrible disillusionment created a "spiritual vacuum" as many expressed it, and soon after the war both Communism and the Christian Church responded to this opportunity. The Communists were rashly hasty, noisy and violent, characteristics the average Japanese disapproves of, and so temporarily lost a golden opportunity of gaining a country superbly prepared already for the glorification of the State above the individual, and the regimentation necessary for a successful Communist régime. What would happen to *Yamato damashii* under Communism is hard to predict.

The Christian church, especially that part of it in the U.S.A., responded to the need by sending large numbers of new missionaries to the country, but these were unable to speak Japanese and so could not do much immediately to fill the vacuum. Of older Japan missionaries there seemed painfully few, while Japanese Christian workers, with homes and churches bombed and burnt, were worn out and often ill from the stresses of war and undernourishment. Many too had been killed both in the army and in bombing at home. Hopes were high at first that Christianity would fill this spiritual vacuum, but it has not yet done so to any great extent. One reason no doubt is an unwillingness for the cost of discipleship. But another contributing cause is the disillusionment the Japanese feel over changes in policy due to expediency on the part of the governments of so-called Christian nations. Unfortunately the words and deeds of our Western governments are far more widely publicized in Japan than the halting words of the missionary.

Meanwhile increasing lawlessness, especially on the part of young people who have had a decade of education more on the American pattern, with no religious instruction, and half digested democratic theories, has made the need to have some

[1] *Five Gentlemen of Japan.*

kind of moral teaching apparent. What more natural than to return to a nationalism which is both inspiring and flattering to oneself? So we are beginning to see Prime Ministers going again to announce important events to the Sun Goddess at Ise, millions of people going to the Emperor Meiji's tomb at New Year, and many demanding again the celebration of the mythical foundation day of the nation when the gods handed it over to Emperor Jimmu.

The idea of the strength of spirit seems to be returning, too. The recent failure of some of the Japanese teams in the Olympic Games brought them the accusation at home that they were "lacking the will to win". There is also a growing popularity for war sagas and autobiographies of war criminals. Most people feel that this is not a revival of jingoism yet, but rather an unconscious attempt of the Japanese to regain their lost prestige and self-esteem.

It still seems true as Dr. Gulick wrote long ago, "No word is so dear to the patriotic Japanese . . . as *Yamato damashii*—in prosaic English 'Japan soul'; but the native word has a flavour and a host of associations that render it the most pleasing his tongue can utter." In the West the teaching of Christianity has so enhanced the importance of the individual that this paradoxically has become the biggest hindrance in attaining the heights of the Christian life. A common definition one hears of consecration is the crossing out of the personal pronoun "I"—"not I, but Christ". Here it seems it must be the "we Japanese" which receives the crossing out—"not Japan, but Christ".

As I was planning this chapter I thought regretfully that I had never heard of any Japanese consciously and deliberately taking this step. However, at that very time my husband returned from a New Year Conference arranged by one of the most flourishing of the Conservative Baptist church groups. While there he heard some of its history. It had come into being only a few years before; and when a number of people seemed interested, the missionary employed a trained Japanese evangelist in the hope that he might eventually become the church pastor. This man when visiting in the homes would first bow to the family god shelves. This naturally brought some remonstrance from the missionary and public discussion of the matter. All but one woman and one young man, a student, sided with the evangelist. The latter turned rather fiercely on this woman and demanded, "Are you a Japanese, or aren't you?" She replied simply, "I am a Christian." What joy there must have been in heaven at that moment! The evangelist left and most of the others drifted away. But from that nucleus of two has grown a strong and virile church, with several daughter churches in the area. It is described by a missionary of another society as one of the most encouraging churches in Japan. The lady acts as a kind of Bible-woman, the young man is now a student of the Tokyo Theological Seminary, and it was through him the invitation came for my husband to go as speaker to the conference. There he took as his subject the Lordship of Christ. At the conclusion nearly fifty out of the more than seventy young people—some after tears and much agony of spirit—rose to promise that from henceforth Christ would be put first in their lives—even before their home or country.

Back in 1920 Uchimura wrote, "Japanese are being converted to the Gospel . . . though somewhat reluctantly. But when they are *heartily* converted . . . when they accept the Gospel of life from *God* (not the missionary) they will become the best Christians, and will be in a position to influence the whole human race." Perhaps this is a mere manifestation of the Japanese spirit of national superiority; but it may well be that what he says is true. At present their ideas of God are far too small. If only they could see who He is, and have a vital consciousness of His presence and power and majesty they might willingly offer themselves a living sacrifice to the Lord of lords in whose service all their fortitude, courage, loyalty and hard work could find its highest expression.

Chapter V

OTHER GODS OF SHINTO

WE have considered already the beginning of primitive Shinto as a mixture of local ancestor and nature worship which eventually evolved into Emperor worship, and in fact the worship of the whole concept of Japan. In order to understand more fully the difficulties which hinder the reception of Christ into the heart and life of many Japanese, however, we must look in detail at some of the practical outworkings of the religions of Japan.

Originally in Shinto anything in the nature of the awesome or powerful was called "*kami*", which unfortunately has been translated into English as the word "god". So when a missionary speaks constantly of "Kami", meaning the true God, the impression in the minds of his hearers may be that of an ancestor, a national hero, a fox, snake, rock, mountain, stream or any of the myriad deities of their pantheon, all of which are known to them as "kami". The word used by Christians for God is *Kami-Sama* (Lord God); but as the *Sama* is used by tradespeople and maids in addressing the master or mistress of the house, and is always used of a guest in the house, it obviously does not convey anything like our idea of God to the heathen listener.

As the aboriginal Ainu were gradually driven out, the invaders formed little independent settlements known as *uji*, meaning a collection of households under one head. The feeling of need for a protective spirit or "kami" made them often choose some outstanding natural landmark of the locality. When the original chieftain died he too was considered as continuing to guard them, and so he also became known as "*ujigami*", or local god.

These ujigami are still a familiar sight today, often holding up the traffic in the busiest sections of Tokyo, for each has its own annual festival when it is paraded through the streets in an ornate palanquin. It is carried by as many men as can lay hand on it, sometimes as many as forty, for all who help are considered to be filled by the spirit of the god. As a matter of fact they are usually filled with *sake*, the native rice wine. There is also an annual children's festival when the palanquin is carried by young boys.

The people who live in each god's area are called *ujiko* (children of the community). Every person in that neighbourhood is expected to contribute to the expenses of these festivals, which of course raises a problem for the Christian. Unfortunately the great number of camera-carrying foreigners who have visited Japan since the war with a desire to understand her culture, has added pressure to make these festivals more ornate and colourful. Some people are beginning to object to this expense, as we see from the following interesting article in the *Asahi* daily paper. "Voices of discontent over donations for festivals are heard in various districts. It would not matter if one need not contribute unless one wished to. But if five or six dignified gentlemen appear with a subscription book, one feels as if one has to make some contribution. 'Keep deities at a respectful distance lest you should offend them' is the creed of weak citizens.

"There are Communities which are advocating that festivals financed by donations should be stopped. A youth organization in Miyazaki has stopped carrying portable shrines, and instead staged a volleyball tournament. A certain shrine in Saga is pushing plans to plant orange trees in the grounds and to use the income from the oranges for the festivals instead of donations."

Such things as this may at least mean one less pressure for the young Christian. The proverb the newspaper quotes, "Keep deities at a respectful distance lest you should offend them" (Confucian in origin), is a very significant one, for these processions have not always been mere shows. In times past if any person during the year offended the god by unsocial or "unexpected" behaviour the palanquin, as it swayed from side to side, might be smashed right through that person's flimsy house. Even in recent years this has been known to happen in some places. Thus one can see why the community feeling is so strong, and why a person is anxious to fall in with "expected" behaviour. In feudal times if they offended too seriously they were banished from the community. If a person were bad enough to be rejected by his own god, obviously no other community would take him in. Thus a man lost his legal status as a person, and was reduced to banditry or begging to keep alive. This centuries-old strength of communal opinion on conduct obviously has a considerable hold on people still, and makes it difficult to live a consistent Christian life.

These local shrines are a real centre of the village, being regarded as places of safety for children to play in. Babies are taken there by their mothers a certain number of days after their birth, and again at the ages of three, five and seven to be blessed. Announcements of importance such as entering school or the army, marriage or a journey to a foreign country are also made to the local god.

From the original communal form of ancestor worship there appears to have developed the idea of the heads of each separate family becoming kami. So ancestor worship appeared in the home, greatly strengthened by Confucian teaching on filial piety, and further strengthened again by the coming of Buddhism to Japan. New and colourful little ceremonies were introduced by Buddhism, giving the home cult of ancestor worship a fresh and emotional attraction. The Obon Festival, the occasion of a three-day visit of the spirits of the dead back to the home, was a Buddhist addition, too. No one seemed to notice that it was a contradiction of the theory that the spirits were there all the time. At Obon, everyone who possibly can returns to the family home. The spirits are greeted with welcoming fires, or even escorted with lanterns from the grave-yards. Various fruits, vegetables and other delicacies are offered at the family shrine while the family all moves into the room with the shrine to sleep at night. At the end of the period the spirits are escorted back. If there is a river or sea available little boats carrying coloured paper lanterns are made, and floated away as it gets dark, making a fascinating picture on a moonlit August night.

After Buddhism became officially accepted, everyone was ordered to have a Buddhist god shelf in their home. There were then two shrines in every house, the Shinto *kamidana* (god shelf) which represented the national ancestors, and the *butsudan* (Buddha shelf) in which were put the name tablets of the more recent family dead. Etsu Sugimoto describes those in her own home telling us that the Shinto shrine represented the Sun Goddess, Emperor and national deities; and was only served by the men of the family.[1] At times of sickness or death in the family this was sealed with white paper to guard it from pollution. The Buddhist one, however, was open at these times, for Buddhist gods gave comfort to the sorrowing, and guided the dead on their heavenward journey. This shrine was bowed to morning and night, and lit up for the evening meal, when they would feel the loving hearts of the ancestors with them. (This in spite of the fact that they were taught that they only came back at Obon!) I have included the above in this chapter because although it appears to belong to the section on Buddhism, ancestor worship has no place at all in original Buddhism. This is merely a Buddhist embellishment of Shinto and Confucian belief.

It is interesting to know what powers or qualities actually are, or were, attributed to these spirits. At first there had been mostly fear in the attitude towards the dead, such as was formerly seen in inland China when the dying would sometimes be placed outside the house. The Japanese in early times used to leave the house in which a death had occurred and build a new one. Gradually, however, with the coming of Buddhism to Japan the feeling for the dead became more tender. All dead Japanese were considered as becoming kami and remaining still a part of this world of the living. After death people were thought to experience an intensification of their earthly qualities; i.e. the benevolent became more good; and the cruel, even more so. They also were believed to have the power to see all that goes on in the home or community, and to give their help and protection. But these powers of theirs could not procure happiness for the dead themselves. *They depended*

[1] *Daughter of the Samurai*, Etsu Sugimoto.

Dressed in her kimono she comes to the Shinto shrine, a pull on the rope rings the bell and there she prays with hands clasped in front of her. After praying she claps slowly and loudly for a few moments, throws in some money into the receptacle just over the barrier and then she goes on her way.

Old Imperial Palace Gardens, Kyoto, Japan.

Old sacred tree with small shrine before it.

wholly on the attention of the living for this. "Each spirit must have its proper shelter, its tomb, of which it can only take possession if the funeral rites are properly carried out; it must have offerings of food, fire, and drink." It is almost impossible for an ordinary Westerner to realize the strength of the hold this belief in the presence of the ancestors has on the Japanese. The educated and cosmopolitan among them claim that it is not worship—that it is only Westerners who call it ancestor worship. One says, "Most of what Westerners name ancestor worship is not directed wholly towards ancestors. It is a ritual avowal of man's great indebtedness to all that has gone before. He is indebted not only to the past, but every-day contacts with people increase his indebtedness. From this debt his daily decisions and actions must spring." Uchimura himself gives us a description of what happened before he left home for study in the United States. "Father bade me address myself to the soul of my departed grandfather before leaving. I bowed my head, and my soul—directed alike to my Heavenly Father and the departed spirits of my ancestors—engaged in a sort of meditation at once a prayer and a retrospect. Our dogmatic (Christian) teachers might have frowned upon us for our conduct, but it was no time to argue then. We loved our God, our country and our forefathers and we remembered them all on that solemn occasion."

I am inclined to believe that it is not worship in the case of the more educated. Certainly it is something much lower than the Christian concept of worship. But whatever it is, it usually proves to be a real hindrance to the development of their Christian lives, and causes them to be the subjects of a great delusion when they believe that their ancestors are present and can help them. They seem to be relegating to their ancestors the prerogative of the Holy Spirit, the Comforter whose work it is to do these things for the believer.

Even in the modern English language newspapers there is constant reference to this belief in the ability of the ancestors to know what is going on. In a recent ferry-boat disaster the newspaper editorial demanded that something should be done to ensure the keeping of safety regulations as well as to "appease the spirits of the dead". Among letters to the editor, too, we have this idea constantly mentioned. One complained of the "inhuman" tax collectors who go to the funerals of well-known people and keep a close watch on the monetary gifts received (unearned income). "Counting the money in front of the spirit of the deceased is a heartless example of bad taxation."

One of the most interesting examples was a violent criticism of a book written by Prince Mikasa, younger brother of the Emperor, entitled *Kings, Graves and People*. In this book the Prince not only made some soul-searching comments on the Imperial household, but also wrote some revolutionary things about the war in China where he served as a major. His critic says, "The Prince has called the Holy war a pillage, assault, arson and rape. Although the blood of our people was shed, and more than two million men have been sacrificed, the great aim of liberating the backward peoples of Asia was achieved. Doesn't his mind see the great future of Japan? . . . He is a fool, coward and double crosser. If the Prince's indiscretion should result in damaging the prestige of the Emperor, who is the symbol of the nation, what face do we have to show our ancestors who preserved our national polity?"

This critic seems not at all concerned as to the truth of what the Prince had said, but only the impression it would make on the Imperial ancestors. It is interesting to note that the feelings of the ancestors seem more important than those of their living descendant whom he terms "fool, coward and double crosser".

Prince Mikasa no doubt causes much heartache among the old militarists for his liberal ideas and democratic ways. He has studied both Marx and the Bible and is said to be a great student of the Old Testament especially. He was even a speaker at the Bible Society meeting when the new Colloquial Bible was dedicated.

For many of the intellectuals, even those professing to be atheists or agnostics, however, the words spoken in the famous Japanese novel *Kokoro* by a sophisticated scholar would probably still be true. "I believed in some corner of my heart that my parents, though they had disappeared from this world, still loved me as they had done while they were alive. Although even at that time (his student days) I was not dull witted, the weight of superstition I received from my ancestors was also hidden in my blood with a strong force, and I think it lies in me even now. I began to feel I should be ashamed to face my dead parents if I did not secure the information about my property. . . ."[1]

There we have revealed I think the main difficulty Christianity has to face from Shinto. Though many followers of Shinto may not worship their ancestors they have imagined in them some of the functions of the Holy Spirit, the Comforter and Helper, and they have given to them the place in their heart which should rightly belong to God. We are therefore very thankful for the promise in the Bible of the mighty weapons at our disposal for the pulling down of strongholds and imaginations.

Apart from the Imperial ancestors and tutelary gods, numerous other deities have been added to the Shinto pantheon. These include such gods as those of grain, storm, wealth, fertility and so on, and they are all included in the term Popular Shinto. In some remote areas there are still evidences of phallic worship. The *Nippon Times* each week gives a short description of some Japanese custom or festival for the benefit of its foreign readers. Not long ago it gave an account of what it rightly termed "one of the most unique festivals" in the country. This is the Hip Pinching Fête on 10th November which takes place in darkness at one of the shrines on the famous Izu peninsula.

Since such things are done in the temples in the name of religion, one can understand the surprise it is to many Japanese to discover what is the teaching of the Christian Church on holiness of life. According to Dr. Natori the Shinto moral code is simply "Revere the Emperor; obey the natural impulses of one's own heart".

Intellectuals despise Popular Shinto of course, yet it is the upper class nevertheless which chiefly claims to be Shinto in faith, rather than Buddhist. It is the ancestor worship aspect especially, that was incorporated in the former State Shrine

[1] *Kokoro*, Natsume Soseki.

Shinto, to which they adhere. There are three important national shrines, the Grand Shrine at Ise dedicated to the Sun Goddess, progenitor of the Imperial line; the Meiji Shrine in Tokyo, a memorial to the great Emperor Meiji to which about three million people went recently to pay their respects; and the Yasukune Shrine, also in Tokyo, where are enshrined all the spirits of the war dead since the Meiji Restoration. There were however 110,000 shrines incorporated into State Shinto by the government before the war, and partly supported by it, the priests being government officials.

These shrines, though originally having their own particular deities became, as a result of government pressure, a mere medium for the worshipper to get in touch with the unseen. The priest would feel free to invoke the aid of any deity desired. This practice no doubt helped to weaken the Christian Church, for it made the idea of one true God, and that a "jealous" one, seem very narrow and undesirable. Further, many of the newer sects which are usually grouped in the Shinto category probably felt more free to borrow various Christian ideas and practices as a result.

Some of these newer sects have made great strides since the war, especially among the lower classes. Perhaps the most important of these is *Tenrikyo* (Teaching of Divine Reason) founded in 1838 by a woman, Miki Nakayama, the wife of a prosperous farmer. On the 9th December that year Miki, her husband and son were all suffering from different pains, one in the feet, another the eyes, and the third the stomach. A Buddhist priest-medium was called in to treat them. At that time Miki went into a trance, and according to tradition became "transfigured by the glory of God". When questioned, a voice speaking through her said, "I am the original and true God who has come down from heaven to save the whole world."

For three days the exasperated husband pleaded with the spirit to leave his wife. But he and the whole family were threatened with extinction unless he promised that his wife could become the living shrine of this god Tenri. When he did that she immediately came out of her trance, and they were all healed.

According to tradition Miki had always been a most exemplary child and wife, full of benevolence to all. But she received much persecution, and frequent imprisonment when she began to teach her new doctrine. Briefly she taught that this is a reasonable universe, that Tenri wills that all men shall enjoy happiness and prosperity. But man, moved by selfish desires and wicked thoughts, suffers misfortune and disease. Man can only progress spiritually by casting out evil. All evils (referred to as "dusts") are related to greed, misguided love, hatred, anger. By gaining mastery of these "dusts" within him, through faith in God and trust in his benevolence, man can at last reach contentment. When union between man and God is perfect, divine favour will cure illnesses, turn unhappiness into joy and save the soul.

Much of this seems to have a Christian sound, and bears some similarity, strangely enough, to the theories put out by Mrs. Mary Baker Eddy at about the same time. When Mrs. Nakayama first began her teaching, however, Christianity had not yet returned to Japan after its centuries of exile, so we may well wonder where she got her ideas. We find that her god Tenri is really a composite deity made up of ten Shinto gods. When she wrote later that he revealed himself sometimes in the form of a single-headed dragon called "Moon", or sometimes as a twelve-headed serpent named "Sun", those who believe the Bible have little difficulty deciding the origin of this religion. The "striving after perfect union between man and god" no doubt is the cause of the demonic possession which is such a characteristic of present-day Tenrikyo devotees, according to a doctor who has worked for some years in Japan. The healings seem genuine, however, and if it is true that many diseases are psychologically caused, it is not surprising that the Japanese with the tremendous pressure and frustration placed upon them by society, should find release in this teaching.

Tenrikyo does a good deal of social welfare work, contributes free labour for public services such as street cleaning, and has a big educational programme from kindergarten to college level. At the headquarters at Nara it has a training school for missionaries where many foreign languages, including English,

French, German, Spanish, Malay and Chinese are taught, to prepare for the conversion of the whole world. It already has over 5,000,000 adherents in Japan, and 530 churches in other countries.

More recently another sect, the House of Growth Religion has arisen and thrived. It has been called the "department store of religions", and has Scriptures which include many quotations from Genesis and John's Gospel, a vocabulary that includes Christian phraseology and practices that involve a form of "Christian Science". It claims that all men are children of God, and that it contains within its teaching the best from all religions. It already has nearly 2,000,000 adherents.

Many of these new religions frankly and gratefully admit to borrowing Christian truths and methods of evangelism. They claim that their greater success is due to their accommodating themselves to the customs of Japan while yet being clear about their own "special advantages", the meaning of which they are able really to get "under the skin of the people". Japanese Christian pastors, they say, are always too difficult to understand, and seem to be merely mimicking their foreign tutors.

The Shinto priesthood is usually hereditary, some families claiming to be descendants of the original tutelary god. There are several kinds, some giving all their time to divination and a kind of witchcraft. Some may have other part-time work such as teaching.

In spite of the divine mission attached to Shinto during the war years it is encouraging to know that even among the priesthood there are those who have found an even greater object of faith than the gods of Japan. One of our English Bible classes has had a Shinto priest attending for some years, and he gives the impression of being a secret believer.

Another became known to some of our workers while doing language study in Karuizawa. A tract had been given to a girl at the station one day. Not being interested, she gave it to her friend Yoko, who was the daughter of the Shinto priest in her village. Yoko *was* interested, and seeing the address of the Karuizawa Bible School on it, wrote asking for further help. A conference was being held there soon afterwards so she was invited to attend, and was converted. Later she entered the Bible School as a student, and made visits home to testify to her family. Her father was not impressed at first, but gradually realized she had something he lacked. Meanwhile a younger daughter was converted, and began a Sunday School in their home. Finally the father accepted an invitation to attend some lectures at the Bible School, to be given by a converted priest. There he was convinced of the truth of Christianity, and later asked for baptism. His home is in a village remote from public transportation, but two carloads of students and missionaries managed to get there to hold a service. He first gathered together all the Shinto and Buddhist paraphernalia he had in his home and shrine, and burnt it in the yard, after which he was baptized. None of the village people would come near, but watched from a distance. As this priest was the headman of the village it was a very big step to take. Later his wife and mother also believed.

Chapter VI

PALE MOONLIGHT OF BUDDHISM

JUST as many of the newer religions have borrowed Christian concepts, the Japanese Buddhists also have unashamedly adopted many Christian ideas. There are now Buddhist Sunday Schools, a Young Men's Buddhist Association equivalent to the Y.M.C.A., and even Christian songs where the name of Buddha has been substituted for Christ. One Buddhist priest near one of our Hokkaido centres had been asked to take some instruction classes for children, and since Buddhism is not a very easy religion to explain he spent most of his time showing them Christian picture stories. The genius of Buddhism seems to be that it can adapt itself to all circumstances. It has very truly been said that Gautama Buddha himself would not recognize Japanese Buddhism as anything which he had initiated.

By the time Buddhism reached Japan it had already taken 1,000 years to cross Asia, assimilating and gathering up into itself like a snowball many of the religious ideas it met on the way. It has been described by Reischauer as "a kind of junk shop containing something of everything, good, bad and indifferent". It already had 5000 volumes of *sutras* (scriptures) but in Japan now 6,771 volumes are recognized by some schools as authentic teaching.

I know of no one who has found a satisfactory and simple definition of Buddhism. One thought he had when he stated it is "the religion founded by Buddha", but the Northern (Mahayana) Buddhism found in China and Japan contains perhaps more that is contrary to Gautama's original teaching than that which agrees with it. As Reischauer says, "There is little that has ever entered the heart and mind of man which does not find its counterpart somewhere in Buddhism."

We have been told by Japanese Christians that whenever

missionaries mention Buddhism or Shinto in their sermons they make mistakes. I can well believe this is so, for Westerners try to find a logical system in these religions which in fact they do not possess, and for almost anything we say that Buddhism teaches, they could claim the opposite. Some Westerners writing on the subject make their ethical teaching seem very high, partly because they read into some of the statements a Christian connotation entirely lacking in the original, or in the modern heathen mind. Perhaps it would be fair to explain Buddhism in the words of a man who for twenty years was a Buddhist priest and who before he became a Christian spent much time in their training schools and also in private study of rare manuscripts in their libraries. This man's name is Taisei Michihata who in 1937 wrote the book *From Buddha to Christ* from which the following is an extract.

"There is no recognized body of fundamental truth in this religion anywhere. If one starts with the idea that it is atheistic it soon seems to be polytheistic. If we shift our ground and think it polytheistic it fades into pantheism; and there are phrases and doctrines in it that seem to indicate it is monotheistic. It is a mixture of spiritual ideas and materialism, of belief of existence and non-existence, of reason and superstition, all blended together in a conglomerate mass. There is no place in it where one may lay hold of it and say 'This is the real heart of Buddhism'.

"It is like a snake. If we grasp its tail, it strikes us with its head and neck; if we grasp its head, it winds its tail about us; and if we take hold of both, it uses its body. Those who only half understand it say that Buddhism is very deep, and that it is very hard to grasp the more profound doctrines; and in this way people are deceived. The truth is, as we have said, that it has nothing solid in it that anyone can really lay hold of, and therefore no one does or can understand it. So if we want to make it at all intelligible, we have to adopt some one line of argument, and reject all the rest of the whole mass of material as false. Every one of the various sects of Japan is doing just this, and the result is that there are many widely differing explanations and commentaries issued. . . . Each sect selects one or more *sutras* as its doctrinal guide, and covers its ears and eyes and acts as if it was determined not to see or hear anything of any of the others.''

Buddhism was first introduced into Japan in A.D. 552 when a Korean delegation seeking help brought, among other presents, some images of Buddha and copies of Buddhist scriptures, together with a letter from the king stating it was an efficacious religion which would bring happiness and good fortune. It was gradually accepted by some in the court circle, and just over 100 years later an official decree was issued ordering the construction of *butsudan*, small Buddhist altars, in all households of the nation. Only the literate could understand anything of the new religion, however, and even among some of these there was a marked revival of the native Shinto during the next century, when the *Kojiki* and *Nihongi* were written. It was then Japanese first began to speak of their ruler as an Emperor, and to enhance their racial importance through the assertion of its divine origin. Perhaps this was a kind of compensation for the obviously superior products of Chinese civilization which the Japanese were importing with great zeal at that time. It is interesting that a similar phenomenon took place when they imported Western culture so avidly in the nineteenth century.

It was not until 200 years later that Buddhism really began to take root in the country. This was the result of the teaching of a man named Kobo Daishi who studied in China and then came home to introduce an entirely new idea—that the chief gods of Shinto were other aspects, or incarnations, of Buddhist divinities. This compromise, so characteristic an attitude of the Japanese mind, and Buddhism in general, met with much approval. In many places rites of the two religions were performed in the same building. There was never a complete amalgamation of the two, however, although many worshippers were unable to distinguish between the two religions; and Buddhism, owing to government pressure, became the strongest element. In the Tokugawa era everyone had to be registered at a Buddhist temple, and family records were kept there. There developed a division of duties in which Shinto deities tended to preside over the affairs of this world, births, marriages, seasonal festivals, particularly rice planting, and victories in battle; while ecclesiastical organization, education and funerals were the responsibility of Buddhism.

The early Buddhist priests, though they were the means of introducing a great deal of writing, art, architecture and other forms of culture into Japan, including some schools and medical work, had little to offer the common man. There was a constant tendency later for them to develop into corrupt, politically minded groups or else to use their time arguing over minute differences in philosophical teaching. It was not until the twelfth and thirteenth centuries that what has been termed a religious awakening touched the country as a whole. It was at this time that three schools of Buddhism were introduced in Japan, and these have continued to have the greatest influence on the country ever since. These three are the Amida, Zen and Nichiren schools of Buddhism. The first two came from India via China. The last is the only one of Japanese origin, though it too had its foundation in one of the ancient *sutras*. Amida Buddhism is the most interesting to the Christian, since it contains the teaching of a salvation by faith. Because it therefore offers one of the greatest obstacles to the Christian faith it must be considered separately in the next chapter.

Zen Buddhism, though known much earlier on the mainland of Asia, did not develop into a Japanese sect until the twelfth century. It was the antithesis of the Amida School, teaching salvation by self-effort, meditation and contemplation, and was much criticized by other Buddhist groups. It has very little of the superstition of the other schools, and appears to be much nearer the original teaching of Gautama who was definitely agnostic. He considered it a waste of time to speculate about the existence of gods; to him this was one of the Great Indeterminates.

For those who are unfamiliar with the story of the founder of Buddhism, an Indian prince known as Gautama, perhaps we should very briefly give the main points of his teaching, as far as it can be judged from existing writings all written after his death. He is said to have renounced his family and wealth, sickened by the sight of poverty, disease and death in the world, and by various austerities sought to understand the meaning of life. Finally "enlightenment" came to him one day as he sat meditating under a tree. We would hardly give the word "enlightenment" to the revelation which came to him, but briefly it was a realization:

1. Of the impermanency of all individual existence.
2. That suffering is inherent in individuality, and it is just due to ignorance that we think of ourselves as individuals.
3. Of the non-reality of an abiding self or ego.

Very soon after his death his followers found this teaching did not satisfy the normal human being, and various deities, many of them Hindu, had to be reintroduced so that today the idols of a Buddhist temple are its main characteristic in most Eastern countries.

Original Buddhism, however, was a philosophy rather than a religion and the same is true of the Zen school. It is this school of Buddhism which seems to have a growing attraction for Westerners. There is a weekly Buddhist English service in Tokyo and Buddhist periodicals are also published in English. Occasionally in the newspaper one sees pictures of Americans becoming Buddhist priests.

Zen promises that by mental discipline the "ultimate reality" can be found in the innermost recesses of one's soul. They seek to attain an intuitive perception of fundamental truth, and a complete detachment from self and personal gain, so that there will be no fear of encountering calamities or adversity. Enlightenment comes when through meditation man's mind becomes a "holy vacancy" and he "absorbs the universe into himself."

The man who brought Zen teaching from India to China once sat staring silently at a blank wall for nine years. Another approved exercise of Zen Buddhism was the attempt to solve certain problems known as *koan*. This was soon dropped in China in the early centuries and has survived only in Japan. Typical examples of such problems are the following. "Two hands when clapped make a sound. What is the sound of one hand clapping?" and "Who is carrying out one's lifeless body?" Some men gave seven or eight years to thinking out one of these problems, and not unnaturally many Western scholars have dismissed these things as "in defiance of common sense" or "a tissue of solemn nonsense". It is only fair however to describe what the Japanese are trying to attain by these means. They say they are aiming at a state of "expertness (muga) when there is no break, even the thickness of a hair, between a man's will and his act". In other words they seek to eliminate the "observer-self", that part of them we might almost call conscience, but which to them, from earliest childhood, has been that constant remembrance of what "the world" is going to think of their every action. As we have seen already, this has made it almost impossible for most of them to make up their minds on any subject, and this has made the more intellectual realize what a handicap it is and seek for some solution. The concentration on these *koan*, therefore was meant to produce supreme frustration, "like a man with a ball of red-hot iron stuck in his throat". He becomes frantic, and finally the obstruction between his mind and the problem, i.e. his observer-self, is eliminated. Suddenly "he knows", or as the Chinese expressed it "he found he was looking for an ox when he was riding on one". The Japanese have likened these *koan* to bricks with which to knock a hole in the wall of *haji* (shame or vulnerability to public opinion) with which their early training has exerted every effort to surround them. Once a hole in this wall has been made one is free as air—one is *muga* (expert) and does not go on solving other *koan*. He has passed beyond the necessity of taking thought about the proper course of action. He need not consider *on* (obligations to others), his energy and attention are solely on the fulfilling of his purpose, he "lives as one already dead".

The follower of Zen has diagnosed one of the greatest needs of the Japanese—or for that matter anyone, the Christian included—namely to be released from the fear of man. Their remedy called *muga* seems very like a travesty of the Christian idea expressed in modern colloquialism as "letting go and letting God" or more scripturally as being dead to self and alive unto God. "I am crucified with Christ, nevertheless I live, yet not I but Christ." The vague "Reality" or Universal

Self with which Zen seeks to be united is neither personal nor moral, however. One who has entered this ecstatic state feels himself no longer bound by the ordinary laws of everyday experience. "He has ceased to think of good or evil . . . released himself from the relative idea of wise and common things." In order to attain this great height of enlightenment he receives the following advice. "Zen seeks only the light man finds in himself. It tolerates no hindrance to this seeking. Clear every obstacle out of your way . . . if on your way you meet Buddha, kill him! If you meet the patriarchs kill them! If you meet the saints kill them all. That is the only way of reaching salvation."[1]

How many have reached this "enlightenment" no one knows. The former priest Michihata says he never met anyone who claimed to have done so, and he himself had close contact with the head of the Zen sect for some time.

While Zen is practised mostly by the upper classes its teachings have had a considerable indirect influence on the whole Japanese nation. It appealed to the military group since it gave them courage in battle, and the aesthetic discipline was easy to follow even in camp. As we have already seen, its influence was strong in the teaching of Bushido. Actually very few Japanese seem to have given themselves to the long years of meditation. It was the Zen monks who were responsible for all the education during feudal times, and they also engaged in some social work. Zen was responsible, too, for the development of the arts, architecture, literature, painting, drama, dancing and also the famous Tea Ceremony, with rules which govern every movement in the making and drinking of the tea—a long drawn out ceremony which is not for the purpose of quenching thirst, but for practising self-culture. Since Zen spurns scriptures and formulas it has been able to adjust itself easily to changing conditions, and still has about nine million adherents.

The Nichiren sect began in the thirteenth century and was the last of the new schools of Buddhism. It is the only one to bear the name of its founder. Nichiren is one of the most colourful and interesting personalities in Japanese history—

[1] Compare Christ's teaching, "If *thy* . . . hand offend thee, cut it off."

one of the few who seem to have held strong and original convictions. His main attack was against the Amida school, however, for he felt they were taking away the glory of the original founder of Buddhism and giving it to another when they preached salvation by faith in Amida. He felt that all the divisions among Buddhists were a serious threat to the religion, and also that all of them were far removed from the original purity of the teaching of Gautama.

There is little evidence, however, that he himself had any clear idea of the original teachings either. In his search after truth he came across the Lotus of Truth Sutra, which was actually written long after the death of Gaumata, but which he decided to adopt as the one and only true scripture. In it he found a prophecy that 2,000 years after his death Buddha would call out of the earth his primordial disciple Jogyo Bosatsu, and entrust to him the salvation of all people in the "Age of the Latter Law". When Nichiren was persecuted by the other sects he became convinced that he himself was this saviour, and he therefore preached with even greater vigour against the sins of his times.

He not only denounced the religious divisions, but was also greatly concerned over the division of the country between the Shogunate at Kamakura and the Emperor's court at Kyoto, and threatened that Japan would be destroyed if these divisions continued. Soon after this the Mongols attacked Japan and were only driven away by a violent typhoon. More storms and devastating earthquakes soon afterwards, bringing famine and disease in their wake, caused people to listen to his words, and his followers to increase in number. So serious were his criticisms of the government and the other sects, that opposition became very strong. The sentence of death was finally passed and he was led out to the sands of Kamakura for execution. One tradition says that a giant meteor appeared and terrified the executioners, another that a special messenger came from the palace ordering his release. From these has originated the spurious claim among his followers that he rose from the dead.

The majority of the followers of Nichiren Buddhism have been from the less educated classes; but during feudal times its teaching appealed to the militant spirit in some, and in the Meiji era it was an important factor in expanding the Japanese Empire. Nichiren's glittering personality, by that time deified, attracted the religious, the patriotic and the intellectuals. Many fanatical nationalists have been members of the sect, which may be compared to the order of the Pharisees. In modern times Nichiren members have played an important, and sometimes violent part in Japanese politics. Though there are only two million members their influence is strong because of their fanaticism. They are usually the hardest to convert to Christianity and we find more actual opposition to the preaching of the Gospel from them than from any other group.

From the remaining sects there has been little open opposition to Christianity. Some Buddhist leaders have claimed that there is no conflict between Buddhism and Christianity—that there is indeed more between different Buddhist sects than between Christianity and Buddhism! But this general Buddhist tolerance, the idea that all religions are "different flowers growing in the same garden", the disregard of logic and confused thinking, the emphasis on the meaninglessness and transiency of all life, have proved a great stumbling block to the advance of a virile Christianity in Japan. Dr. Natori has written, "Take away the superstitious observances of most people not Christians in Japan and their remaining religious belief is all but non-existent. The missionaries' greatest obstacle is the way in which so many people lack a desire to better their situation."[1] The compromise so prevalent in Buddhism, which has enabled it to absorb so much of other religions, causes its followers to say Christianity and Buddhism are just the same. Even Japanese Christians, influenced partly by Western philosophers who are apt to read a Christian connotation into Buddhist phrases, have been deceived in this way. Kanzo Uchimura for instance, can at times write the most sublime accounts of the Gospel such as "When I say I am a Christian, I mean I am a sinner, forgiven only by the grace of God for Christ's sake— that I can boast no good work which entitles me to eternal bliss—that I depend in everything upon Him who graciously

[1] *Historical Stories of Christianity in Japan*, Junichi Natori.

Fishermen in Hokkaido pulling in their nets.

Children's Tent Meeting.

A young Japanese Christian witnesses in the street during the tent campaign.

worketh in me to do that which is pleasing in His sight. . . . I boldly count myself among God's elect by the mercy shown me of forgiveness accomplished in the atoning death of His Son. . . . O the joy, the safety, the perfect tranquillity of being a Christian. God-forgiven sinner: that is my definition of Christian, and that I believe I am."

Yet the following month he writes: "Is there any essential difference between the fundamental teachings of Jesus and those of Gautama? They both stand for unity and peace . . . both teach non-resistance to adversaries, both find in love the only weapon which can overcome the world. We can say that Christianity is the positive and Buddhism the negative view of the same truth." He then quotes Rhys Davis' translation of one of Buddha's reputed exhortations. "Let a man, whether he be standing, sitting, walking or lying down, cultivate towards the whole world—above, below, around—a heart of love unstinted." Whether these were truly Buddha's words is not known; but certainly anyone who has lived in China or Japan, and perhaps India, knows that this aspect of his teaching has never penetrated very far. Early missionaries had great difficulty inculcating the idea of love, and some languages did not even have a word for the concept. Uchimura, too seems to forget what he wrote in his youthful diary of his own experience as a heathen. "I believed that there dwelt in each of innumerable temples its god, jealous over its jurisdiction, ready to punish any transgressor that fell under its displeasure. With so many gods to satisfy and appease I was naturally a fretful child. I framed a general prayer to be offered to everyone, adding special requests appropriate to each." Since there were many temples near his home and it was very troublesome repeating so many prayers he adds, "I would often prefer a longer route with less numerous sanctuaries, in order to avoid the trouble of saying my prayers, without scruples of my conscience."

Again in 1926 Uchimura wrote a magazine article, entitled "Buddha and Christ".

"Buddha is the Moon: Christ is the Sun.
Buddha is the Mother: Christ is the Father.

Buddha is mercy: Christ is Righteousness.
Buddha retires to the mountains to keep himself spotless and
    pure: Christ goes forth to the world to fight the battles
    of faith.
Buddha weeps for the sins of the world: Christ fights to redress
    the wrong. I love and admire Buddha, but I worship
    Christ."

However, that he does not read into those words all that a
Westerner would—who regards mother and father of equal
worth, and the sun and moon on much the same level—is shown
in a further article the following year in which he says, "Even
the teaching of the highest and best philosophers is of earth,
earthy. Man's light in its greatest brilliance is a pale reflected
moonlight, good for *soothing* life's ills, but not for *healing* them.
God's light is sunlight, full of energies, life-giving, shining by
its own light. And where do we find God's light but in the
Bible? And what light so concentrated, sharper than arrows of
steel, as God's words which are His light? Buddhism is widely
diffused light compared with the compact, concentrated light
of the Christian Gospel. Man explains—God declares. The
reason philosophy is more popular than the Gospel, even in
so-called Christendom, is that man loves darkness rather than
light."

These seemingly rather contradictory passages and many
others written by a man who undoubtedly had a deep experience of the regenerating power of Christ, show how the
teaching of Buddhism through the centuries has made it
almost impossible for many Japanese to think a subject clearly
through to a logical conclusion.

We cannot criticize Buddhism without confessing that there
are not a few churches in the West, bearing the name of
Christian, which have little within them having any resemblance to New Testament Christianity. Buddha must have
been a man of great personality and sincerity, and he produced
an ethical code which no doubt shone as a ray of moonlight in
the darkness and chaos of those days when men had forgotten
God and His commandments. Nevertheless his confusion of

thought and inability to think a matter logically through—
(as for instance, if there is no *ego*, or individual self, who or
what is it that has to have the right views, aspirations and
effort, which he had taught were necessary, who or what
is it that was "enlightened" in his case?)—were no doubt
largely responsible for the extraordinary and utterly diverse
developments of his teaching in after years at the hands
of his followers. Japan has to thank Buddhism for most of
her art treasures, and for almost all of the few buildings of any
historical importance which she possesses. The pale moonlight of the knowledge of an ethical code, without the power
to live up to it, is however completely eclipsed, I believe,
by the darkness of mind and confusion of thought which has
resulted from centuries of training in Buddhist philosophy,
and which, it appears, will take long to dispel entirely even in
the regenerate Christian in Japan.

Chapter VII

A PSEUDO SALVATION-BY-FAITH

AMIDA Buddhism, which teaches that salvation can be obtained through faith in another, seems to have developed much more in Japan than elsewhere. In one part of China at least, the emphasis seemed to be largely on the accumulation of merit through good works, vegetarianism and so on. Nothing in the Amida school seems to resemble the original teaching of Gautama, and there has been much speculation as to its origin.

The man who brought back the germ of this idea to Japan had studied in China during the seventh century when Nestorian influence was penetrating China. He is said to have lived only a quarter of a mile away from a temple where Nestorian teaching was known. There is no evidence that Amida (or Amitabha) was ever a historical person. The whole idea is based on a very flimsy foundation. In eternity Amida is said to have refused Buddhahood "unless all that call my name shall be born in my Pure Land." . . . "And he took Buddhahood, therefore whoever calls his name shall go to the Pure Land", is the conclusion of the originators of this school of thought. The Formula, "Oh Save, Amida Buddha" repeated with faith is believed by some sects to save, though in the earlier days the need for works too, was stressed. Shinran, a disciple of the man Honen who introduced this teaching to Japan, gradually claimed that this formula was a thanksgiving for salvation already attained. He developed the idea of salvation by faith alone, for the good and the bad, involving a new birth. The equality of all believers was taught, no distinction being made between priest and laity, and he abolished celibacy for priests.

There certainly seems to be a Christian ring about much of this and it is fairly obvious that Amida is either a corruption of the historic Christ, or else that the whole idea is the product of wishful thinking on the part of needy man who realized his

inability to save himself. Many attribute these Christian ideas
to Nestorian influence in China, but there are some Japanese
Christians who do not hold this view. J. Funaki for instance,
suggests that the Nestorians did not have this evangelical
emphasis in their teaching. Furthermore, although the phraseology seems to be the same to us, it has quite a different connotation to the Japanese. He pointed out that there is no idea of a
righteous God forgiving sin. The evil in this life is thought by
the Buddhists to be the result of wrong action in a former life,
so there is no feeling of personal responsibility. Amida moreover is not omnipotent. He has no power to intervene in this
life, and can only affect life after death.

Actually the idea of Amida and his Western Paradise is
found in a sutra appearing long before the Nestorian influence
of the seventh century. Its origin is shrouded in obscurity,
for nothing is known historically of that period between 200
B.C. and the first century A.D. when Northern (Mahayana)
Buddhism developed. Since Buddhism travelled to China
during this period via northwest India and then Central Asia,
the solution to this mystery lies somewhere there. Greek influence was known in those northwest areas when Alexander
the Great advanced that far. There is the possibility that the
apostle Thomas went that way into India, and that therefore
some Christian ideas were incorporated into Buddhism at that
time. It is interesting that both the Roman Church and
Buddhism have many externals in common. Xavier and his
companions were quick to recognize this with annoyance when
they arrived in Japan, thinking the Buddhists had copied
these things from the Church. Probably both Romanism and
Buddhism were influenced by even earlier pagan practices.
These similarities include such things as the use of halos,
rosaries, masses for the dead, the use of incense and the formation of a main altar with two side altars, and the worship of the
virgin and child statue which is very similar to the Buddhist
Goddess of Mercy.

At any rate, whatever its origin, the two great reformers
Honen and Shinran found in this idea of salvation through the
help of another something which would appeal to every one,

however poor and unlearned. Even women, who before had been considered impure and unworthy of obtaining Buddhahood, were offered this salvation. The Amida sects have therefore proved the strongest branch of Japanese Buddhism, having about twenty-two million members.

Since salvation from Amida is so easily obtained we can realize part of the reason why so many Japanese register decisions to accept Christ after attending one or two Gospel meetings, and later fall away. Having been brought up on this easy doctrine they usually have not the slightest conception of the radical change in their lives which will be required when they take the name of Christ, and it is no wonder that many forsake this for the easier way. I am sure, however, that Westerners and Japanese Christians of long standing, are continually reading into Buddhism much more than those who are within its fold actually experience. Uchimura writing in 1915, after being a Christian about twenty years, states, "Thirteen million of my fellow countrymen who profess the Jodo form of Buddhism are my brothers and sisters in faith. They take the same attitude to their Amida that I take towards my Jesus the Christ. Change but the object and they are like me and I like them, and faith being the human side of religion, by faith we are united in religion, and not by the object of faith." A few years later, however, he has learned a little more truly and writes, "Faith by itself does not save. It is the object of faith which saves. It is the Lord Jesus Christ who saves, not our faith." Most Buddhists, however, do not even believe in a power higher than themselves; and it is only the most simple minded among Buddhist followers who achieve a real faith in Amida which approximates in any way to the Christian's faith in Christ—and for them the object of their faith has no basis in fact. However, praise God, there are those who have truly entered the light, even from the spiritual darkness and intellectual confusion of a Buddhist temple. Taisei Michihata, the ex-priest to whom reference was made in the previous chapter, is a wonderful example of one who found in Christ what he had sought so long (earnestly but unsuccessfully), in Buddhism. Because it reveals so much at first hand of

the procedure, and ethical teaching, and practice of Amida
Buddhism, at least during the early part of this century, I am
devoting the rest of this chapter to a brief account of Michihata's
early life and conversion.

He was the son of a priest, but his parents died when he
was very young. He was adopted by the priest of a temple in
the next village, while his elder brother carried on at the old
home temple. He himself became a priest when he was six
years old, and soon after the ceremony of receiving the tonsure
he was awakened one night by a female form which said,
"You must always be filial to your parents; and next to that,
you must be earnest in your religious life." This heavenly
vision made a great impression on the little boy, and he
attended to his duties seriously, helping with the temple rites
and funerals, and visiting adherents and reading the sutra
before their family shrines.

He studied Buddhism deeply, and had written two commentaries even before he went to the priests' training school as
a young man. His life became very unhappy, however, for the
old priest, a man over sixty, suddenly brought a woman of
ill repute into the temple, and eventually had three children by
her. The adopted boy, no longer needed to carry on the family
name, was therefore treated with much cruelty. He tells us
how much harder to bear was this injustice than any self-
inflicted austerities. It was this trouble which was mainly
responsible for leading him into such a deep study of his
religion as he sought there to find an answer to his problem.
At fifteen he preached his first sermon, and even offered to go
as a chaplain in the Sino-Japanese war—the only priest to do
so in his area—but he was turned down because of his youth.

In his early teens the old priest had advised him to start
drinking, in order to attract people to himself and the temple.
All their religious services were just a commercial proposition,
and the amount of money each temple contributed to the headquarters of the sect determined its rank. Drink became his
master, and it was only the power of Christ which finally
delivered him from it, after many years of ineffectual struggle
in his own strength.

The unpleasantness at home was becoming so acute, however, he finally decided to commit suicide. As he searched the sutras for help and comfort in his distress he found only cold reason or subtle philosophy. Seeing no hope in this life therefore he began to seek it in the next. He found a book by Genshin, a monk who was highly thought of in both China and Japan, who had helped lay the foundation of the Amida teaching. The book was called *Gaining Paradise by Prayer to Buddha*. The last chapter urged the attainment of Paradise through committing suicide by throwing oneself down from some height. It stated that if a person were to make a vow to renounce the world and to attain Paradise, set a day, after giving himself up wholly to Amida, throw himself into the river or sea, he would be welcomed by twenty-five Boddhisatvas seated upon purple clouds, and would be immediately received into Paradise. When one of Gautama's disciples, weary with this life, had committed suicide, the great teacher had said, "If one commits suicide in order to be born again in a different body it is sin: but if it is for the purpose of gaining 'Nirvana'[1] it is not sin." He also found a promise that if one practised the required self-discipline faithfully, one would be rewarded with a vision of Amida in the sky.

Michihata thought he would like this double blessing, so decided to practise the self-discipline first, and then commit suicide. The prescribed discipline was that every day for ninety days one must purify the body with cold water three times, and repeat the invocation to Amida 3,000 times. This, with all his temple duties and kitchen work kept him very busy, but at the end of the ninetieth day the carefully planned moment came, and, with an invocation to Buddha, he jumped into a ten-foot well. There was little water in the well, however, and he recovered consciousness almost immediately. With bitter disappointment he found himself still in this present world, without even having seen a vision.

He then decided to do a second ninety days of preparatory discipline and at the end of this he climbed a pine tree and tied his girdle to it, intending to hang himself. Just as he was

[1] State of non-existence of the individual—the Ocean of Oneness.

about to do so he heard a voice saying "Stop! Have you forgotten the vision?" He was completely taken aback, for there was no one near: yet the voice had smitten his ears with tremendous force. As he thought things over he became convinced that he was in the hands of some higher power. But what was that power? Try as he might he had not been able to get the vision of Buddha or Amida the books had promised him, and he realized these were just imagination and lies. Yet the voice he had heard was real, and he knew the time for him to die had not yet come, and he must probe further into the spiritual realm.

He still had a long way to go in his search. The most logical place seemed the priests' training school, but he was disgusted with much that he saw and experienced there. Although there were lectures on the Buddhist doctrines and an oral examination at the end, the questions and answers for this were written out and distributed to the students a week beforehand. There were also certain rites to perform, one of these being purification by pouring three large buckets of cold water over the head each day. Before each bucket was poured there was a short prayer to be said, the first "I cleanse my body that I may fulfil my vow to all living creatures, with my body and soul purified without and within". The second was "May my senses be made pure and holy" and last "May my deeds and words and will bring forth that which is pure and holy". This sounds very laudable; but few priests went through it with any serious purpose, many of them inventing and repeating parodies on the prayers. Since twenty or thirty were engaged in this at the same time it was impossible for the head priest to see and hear all that went on. Some only put a little water in their buckets while others engaged in horse-play. When they were supposed to repeat the invocation to Buddha they changed it to "Hail fried bean-curd" a sentence with similar sound in Japanese. When he eventually went to a Christian Bible School, Michihata was very impressed by the difference in spirit and moral character between those he found in training there and those who had been his fellow students in the Buddhist training school.

There was a further rite in this training period called "Entering the Sanctuary" in which the candidates were called up before the altar and given the ten commandments on a scroll. Although Buddha had only given eight of these, any other two were usually added in Buddhist ceremonies to bring the number up to ten. Yet even at the time of this rite priests ate meat and drank wine, although both these things were forbidden by those very commandments. The priests evaded this prohibition by saying it was not drinking if the wine were served in a rice bowl instead of a wine cup. Because few cared to keep the commandments during their lifetime the practice had arisen of reading and explaining them to the corpse at funerals instead! While still a priest Michihata could see the folly and weakness of this. Yet if he tried to preach some of these things to the living, the numbers attending the temple would drop. Once when he had begun a discourse on the first five commandments, one of the men in the congregation called out "Quit that stuff! We don't want to hear that". So he obligingly switched to the moving tale of "The Thirteen Bells of Nara".

Dr. Natori also has an interesting passage about the difference between a Christian and a Buddhist sermon. The missionary, he says, may often begin by asking the audience if they are really happy, if they have an assurance of eternal joy that makes them want to sing. The listeners are amazed at such a strange approach, for what they hear in the village temple is something along the following pessimistic vein. " 'Man is no sooner endowed with a body than he is possessed by the five lusts, the desire for fair sights, sweet sounds, fragrant smells, dainty meats, and rich trappings. They become his very heart, and it being a law that every man follows the dictates of his heart, in this way the body, the lusts of the flesh, the heart, and the dictates of the heart blaze up in a consuming fire. "Alas for the miserable world!" said Buddha.' Other Buddhist sermons centre around a sentimental story of wicked badgers and kind Buddha and the like."[1] From this we may gather that there is no emphasis on personal responsibility for sin and lust. Though it may be pessimistic it is not

[1] *Historical Stories of Christianity in Japan.*

calculated to produce any feeling of guilt or need to reform.

Michihata tried a period in another training school where the immorality of the other priests was a constant pain to him. He tried retreats where he sat naked for fifty nights in a temple room reading the sutra while the mosquitoes sucked his blood. At last he decided the only way was to study by himself, so he went to visit a temple with a very valuable library, where one of his uncles was head priest. Here he spent his time in research into the origin of Buddhism in general, as well as his own sect. It became clear to him that it was only a negative religion denying the existence of any being higher than man, and with no belief in the immortality of the soul.

Soon after his return to his own temple his stepmother put poison in his food, which he detected just in time. He therefore hurriedly left home and tried travelling with a head priest of his own sect on a preaching tour in Hokkaido. Later he worked with the heads of the Zen sect in the south, hoping to get some spiritual light from them. He found to his disappointment that while they preached of "faith, self-respect, reverence, moral improvement and progress, under cover of all this fine talk they were giving free rein to lusts of every kind". He found no one of really high character during all this time.

It was while he was working with one of the priests of the Zen School that he attended his first Christian service. He happened to hear some of the preliminary street preaching, and when he went in to the service he was immediately impressed with the earnest and reverent spirit of the meeting and the obviously high character of the pastor, and of the missionaries whom he met later.

From that time he occasionally visited a number of different churches, Roman Catholic and Protestant, in the big city of Osaka, always changing into a Western suit so that no one would know he was a priest. Michihata was particularly moved one evening at a prayer meeting he was attending, to hear one of the laymen pouring out his heart in thanks to God for saving him from drink, and praying for help in his business life, where drink is so incessantly pressed upon all. This really amazed him; for he knew that he, a priest, could not overcome the craving for drink, though he had often tried to do so. Yet here was a despised layman who had conquered this lust. He even began to pray to Buddha and Amida the way he heard the Christians pray, but it just did not seem to fit at all, because he did not in fact believe in their existence. He tells us that the prayers of most Buddhist priests are more in the nature of incantations.

He began comparing the two religions in a methodical way, studying the Bible; but he nearly went out of his mind during this time of conflict. Among other efforts at finding the light he fasted for a week on top of a mountain. Finally he found what he was seeking. It was 28th May, 1910, the anniversary of his father's death. After going through the usual rites for the dead, he gave himself up to meditation, and finally turned to the Bible. It opened at Luke, chapter 15, and as he read it over many times he came to realize that he was the lost sheep. Suddenly he felt someone calling gently "Come unto me all ye that labour and are heavy laden, and I will give you rest", and he knew it was the voice of Jesus the good shepherd. "In that instant", he writes, "my heart was so filled with gratitude and joy I could scarcely speak . . . and I put my face down on the Book, my eyes overflowing with tears of joy. I seemed to be filled with various emotions: gratitude, joy and conviction of sin. The light of God's Word shone into my very soul. I was filled with the fire of His Holy Spirit. I stood up new-born in the Kingdom of God. I knew I had attained salvation, I had grasped a real faith. I had gained that for which I had sought so long. I danced about, waving my arms for sheer joy, not knowing where I trod."

The next day he hurried to Osaka to call on the pastor of one of the churches he had visited to tell him what had happened. The pastor's first comment was, "You have already been baptized with the Holy Spirit, so you are certainly ready for baptism with water at any time." When it was learned that he was a Buddhist priest, however, and not only head now of his own local temple, but also deeply involved with the head Zen priest in organizing the building of a memorial to the casualties of the Russo-Japanese war, it was obvious he could not be baptized while still engaged in this work. His relatives and temple adherents were naturally very much against such a step. His wife in particular was strongly opposed since he had always lived in a temple and had no qualification for earning a living by any other means—unemployment always being a major problem in Japan. He could not think of anything to say in reply to his wife, so continued as usual every morning and evening reading the sutra, and performing all the prescribed rites; but when these were done, going to his study and reading the Bible, singing hymns and praying in the name of Christ. He says, "It was certainly an inconsistent sort of life. But even under such odd conditions my faith became stronger and stronger, and I was more and more conscious of God's mercy."

At last one evening he was reading his Bible and came to these words: "He that spared not His own Son, but delivered Him up for us all, how shall He not with Him also freely give us all things?" This wonderful truth came home to his heart, and he hurried out to his wife in the kitchen and read her the passage saying, "Look here! The Bible says God has promised to take care of his people. . . . If I had had sufficiently strong faith from the beginning I could have made the change at any time. One who has strong faith does not mind pulling a cart or a rickshaw or even doing rough manual labour. We will leave this place tomorrow, trusting everything to God."

So they left the temple and on 7th November, 1910 he was baptized in the North Side Presbyterian Church, Osaka. The pastor, recognizing in him a great power for the Gospel persuaded him to enter Bible School. His Buddhist friends could not understand him changing his faith, and concluded that he must be getting rich now that he was in contact with foreigners. When they found out he had given all his silk robes to his brother, and was living a very simple life over a Gospel hall, his priest's cotton robes dyed and made over into ordinary garments, they changed their minds, and decided there could not be much in the new way of life after all. It was mainly for this reason that Michihata determined when he graduated to be an independent evangelist. Writing twenty-five years later, after a fruitful time of service both by preaching and writing, he testifies that God has met his material needs during all that time.

Chapter VIII

THE SENSE OF SIN

AS we study the religions of Japan it soon becomes clear that their ideas of sin fall far short of the Biblical conception. In both Chinese and Japanese the same character is used for the word "sin" and to them its essential meaning is the same as our word "crime". Missionaries in both countries have to explain carefully its scriptural meaning of disobedience to a holy God.

The Shinto gods were all good-bad in character. The sun goddess's brother in particular acted in a frankly indecent and outrageous manner, but nevertheless is one of the most popular gods, and receives worship even now. Others are considered the special protectors or patron saints of thieves, and prostitutes, as well as travellers, fishermen and other classes of people. Etsu Sugimoto describes them as "our jolly and helpful Shinto gods", none of whom they feared, and adds "our man-made laws of convention have had more power in moulding the lives of the people, and have left a more lasting stamp on their souls, than have our gods".[1]

The scholars Mabuchi and Motoori, who were largely responsible for the revival of interest in Shinto and nationalism in the seventeenth and eighteenth centuries, insisted that the early Japanese emperors and people "conformed intuitively to the natural principles of righteousness revealed in the universe". Motoori claimed that "moral ideas are implanted by the gods and are of the same nature as instincts. . . . Since the Japanese people are naturally and unerringly upright in their practice, they require no special system of moral instruction."

They argued that the Chinese were therefore inferior to them because the latter *did* concern themselves about morals, and blamed foreign intercourse for any lack there might be in

[1] *Daughter of the Samurai.*

modern Japanese conduct. One of their earliest poets wrote, "Japan is not a land where men need to pray, for it is itself divine". The Japanese in general have never recognized a conflict between good and evil. Human nature, Japanese at least, is naturally good, and it only needs to clean the windows of its soul, so to speak; it is like removing the rust from the blade of a sword, and man's essential goodness will then shine forth again. Dr. Nitobe tells us that the mirror, one of the sacred emblems in Shinto shrines, typifies the human heart "which, when perfectly placid and clear, reflects the very image of the deity". It is a common belief that man has a gentle and a rough soul, and both are good—but suitable for different occasions. As someone has said, the Japanese have "the incapacity to discern, or reluctance to grapple with, the problem of evil". They are not alone in this reluctance of course, it is common to most human philosophies. Strangely enough, although Shinto officially does not recognize sin in man, it does provide an annual purification rite which may just be for the purpose of ceremonial cleansing—but which has a substitutionary aspect strangely reminiscent of the Hebrew scapegoat. Here is the ceremony as described in one of the daily newspapers by Setsuo Uenoda. "The Japanese people will observe on 30th June the ceremony known as *Oharai* or Great Purification, to clear and purify their bodies and souls from sin and defilement. . . . At the Imperial Palace the Emperor and Empress will observe the ceremony at the Shinto sanctuary in the compound of the Palace.

"The ceremony may differ more or less according to the tradition of each shrine. For instance at the shrine in Kamakura the shrine distributes among the people in the city, a few days in advance, paper cut-outs in the shape of human beings, known as *hitokata*. Each family is given as many cut-outs as the number of its members. Each person must write his name, age, sex, etc., on the paper, and then blow his breath over it, symbolizing that his sin and defilement have been transferred to the paper.

"Late in the afternoon of 30th June the cut-outs thus filled out and collected are burned in the compound of the shrine in an impressive ceremony symbolizing the destruction of sin and defilement. Some shrines take the papers to the seashore and cast them into the sea to have them carried away by the tide.

"The *Oharai* is an expression of the Shinto religious faith, as well as a Japanese racial trait of love of cleanliness. The rite is a simplified form of purification by taking a bath. There is no religious significance in bath-taking itself, but psychologically it is an act of purification that washes away not only from their bodies but souls, all the dust, weariness, vexatious thoughts and feelings, and makes them feel almost elevated from the world of sin and defilement."

It seems obvious from this last paragraph that the cleansing is not that sought by a repentant sinner conscious of his responsibility and guilt, but rather a removal of something contracted from outside the individual. It is interesting that Uenoda adds at the conclusion of his article that the rite "had its origin in a Japanese myth" and was practised in the early days of antiquity. The ceremony was not carried out through the centuries of civil war but was "definitely revived in June 1871". One cannot help wondering if this revival was due to the influence of the coming of Protestant missionaries to the country, and a desire of the Japanese to show that they too had a remedy for sin in their culture. This remedy is so easy and cheap, however, that it is not calculated to produce any abhorrence of sin. It is only when we see the tremendous cost of our redemption in the death of Christ that we have a real comprehension of the pollution of sin.

While it is often difficult to know what beliefs are due to Shinto, and what to Buddhist teachings, since the latter has absorbed so much of the former, it does not appear that Buddhism, in spite of its commandments, produced any greater sense of sin among the people. There does not even appear to be general agreement as to what these commandments are. The first five are given as prohibitions against (1) the destruction of life, including animals and insects, (2) stealing, (3) adultery, (4) falsehood, (5) the use of intoxicating drinks. But it seems as if the idea of having ten commandments must have been borrowed, for Michihata lists only three more: (6) covetousness,

(7) anger, (8) scornful speech. He concludes, "then two more of some kind are added so as to make the number up to ten".

Reischauer, however, gives us the following: (6) Eating at forbidden hours, (7) frequenting worldly amusements, (8) using perfumes or ornaments, (9) sleeping on a raised couch, (10) receiving gifts of money.[1] It seems probable therefore that different sects chose their own code of discipline, and few took the keeping of these commandments very seriously.

So it is evident that the Japanese have no final standard of right and wrong in either of their religions. Some things may be right in some circumstances but wrong in others; there are no absolute values.

There is no root word for either "good" or "evil" in their language. People are basically good, but acts in certain circumstances are good or bad. When I first started teaching Bible stories in English at a girls' high school in Japan I thought I was giving a very easy question by asking, "Was Cain a good man or a bad man?" I could not understand why no one would answer it at first in any of the six classes, for the standard of English was high and they studied Hemingway, Carlisle, Huxley and many other English authors in their reading. I have realized since, however, that it was probably because the whole concept behind the question was foreign to them. Although Buddhists use some of the same terms as Christianity, their meaning is often quite different. They do use the terms "good" and "evil", and when Western scholars and philosophers describe the religion and its ethical teaching it appears to have a high standard, and be much the same as Christian ethics. What the Buddhist usually means by "evil" is ignorance, and by "goodness" knowledge. For them evil is an effect, not a cause, the effect produced by ignorance or error. In other words "the wages of ignorance is suffering", rather than "the wages of sin is death".[2] That is why their aim is "enlightenment", to produce scholars rather than saints.

Many thoughtful Japanese have realized their lack of an adequate moral standard, and some have theoretically adopted

[1] *Studies in Japanese Buddhism*, A. K. Reischauer.
[2] Ibid.

the Christian ethical standard, without taking the step of becoming Christians. The Quaker missionary Mr. Gurney Binford tells us of a schoolteacher who once came to visit him, saying he was seeking an effective basis for moral teaching. Mr. Binford asked, "What moral teachings do you have?" The teacher replied, "Oh there are books on ethics which are our guide for moral instruction, but somehow there seems to be something lacking. They do not bring more than conformity to custom."

Again a woman patient in a hospital realizes something is wrong in what she has heard over the radio, and writes to a Japanese newspaper about it.

"Editor:

"A well-known writer, during a family programme broadcast over Japan Broadcasting Corporation network recently, commented, 'They say that I often write novels about the love affairs of married women. But I believe there is nothing so single-minded, pure and beautiful as the romance of a married woman. In the old days the love affairs of married women were regarded as being sinful. From now on, however, I think that it will be all right for married women to indulge in such affairs more freely.'"

Although she does not approve of this, she does not really know why. She calls it "the expression of such careless views", rather than immoral, and fears that if there is no marriage in society people will be the same as animals. In other words people would not be conforming to age-long custom.

The morals taught in Japan up to the time of the war were chiefly concerned with "obligation" *on*, and "duty" *gimu*. Everyone passively incurred "obligation" from the Emperor, parents and teacher, and this involved "duty" to be paid (though it could never be repaid in full) to the Emperor (formerly the feudal lord) known as *chu*, to parents and ancestors *ko*, and to one's work, *nimmu*.[1] These duties are compulsory and universal, and are obligatory irrespective of the worthiness or otherwise

---

[1] For greater detail read *The Chrysanthemum and the Sword.*

of the lord or parents. In reality the moral code of the Japanese
one might almost say is "Might is right". There is a well-known
proverb "The Emperor's army if you win, the rebel army if you
lose". If you captured the Emperor you were "good" or "right".

The Japanese very early in their racial history must, like
many other nations, have lost or rejected the concept of one
supreme and holy God who has given a revelation of Himself
and His will to man, and to whom they will one day have to
give an account of their actions in this life. Because of this, and
since custom, or loyalty to the ruling power, are the only
standards recognized by them, there has developed the
phenomenon which sociologists term the Shame culture, rather
than Guilt culture with which we are so familiar in the West.
Even in the West, however, shame is also experienced, and in
the proportion in which God is ignored or forgotten in the
individual life the Shame mechanism takes over increasing
control. When people are well taught that God has declared
some things are wrong, and others right, they develop a conscience which feels guilt if they do the wrong things, even if no
other person knows about them, and often a real relief is
experienced in confession of the sin. Their self-respect is
damaged when conscious of doing something sinful or mean,
even if it is not known to anyone else. The Japanese idea is
completely different. To them self-respect means only circum-
spection in behaviour. They have the expression "to double
self-respect with self-respect", and its meaning Ruth Benedict
tells us is "to observe extreme caution". They even say, "If
there were no society one would not need to respect oneself".
Another proverb is to the effect that one need not feel shame
when away from home—that is, where you are not known
personally. Unfortunately many of the military forces stationed
in Japan and other countries appear to act on this latter
principle too, so the Japanese find it hard to believe sometimes
that Christian principles mean very much to us in the West.
Indeed it seems that in some ways the Japanese are more
honest than we are, for since they have no absolute standard
and believe it right to follow natural instincts when these
do not conflict with their duty to the Emperor, or with custom,

they can frankly state their motives and actions. We on the other hand, unless we seek constantly the mind of Christ, seem to develop a strange capacity to blind ourselves to the degree in which our conduct fails to conform to our ethical standards.

Shame involves an audience, and the supposed or actual criticism of others. This of course may also be experienced by those brought up in a Guilt or Christian culture, when found doing "the wrong thing" socially, such as wearing inappropriate clothes at important functions and so on. Here there is no sense of guilt, but it can nevertheless be an extremely unpleasant feeling, nor can it be relieved by confession. Since this shame is the only response Japanese have been trained to cultivate one can realize why "face" plays such an important part in oriental life, and why the gospel of forgiveness of sin does not appear to meet their need. In China we were all much aware that stealing, which was so prevalent, was only considered bad if it were discovered and punished. This attitude seems to be coming more prevalent in the West too, unfortunately. We knew a man who was jailed for a few days for drunken driving, and he and his friends were filled with the sense of shame over the imprisonment, while apparently having none for the drunken driving—because they just did not regard that as "sin". In Japan, stealing by individuals, apart from organized gangs, seems rare, and I once asked a college student in one of my Bible classes by what method their children were taught not to steal, since it struck me it must be very effective. She thought a moment and replied: "We are told that our families will get into trouble if we do." This is certainly true, for not only would there be the immediate shame experienced at the trial, but in Japan any experience with the police is likely to be entered on the family record. This important document has to be shown by any member of the family applying for a job, or may be called for when a marriage is arranged and on other important occasions. So this sanction is a very strong one. Of course we use the fear of consequences as a deterrent in the West too, but in Christian circles at least it is also taught that stealing itself is wrong, that God has forbidden it, and that it is doing an injury to the person from whom a thing is stolen. This produces the consciousness that whether anyone discovers the theft or not, it is still wrong, and furthermore is known to God.

Since the Shinto and even most of the Buddhist popular deities are amoral, they obviously are not very troubled by the wrong behaviour of their devotees, and usually only receive prayers for good luck. Michihata says that in non-Christian religions prayer for cleansing from sin is very rare, for "forgiveness" has no meaning. In Japanese the word used for forgiveness means "to allow"—it doesn't matter if you do it—which is really almost the opposite of the idea of God's forgiveness. A Japanese teacher was asked by a friend of ours how you can make clear the difference between the two ideas, and it did not seem that the teacher could see there was any difference. When the more philosophical Buddhist, who recognizes no Being outside himself, engages in prayer he will find he is actually confessing to, or worshipping himself, so Michihata discovered, and obviously the idea of seeking forgiveness would be incongruous and unnecessary.

It would seem then that since there is not only an absence of any absolute moral standard, but even an actual teaching that there is no such thing as sin, the task of bringing the message of the gospel of forgiveness of sins through Christ would be a difficult and a thankless one in Japan. The glorious fact remains, however, that these people were created by God, with immortal souls which are capable of a consciousness of sin, despite many centuries of cultural teaching to the contrary. Amy Carmichael in her letters tells of a proud old grandfather in a family who, after hearing the Gospel, told them that for fifty years he had been a slave to sin, and after three days of struggle he was ready to humble himself before God and man, and confess himself a sinner.

Again, some time ago at the Kobe Mission Hall, run by workers of the Japan Evangelistic Band, a man as he passed down the street just heard the words: "The blood of Jesus Christ, God's Son, cleanses from all sin." Then immediately, for the first time in his life, he became conscious that he was a sinner, and needed cleansing, and he accepted Christ that night.

Early this year I witnessed another striking case of consciousness of sin. I was at the Woman's Union Missionary Society home in Yokohama one Sunday afternoon when a young man came to the Bible Study Class there and told the workers he wanted to accept Christ that day, for every night as he went to bed he thought of all the sins he had committed and could not stand it any longer!

So we rejoice that there are those who do feel consciousness of sin in their lives, and are glad to avail themselves of the offer of salvation. More is needed, however, than to feel the need for forgiveness in a moment of emotion at a Gospel service. There must be a whole-hearted acceptance of the fact that there is only one God, whose standards must be ours, and that seems to be the most difficult thing to obtain in Japan. No doubt the Amida teaching is largely responsible for this, but many make a decision for Christ and want forgiveness of their sin, without having any conception that they must strive to overcome sin in the future and conduct their life according to God's standards. Their reaction often is "We Japanese don't think that way", and they feel that Christianity should be adapted to their customs just as Buddhism was. For example one writer chides Christianity thus for trying to bring in temperance. "It is a great mistake to stop 'sake' drinking in Japan, where the marriage ceremony consists of drinking 'sake', and bottles are offered daily to shrines and ancestors. Since it is traditional, it is no disgrace in Japan to become fully drunk. On many occasions persons who fail to do so are regarded as unsociable. A state of complete intoxication may even be said to be one of the social requirements."

Even if they do recognize a certain standard to be God's will, their own will to keep it is often weak and Kanzo Uchimura said the main reason for the falling off of Christians was that they could not meet the strict moral requirements of Christianity. However, I do know personally of some who have experienced a real conviction of sin, and now, several years later, are serving God and seeking to teach others of Him. One is a

man who had been a boxer, but had had to give this up because
of permanent injuries to his head and eyes, and had taken to
drug peddling. He had always been a misfit, and had often
played truant from school. Now he became in constant fear
of the police, as well as others, and was afraid to walk straight
round a corner for fear of finding some of his enemies lying in
wait for him. He did attend one church service, where he heard
a talk on the Ten Commandments, but he felt that he had
broken them all, so there was no hope for him. Later one of the
missionaries had an advertisement of his services put in the
local newspaper, and someone brought this man along. The
book of Romans was being studied just then, and at first it
only deepened his sense of hopelessness, but finally after much
study he received assurance of salvation. His dishonest practices, idolatry, drinking and smoking were all immediately
given up, and a great urge has come upon him to preach the
Gospel to others.

Lastly I will give the testimony of one of the students at the
Tokyo Theological Seminary with which my husband and I
have been connected most of our time in Japan. "It was in
January 1951 that I was saved, I who was filled with filth and
had nothing to recommend me, was saved by the mercy and
grace of the Lord. For some time before that I heard about
God who created the whole world, who was alive, and who was
interested in man. This was quite surprising information. At
another meeting God made me realize how wrong my way of
living was. It was then that I knew I could not live without my
sins being forgiven by Christ through the Cross. In this way the
Lord cleared the dark clouds from my life, but He had something more for me. From 2 Cor. 5: 14 and 15 He showed me
what He required of me, and how I could fulfil the requirements. Through these verses I knew that the Lord was calling
me to live for the One who had died in my stead, and that He
was calling me into the ministry of His Son."

Chapter IX

THE FEAR OF DEATH

THE fear of death, or of what may happen to them after death, is responsible for many people accepting Christ as their Saviour in the West. Not long ago in a survey among the students of a well-known Bible School a very high proportion admitted that this was the primary reason for their becoming Christians. Among the Lisu tribespeople of western China, with whom I lived for some months, the greatest appeal in the Gospel was the news of the Resurrection, and the certainty of a life after death. One of their evangelists told how when a little boy, someone in his family had died and he had been filled with terror for years, wondering what happened after death. Some of his people were even known to weep themselves blind over the loss of a child. Missionaries in other countries, too, such as the Philippines, have told how the good news of life after death has been received with joy, and the exclamation "This is what we have been waiting for".

It seems the peculiarity of Japan, however, according to many writers, that the people are not even interested in this subject. Someone has said they are "optimistic in this life, and indifferent to the next world". Ruth Benedict writes "The Japanese have always been uninterested in fantasies of a world of the hereafter. Their mythology tells of gods, but not of the life of the dead. They have even rejected Buddhist ideas of differential rewards and punishments after death."[1] When Amy Carmichael was a missionary in Japan she once sought to stir the people to concern by asking "Are you ready for the next life?" The answer she received was: "We are not ready for this life. How then can we be ready for the next?" A Chinese evangelist who visited Japan recently said he heard a Japanese pastor say the Japanese are not interested in going to

[1] *The Chrysanthemum and the Sword.*

heaven because their ancestors are not there. After Etsu Sugimoto adopted the Christian faith she sometimes took her mother to church with her, but although the latter believed the Christian teaching she heard to be true, she said she could not become a Christian because it would not be right for her to go to a better place than that of her dead husband.

It is easy to see how this attitude had developed when we remember the early Shinto teaching that all Japanese become *kami* and that their spirits are still around in the land of the living. During wartime, Shinto taught that the soul of a slain soldier would instantly be transported to the sanctuary of the Shrine for the war dead in Tokyo and would become a tutelary deity. The Emperor Meiji once wrote a poem with the same thought: "The souls of heroes whose bones whiten in foreign lands have even now returned to the capital." Soldiers bidding one another farewell before going off to battle would say "Meet you at Yasukuni", meaning their souls would meet at the Shrine in the homeland.

Their cult of shame (rather than guilt), an intense chagrin at a social *faux pas*, obviously has no place for a future punishment of these mistakes in an after life. Buddha had taught that there were some Great Indeterminates, one of which we have mentioned already—whether there were gods or not. Others were whether the world in its real substance is eternal or not, whether the soul is the same as the body or different from it, whether a man exists in any way after death. Since these were indeterminates it was a waste of time for man to consider them. Many modern Buddhist scholars agree with this view which, since no amount of meditating on the part of man can provide the answer, would be a very sensible one, were it not that God has given us a revelation about these things in the Christian Scripture. Buddha in his wisdom could not escape the feeling that it *did* matter whether one's deeds were good or bad, however, and he developed the doctrine of Karma, which to us and the common peoples of India has been known as the concept of transmigration of the soul. Since Buddha did not believe in the soul it is difficult to know what he did mean by this doctrine. It seems to be a kind of impersonified will to do good or bad which continues in another living being after one's death, since all are "bound to the wheel of life" until their enlightenment.

Obviously not many people could be satisfied with such an abstruse concept. India was already familiar with the idea of heaven and hell, and Northern Buddhism developed this and other ideas more understandable to the common man. By the time it reached China it had many elaborate descriptions of hell, one especially obnoxious part being reserved for women. We found in China that the women particularly seemed greatly concerned to accumulate merit in this life by means of vegetarianism, etc.

In Japan, however, this idea did not find acceptance at all, probably due to the already existing Shinto concept that they were all descendants of the gods, and all teaching on hell was dropped except as tales to children. Etsu Sugimoto speaking of Buddhism says, "as a rule this is not a religion of fear, although the evil spirits of the hells as pictured in ancient Buddhist books are fearful indeed, but even they allow two days each year to climb to a higher plane. Thus to a Japanese even the sad and puzzling path of transmigration leads at last to a final hope. Buddhism in its ages-long journey to Japan seems to have dropped many of its elements of terror or else they were lost in the goodly company of our jolly and helpful Shinto gods. Not one of these do we dread, for in Shinto even death is only a floating cloud through which we pass on our journey to the sunshine of Nature's eternal life."[1]

Perhaps her extensive contact with the West, or the scholarly background of her samurai home made Etsu Sugimoto aware of the idea of transmigration. Other authorities state that most ordinary Japanese have no knowledge of this theory, or at any rate do not think of applying it to themselves, for as soon as their relatives die they are called "buddha" and their names are put in the *butsudan*—Buddha shelf—of their home. Japan is I understand the only Buddhist country which uses this term.

With the comforting assurance that one will become "kami" or "buddha" at death, and will remain in the environs of

[1] *Daughter of the Samurai.*

Japan to guard and protect one's descendants, it is not surprising if the average Japanese does not show much interest in other people's views of the after life. Furthermore the great frequency of suicides (in 1954, the latest statistics available, Japan once again had the world's record) seems to confirm the idea that the Japanese do not have much fear of death. In the story of the priest Michihata, we learned that certain Buddhist writings actually recommended suicide, and Dr. Nitobe tells us that Bushido got its disdain of life and friendliness with death from Buddhism. In fact the committing of *hara-kiri* as a means of maintaining one's honour went to extraordinary lengths. "The glorification of *seppuku* (more polite form of *hara-kiri*) offered naturally enough, no small temptation to its unwarranted committal. For causes entirely incompatible with reason, or for reasons entirely undeserving of death, hot-headed youths rushed into it as insects fly into fire."[1]

Since the introduction of a criminal code much of the purpose of *hara-kiri* has of course disappeared, and one rarely hears of its performance now. Ordinary suicides, however, occur every day, drowning, jumping off heights such as bridges or department store roofs, or the use of gas or sleeping pills being the favoured modern methods. Often a couple in love, knowing their families would not agree to their marriage, commit suicide with the idea of being together in the next life.

Suicide to help relatives seems another favourite theme. Not long ago in our newspaper under the caption "Kin commit suicide to meet Papa's debts" we read of the wife and two daughters of a business man in financial difficulties whose bodies were found in a gas-filled room. In a note addressed to her husband, which enclosed the insurance policies for the three, the wife had written, "In two years you can obtain the insurance money, even in deaths by suicide. Please use it to recover your business".

Again a newspaper editorial commenting on a new car liability insurance law, recalled that when several years ago the city of Sendai set compulsory indemnities for anyone struck by its streetcars, there were so many attempted suicides (so

[1] *Bushido.*

that relatives would get the money), that the transportation system had to be saved from financial ruin by a new city ordinance against would-be suicides.

A missionary we knew had an unpleasant shock, after leading a girl with tuberculosis to the Lord, to find when he went to visit her a second time that she had committed suicide. She had left a note saying how happy she was that she could now go to be with Christ, and evidently felt this was a good way of relieving her family of the trouble of caring for her.

Probably the majority of modern suicides in Japan are for the same reason as in other countries—an inability to cope with the difficulties of life; but a newspaper article on the subject points out that whereas in Denmark and Austria (the countries with the next highest rates to Japan) those committing suicide are usually the aged, in Japan they are mostly young people, especially women. Older children in Japan will occasionally commit suicide for not passing appropriate examinations, especially entrance to a university. A high school girl drank poison in the science laboratory recently because "she could not understand why she was alive." The most frequent in Japan, however, are the suicides of mothers with young children and the newspaper states this is not mainly from economic causes but from painful human relations, either with the husband or the mother-in-law. As the children are usually regarded as the possession of the whole family, rather than of their own mother and father, perhaps the mothers hope in this way to obtain possession of their children in the next life, just as the suicide lovers hope to continue to be together. Or perhaps it may be a revengeful desire to deprive the mother-in-law of the children.

Then comforting views of the after life in no way help to hasten men into the kingdom of God; but there is one aspect of the fear of death which as we shall see is the greatest hindrance to Japanese people becoming Christians.

In spite of claims to the contrary it appears that in the early history of Shinto death was feared, and when a person died the family abandoned their hut to the corpse, and moved elsewhere. The most primitive Shinto idea of pollution was associated with death, and not until Buddhism was introduced did

the Emperor stop moving his capital at the death of his pre-
decessor. The Buddhists as we have seen transformed and
softened the idea of death in the family, besides which they
took over the responsibility for funerals. In fact, after the
Christian persecution of the Tokugawa Era everyone had to be
registered by law at a Buddhist temple, and the priests had to
examine every corpse for any outward symbol of the Christian
religion.

It is probably partly due to this fact that the law-abiding
Japanese people still feel they must be buried in the Buddhist
manner, and partly no doubt to definite Buddhist teaching to
that effect. While the average Buddhist priest seems very
tolerant of, or even uninterested in, the beliefs of his adherents,
he is interested in being kept alive and able to maintain his
temple. Like Roman Catholics, the Buddhist priests were
shrewd enough to see that through death they could be sure of
an unfailing income. They therefore managed to make it clear
that though everyone could become "kami" or "buddha", the
appropriate ceremonies and masses for the dead were necessary
to ensure the comfort of the spirits, and relatives who failed to
supply these should naturally be considered inhuman in the
extreme. One of our missionaries had the sad experience of
seeing a boy who had attended a Bible class taken by the
police, because he stole some trivial thing in order to buy a
lantern for his dead mother at the Obon Festival. Olga
Abrahams tells of their servant-maid who accepted the Lord,
but was told by her friends that she was embracing a foreign
religion unsuitable to a loyal Japanese subject. Then she had a
dream in which her dead father appeared to her, begging
that, in token of her loyalty and affection, she would at least
offer him flowers if she did not give him food. With the great
Obon Festival of the Dead near at hand she felt she must
take part in the customary rites of ancestral worship. Hence we
find that though a number of individuals are glad to accept
Christ as Saviour, they are bound by fear when it comes to
destroying the family god shelves or refusing a Buddhist
funeral for a relative. Some have even been known to revert to
Buddhism in old age, after years of at least nominal Christianity.

This is not the only aspect of the problem, however; there is another of very practical importance. I once heard a missionary at the end of his first term of service declare, "The best way to begin evangelistic work in an area is to buy a burial ground!", and he was not being facetious. Japan is a small and over-populated country, and every bit of land is valuable. In some districts the only legal burial place is in the Buddhist ground.

So we see by what ingenious devices the Mighty One has sought to entangle his captives, and also deaden their God-given instinct of fear of death so that they do not respond to the usual stimulus of the warning to "flee from the wrath to come". The Bible suggests that most of those who are in bondage to Satan do fear death, however, and my husband made enquiries among some of his students at the Seminary, and other University Bible classes, asking if they thought the average Japanese was not afraid of death. All said they did fear death. Some who had had experience of the army said that men were prepared to lead suicide bayonet charges because they were liable to be shot from behind if they did not, and one might therefore just as well die in glory as in disgrace. In other circumstances, too, it is often only that their fear of man and public opinion is even greater than their fear of death. Even though their false religions have sought diligently to blind them, at the moment of death it seems that many do experience fear, as medical missionaries and others have found. Some of those engaged in rescue work before the war had a small hospital for the girls who were too diseased to be of any further value to their masters, and one of them has told me of the very obvious difference between those who had accepted Christ and those who had not, when the time of their death approached. One girl who had been rescued soon after she had been sold by her father, became a nurse to the sick ones after her conversion. She would sometimes plead with them till two or three o'clock in the morning, afraid that they might have the horrible experience of dying without Christ during the night.

Michihata gives us further light on this question as to whether the Japanese are really impervious to the fear of death. Whatever their culture may teach it seems that at the moment of death it does not bring them much comfort. This is brought out in his description of his first Christian funeral during his time in Bible School. "The formal part of the ceremony was soon ended and the lid of the coffin removed so that the relatives and friends might bid a last farewell. I moved forward . . . then as I saw the face of the man a sudden wave of emotion swept over me. It did not look like one who had passed through the gates of death. He looked like one lying there in peaceful sleep. There was not a trace of suffering visible anywhere, he even seemed to be smiling!

"While in the temple I had conducted funerals without number . . . at first I had a sort of morbid curiosity in regard to the dead . . . but in the end I came to loathe these services so deeply that the very mention of a funeral made me shudder. For some centuries now all Buddhist priests have been accustomed to open the lid of the coffin at the time of the funeral, and perform the ceremony of bestowing the tonsure on the deceased. Then they repeat the masses for the dead which include the words 'Leaving this world of change where true thankfulness and affection never come, pass on to the realm of peace where true love and gratitude ever abide'. This is repeated three times, followed by the invocation to Amida. The whole ceremony only takes about ten minutes, but during that time the priest must look almost continuously at the face of the corpse. Usually the head has been shaved roughly, the body wrapped in a single garment, the knees are drawn up under the chin and the face has an expression like that of a person in a sleep filled with fear, and without hope. It is a sight one does not care to look upon a second time. This is why I came to have such a dread of it all. . . . When I looked at the face of Mr. Watanabe that day, however, it was entirely different from anything of the kind I had ever seen before. The peace and quiet of his whole countenance stirred my soul to its very depths . . . and with it came wonder at the power of God who could make such a marvellous man out of an ordinary human being."

In spite of Shinto teaching it appears that some, especially the elderly, do have a little feeling of insecurity about the future, and the Buddhists do not miss the opportunity to help those adherents who have the money to pay for it.

Fear of death, however, and even a Buddhist funeral, have been the means of bringing some to Christ. Cremation is now obligatory in Japan, and it is the gruesome custom for the next of kin to have to pick the bones out of the ashes with chopsticks. Buddhist priests will only attend this last ceremony if they are well paid, and the fact that an Anglican missionary attended this when one of his Christians died, and refused any payment, was the means of the entire remaining family becoming Christians. Miss Anna Gulick told me she had assisted one of her Christian girls in this unpleasant task when her remaining parent had died. This girl said afterwards what a strengthening this had been to her faith, and that she had never loved the missionary so much as since she had done this great kindness.

While we were visiting the home of a Chinese couple in Tokyo I heard another very moving story of a man who through fear of death finally found Christ. The occasion was the celebration of the birth of a boy, after having three daughters. About twenty Chinese friends were there as well as two missionary couples and the local Japanese pastor and his wife. After the host and hostess had given their testimonies of God's goodness to them the Japanese pastor got up and said (in English) that although he had not understood a word of their Chinese he had felt God's blessing there and would like to give his own testimony. He had been born in Nagano prefecture, twenty-two miles from its capital city, and was the seventh child in the family. His father was Shinto in belief, his mother Buddhist, and his favourite eldest brother Confucian. When he was sixteen this brother had called him one day and told him the most important thing in life was peace of heart. Soon after this the brother died following a very short illness. This was a great shock, and he began to study religion to find out where his brother was, but was soon disgusted with Shinto superstition. In Buddhism he could find nothing clear, nothing definite, nothing which gave any hope.

The next year two sisters died, then his father, then mother and remaining brothers, till there was only himself and an older sister who was sick from pleurisy and rheumatism. He himself was due to enter the army when he was twenty-one, but was told he was too sickly and was sent home.

Then on 12th March, 1903, exactly fifty-three years ago that day, he had visited a store in a village five miles from his home. There he saw a man reading a book very intently, and he asked what it was. When told it was a Bible he asked what that was, and heard that it was a book given us by God who created the world, the one true living God. This was what he had been looking for! He stayed for two hours asking questions, and finally, knocking his head on the floor three times, begged to borrow the Bible. The man said he was a Christian and must read it himself, but he lent him some of the Gospels. He took these home and read them straight through to his sister, and as he read of the Crucifixion and Resurrection he believed. Next morning as he went outside everything, mountains, trees, rice fields, all seemed new—the work of God. Suddenly he noticed the chickens and called them to him and said, "Do you know there is a living true God?" When he went into his sister's room he found her believing in God and healed in body. She said they must get a Bible of their own. So he walked into Nagano city, twenty-two miles away, but could find no Bible. Then he walked to Tokyo, over 100 miles, for there was no railway then, but could not find a Bible. He had never heard of a church, so only looked in ordinary book stores. He went home, saved up some more money and did the three-day walk to Tokyo again, still without result. After making a third visit he found a copy of the Bible in a second-hand store and went home rejoicing. He began witnessing for Christ, and several years later went to the United States for training in the ministry. He is now very strong and healthy looking and appeared at least fifteen years younger than his seventy-five years of age.

Perhaps we can end this chapter with the brief stories of two Japanese who really did not fear death when their time came. One is told by Miss Dorothy Hoare who was a missionary of the Japan Evangelistic Band. One of their Christian women had a daughter of fifteen who was very sick. "But she was so happy as she was dying that her very face shone, although she had had a long, trying illness." After she stopped breathing the younger children left her bedside, but her father and mother still sat praying. Suddenly she opened her eyes and in an energetic voice said, "I have come back again." Her mother said, "God has given you back to us." Then the girl said, "I saw the Lord Jesus standing and smiling." Her mother asked, "Didn't He take your hand?" She answered, "No, I didn't get as far as that." Then while her parents continued praying she went to be with the Lord.

The other story is told by Miss Irene Webster-Smith, whom God used to win to the Lord some of the war criminals in Sugamo Prison, before their execution. One day an American army officer came up to her and said, "I am a medical officer, and I want you to know that I was with two of your friends this morning when they paid the death penalty. After midnight struck these men came out of the inner prison, their Testaments clasped in their manacled hands, singing *Nearer my God to Thee*. Back in their cells the other prisoners were singing *God be with you till we meet again*. These two men knelt down there on the drop floor and with praise and thanksgiving, their faces radiant, commended themselves to God. Because of what I saw there in the early hours of this morning I came to find you, as I wanted to be able to meet my Maker as these men met theirs." So she had the joy of leading this young man to Christ too.

It is traditional for most Japanese to write a poem on the last day of their lives, if they know death is certain. One of these two, a general, wrote, "The call for the execution is as sweet as the voice of angels, Now I start on the journey to the kingdom of God." He also wrote Miss Webster-Smith a letter which said in part, "Thank you very much for your guidance to lead me to Jesus Christ. . . . Today I am going back to the Eternal Life under the feet of God. It is a joy which exceeds all. I am so grateful that I can go to Him in such peace and as a child of God. We sang these hymns (*What a Friend we have in Jesus*; *What can wash away my stain?*; *Face to face with Christ my Saviour*, etc.) this morning from the bottom of our hearts until tears ran down. How happy we are to go back to Jesus, saved by His graceful hand. . . . I cannot thank you too strongly for the great love of Jesus Christ. I pray you would work harder for Jesus Christ and also take great care of your body. May the mercy of Jesus Christ abide with you. Amen. 9 p.m. 11th February. (Signed) Hideyoshi Ishizaki."

Chapter X

JAPANESE LANGUAGE—THE ART OF CONCEALING THOUGHT

IN spite of much research the origin of the Japanese language remains a mystery, for it appears to show no kinship with any of the main groups classified by modern philology. Various foreigners have attempted to establish a relationship, some to Korean, and some to the Oceanic Island group; but most Japanese scholars consider these men's knowledge of Japanese was too limited for their data to form convincing proof. Although some Japanese have had a real desire to find the solution to this problem, the strong nationalist element in pre-war years discouraged research along this line, since the apparently unique character of the language gave weight to the theory that they were directly descended from the gods. For the same reason the study of anthropology was also discouraged, and history was rewritten with the purpose of establishing the divinity of the race. Xavier after a little time in the country claimed that the language was invented by the devil, and many missionaries since have felt inclined to agree with him as they have struggled to master it!

Whatever its origin, it would be true to say that the Japanese language is one of the worst media imaginable for the presentation of the Gospel, or for that matter any exact science. When modern education began at the Meiji Restoration, classes were taught in English or German in the universities, and there was even talk of adopting English as the national language, so the following newspaper editorial informs us: "Some ninety years ago . . . the suggestion was seriously considered that the Japanese language should be abolished in favour of English. The idea is not so incredible as it may sound. What may seem surprising is that back in those days people were that far-sighted in estimating the language barrier.

"It is no less true today that the Japanese are peculiarly handicapped in international communication. No matter how much we may want to join . . . the international community, our language is a strong isolating factor. There is no other language like it. The most bilingual of us know that shifting from Japanese into English is like moving from one world to another.

"Indeed it does seem that abolishing our traditional tongue would be a logical move. But practically of course there is as much chance of accomplishing that as there is of changing human nature. Not to mention the fact that it would be cultural suicide."

From early times the Japanese seem to have been aware of the deficiencies of their language, judging by the vast number of borrowings there have been from other languages, especially Chinese during the fifth to the ninth centuries, and English in the last. There are said to be over 5,000 English words adopted into the language now, and there are also some German and Portuguese. The Japanese had no written language of their own, so borrowed the Chinese ideographs around the fifth or sixth century. Sometimes the Chinese character was just used as a mere sound or phonogram, sometimes it was used to express the same idea as the Chinese symbol; though it might then be given the Japanese pronunciation for that idea, or it might retain the Chinese sound. In early days this usually followed the south China dialect; but later there was more contact with the northern Chinese and their pronunciation was also adopted, so that now one symbol or character may have as many as five or six completely different pronunciations.

Only about 1,800 of these Chinese characters are now in common use, and they are used for nouns, and also the roots of verbs and adjectives. There are also two other forms of Japanese writing, a kind of syllabic script, each consisting of fifty-one symbols. One of these is used for expressing verb endings and parts of adjectives as well as all prepositions, the other is used for writing foreign words (other than Chinese) which have been adopted into the language. All Japanese sentences could be written in this much simpler script; but since many words have the same sound it is easier to understand quickly if the Chinese characters are used. One famous example of many words with the same sound is the sentence *Gozen ga gozen ni gozen o gozen meshiagatte gozensoku ga gozenkaishita.* (The honourable master ate five bowls of the honourable rice in the morning and was cured of asthma.)

Japanese grammar has some very long and complicated auxiliary constructions, especially the verb endings which denote tense; voice; negation; causation; potential and tentative ideas; and degrees of politeness. The very length of the words is quite a handicap to the foreigner trying to learn it. A Chinese friend in Tokyo once remarked that whereas to say "good morning", or "thank you", takes two syllables in Chinese it takes nine and eleven respectively in Japanese. Another Chinese lady added in one of their beautifully neat four character phrases, "Their words are many, but the meaning is small." A Japanese, Kanzo Uchimura, has this to say about it: "Our language—what an unwieldy thing it is! And the wholesale introduction of Chinese characters was necessary before we could express our own thoughts."

A further serious complication for the Westerner trying to learn it is that Japanese is a "respect" language, made to express grades of social distinction very exactly. For instance I have been told there are ten different words for the personal pronoun "I"—one of them used only by the Emperor when referring to himself. Both the root and the ending of a verb may change according to whether one is using the honorific, the humble, the polite or plain style of speech if speaking; in writing, other forms again may be required.

A missionary, who is now doing some translating for the Japan Sunday School Union, discovered there was a choice to be made from nine styles of Japanese, each differentiated by the types of words used and the grammatical endings and particles. Women's language differs from men's and is not found in text books or descriptive writing. This has to be learnt at home, and one of our teachers told us that her grandmother had been teaching her how to speak until the age of twelve. It is the women who are said to have been responsible for all this social differentiation during the Tokugawa era, and even today they are still very proud of all their flowery phrases which mark them as being well-bred. This "respect" element in the language makes it more difficult for a foreigner to learn it in conversation with people. Except for one or two set honorific phrases, in China one could answer a question by using exactly the same words in a positive or negative order. In Japanese one often has to use an entirely different verb, and remember to drop off the honorific ("go" or "o") in front of the noun, if it is anything connected with oneself.

Through the years a good number of missionaries are said to have returned home because of an inability to get the language. However, it is not the mere technical difficulty of learning the language which is the only trouble. The effect of one's stumbling efforts on the Japanese is also a real handicap. One of Xavier's companions, Fernandez, did attempt to learn the language but according to one writer "used his Japanese more to the amusement of his hearers than their conversion". However, that was before the ladies got to work complicating the language socially and now the foreigners' efforts seem to produce more pain than amusement. While we were in our first few months of language study the Japanese leader of one church group came to give us an orientation lecture and among other things he said, "If you cannot speak very nicely in Japanese, always use an interpreter." This was not very encouraging for us, since Mission policy did not provide for the use of interpreters. In China, of course, there would have been few qualified interpreters available except in the coastal provinces where we had little work. Usually our stumbling efforts to speak the language there were greeted with encouragement and pleasure by the Chinese; but in Japan it seems to cause the people real discomfort and pain to have their language misused. For teaching in the Seminary for example, my husband and others at first wanted to try to get their lectures into Japanese but were dissuaded from making the attempt by being told that lecturing required a special type of language. One or two who did try it had an almost rude response from the students. The principal said that even Nisei (Japanese born in the United States and

Canada) who had been through a Japanese university and so could understand and converse freely in Japanese, "of course would not attempt public speaking". We have heard of Nisei missionaries who after five years out here have only helped a little in children's meetings, and who would not *begin* any public ministry until they had reached the point in the Language Study Course where most Westerners usually stop studying. We can understand something of the reason behind this when we read the following letter which appeared in a newspaper some time ago:

"Editor:
"What is unpleasant to hear on the radio is having a foreigner or a Nisei-like Japanese appear as master of cere-monies. I doubt the common sense of those who draw up such programmes and who are satisfied to sell such impure Japanese.
"Although commercial broadcasting is a private enterprise, I think radio has the duty, from a social and ethical standpoint, of spreading correct, standard Japanese.
"Let's drive affected Japanese-imitating Nisei from the air. Innocent children who are unaware of the kind of language being used readily imitate such speech. Just listening to it gives the impression that Japan is a colony."

The principal of the Seminary told us that he only knew of three missionaries who could speak Japanese acceptably in public, and two of these were children of former Japan mission-aries. We heard of one missionary who had been out here many years who went to take a week of meetings in another place and after the first night was asked to speak through an interpreter. My husband followed another man who had been taking some meetings at a certain place. This man had also been out nearly twenty years and most foreigners consider him very fluent. The students there, however, were surprised when they heard how long he had been out. "It would have been very good if he had been out here two years," they said, "but for twenty years—no, it was poor Japanese."
We once asked a fine Christian girl who does quite a lot of

interpreting what she thought was the best thing for a foreigner to do. She considered a moment and then said she thought interpreted messages were better unless the missionaries' Japanese language was very good. She had listened to some and had no idea of their meaning at times; although they might sound fairly fluent and have a wide vocabulary, if they left out some of the little particles then the Japanese had no idea of the subject and object, and could not get the sense.

One of the reasons for the desire for interpreted messages may be that there are always some who want to improve their English, and it is interesting that women at least do not always agree with the foregoing view. I heard of a Swedish lady who was told by the Japanese pastor that she must use an interpreter so that the message would be in language worthy of the Gospel. But the women of the church said they found her stumbling Japanese easier to understand. While we were doing language study we were up in a small mountain resort where the little Japanese church was without a pastor for some months. Our teachers who attended this church suggested that some of our men should preach there, so David Hayman and my husband prepared some simple messages with their help. Having already heard the other opinion expressed I asked one of the teachers afterwards if it would not be better for the messages to be interpreted, but she replied that this simple language could "enter the heart", and she herself had been blessed from it. We realized what a welcome change this must have been when a new pastor finally came to the church, straight from Seminary. When we asked what his first sermon had been about the teacher told us it was on "negative nihilism and positive nihilism"—this to a little mountain church where most of the small audience consisted of women! Another student from that same Seminary had gone to a church in Hokkaido with which we had co-operated and his first sermon in the little fishing town was on the three authors of Isaiah!

It is constantly impressed on the Japanese in their upbringing that they must appear learned, in fact it seems to be a compliment to a teacher to tell him you do not understand. In a discussion in one of his Bible classes at the Peers school a student asked my husband if it was hypocrisy to tell a teacher you failed to understand what he had taught when you really did—with the idea of making him feel pleased! A British writer also tells that when he began teaching in a Japanese university he was told to deal with some things which would be above the students' heads. It was salutary for them to find there were things they did not understand, and it would be good for his prestige. For the same reason you find all kinds of most difficult English books on the high school and university curricula, the idea being that if anyone is known to teach such a difficult book he will be much respected—whether his students understand him or not.

This idea probably had its root in Bushido, or even further back in Buddhism, for Dr. Nitobe tells us of a saying, "Only a pomegranate is he who when he gapes his mouth, displays the contents of his heart." He continues, "To give in so many articulate words one's inmost thoughts and feelings—notably the religious—is taken among us as a sign that they are neither very profound nor very sincere. It is truly jarring to the Japanese ears to hear the most sacred words, the most secret heart experiences, thrown out in promiscuous audiences. Speech is very often with us 'the art of concealing thought'."[1]

The Japanese bishop quoted earlier also tells how he warned a group of vising American church dignitaries that the Japanese people would not say all they felt, or even all they should say. "They would be inclined to say half of what they have in mind, and expect him to guess the other half. If he failed in this he would be in danger of being considered stupid. This somewhat fundamental difference in psychology may be illustrated by saying that Westerners speak in straight lines while Japanese speak in curves. Straight lines are obvious, curves may be complicated."[2]

So the Japanese pastor and evangelist is faced with a hard choice, and has to be prepared to "make himself of no reputation" if he is going to make the Gospel plain for all to understand. Yet the situation is not as simple as that. It is not only his own reputation which is at stake—it appears to be that of the

[1] *Bushido.*   [2] *Japan Speaks for Herself.*

Gospel too, because of this insidious impression left by the teaching of Buddhism which implies that anything simple and easily understood is not worth much. However, they should be able to see by now, from the growth of some of the new sects, that people do need something they can understand. Even the sophisticated scholar in the novel *Kokoro* says, "I believe that commonplace ideas passionately expressed are more effective in real life than the original inventions of a detached intellect. It is the heat of the blood which impresses us; for, in addition to the words which reverberate in the air, the emotion by its intensity pierces the soul."

If that is true, even in Japan, of "commonplace ideas", how much more should the simple, yet life-giving Gospel be proclaimed passionately and with an intensity which pierces the soul, instead of being given as a detached and elaborate lecture —a stone instead of bread—to the congregations of Japanese churches. We in our limited experience have only known four or five Japanese pastors who really "get through" to their audience. The coming of Billy Graham to Japan for his brief conference with the pastors was, I believe, a real help to them, for his world-wide reputation, and success in other Asian countries, made them willing to listen to him when they would not to a mere local missionary. When it comes to the Gospel, the revelation of God to man, how can we "half" say it? The Japanese may be trained so that they can guess the unseen things of ordinary life or poetry, but they cannot guess the revelation of God. His thoughts are higher than our thoughts. Even Buddha himself realized we cannot discover anything about God by our own thoughts. So there are times when the missionary and the pastor need to speak plainly and simply and fully.

Even with the desire to do so, however, this is not an easy thing to accomplish in Japanese. In one of his homiletics classes at the Seminary my husband said something to the effect that the preaching of the Gospel must be "clear and definite". Silence followed while the interpreter frowned a little anxiously. My husband repeated the sentence, and still there was silence. Finally the interpreter said, "We all know what you mean in

English, but it is hard to put that into Japanese." Of course a foreigner can find both the words "clear", and "definite" in an English-Japanese dictionary, and could choose one from the number of Japanese equivalents and put them in the appropriate place in a sentence. But the impression made on a Japanese listener would usually not be nearly so clear as the foreigner imagined. Most words have several meanings—that is their beauty. Clearness and definiteness are not characteristics which are favoured, except to denote social inequalities. One Christian leader has told us that it is extremely difficult to express in Japanese the differences between orthodox and Barthian or even liberal theology. My husband was helping to get a statement of faith in Japanese for a certain organization recently, and there they experienced the same difficulty. Some beliefs had to be expressed both positively and negatively to try to get the idea across. Some friends of ours who train young church people in evangelistic team work thought they would have some texts and slogans around the walls of the work room where the students prepared flannelgraph and other material. One was "No child is too young to come to Jesus". They asked some of the Japanese—most of whom were at university and one a seminary student—to translate this. After much discussion they decided it could not be put into Japanese which would not be misleading, and might even sound as if children could not come to Jesus. Another missionary writing to her friends asking for prayer in language study said, "If you had attended a recent teachers' meeting at the College you would understand what we are up against. The main portion of the three-hour meeting was spent in discussion (by the Japanese teachers, not the foreigners) as to just which Japanese words were correct in certain places in the College Handbook. Even the Japanese have trouble with the language."

Frank Gibney has called it "an oblique, devious, allusive language"[1] and because of this it seems that for really getting the meaning across interpretation is best for teaching, and even sometimes for preaching. One of the students at the Seminary once remarked that a missionary teacher can say in ten minutes

[1] *Five Gentlemen of Japan.*

what a Japanese takes an hour to say. For soul winning and making real friends, however, a good knowledge of Japanese is essential. In the cities at least, the missionary finds constant discouragement in using the language, especially if he is thin-skinned, but also because so many Japanese know English, and even if one asks a question in Japanese the answer will often be given in English. On the other hand he will meet with criticism if he does not use Japanese. Uchimura, after criticizing Japanese for its unwieldiness, later has even stronger criticism of missionaries for their lack of it. Writing in 1916 he says, "There are English and American mission-aries who have been twenty, thirty and even fifty years in Japan who cannot speak respectable Japanese. The reading capacity of missionaries is next to nothing. I know no one who can read ordinary Japanese literature in the original. No wonder they cannot understand us, and still remain utter strangers to us. The fact that they despise our language is a sure evidence that they have no true love for our souls."

The missionary therefore must just develop a thicker skin and do his best, knowing that he will be criticized either way, for few people can reach the stage of speaking "very nicely" without first speaking rather badly for a long period. In spite of the clumsiness of the foreigner, and the difficulty even the Japanese have with their own language, and in spite of all the training in appreciation of the complicated, there are those who have heard the Gospel in its simplest terms and have not been repelled, but have received it into their hearts. One of the most convincing cases I have heard of is the woman mentioned in chapter four whose answer to the Japanese evangelist's question as to whether she were a Japanese or not was "I am a Christian". At the time of her conversion she was an English teacher in Yokohama and, I believe, had been a nominal Christian for some time. A big evangelistic service had been planned in Yokohama, primarily for the American forces, but it was open to the public, and some of her students had asked permission to go in order to hear some English. At the end of the service an appeal was made and some of the girls expressed a desire to go forward. The teacher felt responsible for them, so decided she had better go along with them. The preacher knowing no Japanese was rather at a loss how to deal with these enquirers, and just kept repeating in English "Jesus died for you". As this lady stood there with her students, suddenly the truth of these simple words burst into her soul; and, with tears in her eyes but joy in her heart, she accepted the Saviour revealed to her by those simple words. She had heard many Christian sermons before, but the truth had never been clearly revealed. Now, for the first time, she was given a foretaste of the life which is eternal.

Chapter XI

A BLUNTED SWORD

THE sword has always been the most highly honoured
weapon in Japan, and their swordsmiths are said to have
been the best in the world. One of them, Kokaji Munechika,
who lived in the eleventh century, regarded his work as sacred,
and whenever he finished a sword he cleaned his place of work
and offered sacrifices to the forge, thus giving rise to a special
festival for metal workers. In a land where the sword is so
highly thought of it seems particularly tragic therefore that
until now the Sword of the Spirit, which is the Word of God,
should in Japan be so blunt a model of that two-edged blade
intended by its Maker to penetrate the depths of the hearts
and minds of men.

"The entrance of Thy words giveth light", sang the psalmist,
probably speaking from personal experience as well as by
inspiration of the Spirit. For this reason it has always been the
aim of Protestant missionaries to produce the Bible as soon as
possible in the native language of their converts: Japan was no
exception. In 1872 at the first missionary conference ever to be
held there, a committee was formed to undertake the translation
of the entire Bible; and Dr. J. C. Hepburn, a Presbyterian
missionary, was appointed head of this committee. He was
one of the very earliest missionaries and had landed in Japan
on 18th October, 1859. Although a medical doctor, Hepburn
was a gifted linguist, and after two years in the country, he
attempted the first translation of Matthew's Gospel. Official
prejudice against and fear of Christianity, were still so great,
however, that his teacher refused to help in this and left him.

According to Mitsuzo Goto, a professor at the Japan Christian Theological Seminary,[1] in an article in *The Bible Times*,
this first missionary committee planned to produce a colloquial

[1] Run by Independent Board for Presbyterian Foreign Missions.

translation "but the Japanese pastors who were assisting in the translation, influenced by Buddhism and Confucianism, objected. They felt that 'Religious script in an easy language would not be appreciated by the Japanese people', and they insisted that the characters found in the Chinese Bible should be used."

Finally the Japanese translation of the Bible was completed with the meaning being given in Chinese character, and the pronunciation, at the insistence of the missionaries, was put in the Japanese syllabic system at the side. Time has proved the latter to be a wise precaution since some of the characters used in the Old Testament cannot be found in any Japanese dictionary, but Mr. Goto tells us that these syllabics are so small that no middle-aged person can read them without a magnifying glass. This first translation of the Bible was completed in 1888 and presented to the Japanese nation with these words: "May this sacred Book become to the Japanese what it has come to be for the people of the West—a source of life, a message of joy and peace, the foundation of a true civilization and of social and political prosperity and greatness."

Like all first translations this was found to contain errors, and accordingly from 1909 to 1917 a revision was made of the New Testament by Japanese scholars who understood Greek and Hebrew as well as English and German. The Old Testament, however, remained as it had been in the original version.

This was the translation which was in use when we arrived in Japan in 1952, and it was a great shock to new missionaries to be told that there was scarcely a verse in the Bible that a child of twelve would be able to understand, and that there was much no adult could understand either. Even the revised New Testament of 1917 was written in the classical style, and some described this to us as being as different as Chaucerian English is to modern speech, others merely that it was the equivalent of Shakesperean English. The Japanese language has changed tremendously in the last fifty years, both in noun and verb forms, so much so that one of our teachers told us that her father can hardly understand the radio-news broadcasts, while she herself finds difficulty in understanding a tract

Bridging the moat into Hirosaki Castle.

A Japanese Buddhist priest exhibiting charms at the entrance
of the shrine at Nikko.

Mt. Asama, viewed from Karuizawa.

written by one of her father's contemporaries. Even in the last ten years there have been so many changes that the few Japanese troops who have recently returned to Japan, after living in hiding in the Philippines ever since the war, say they had difficulty in understanding their own people at first.

It will be readily understood therefore how incomprehensible the Bible was to most of the younger generation who no longer study the Japanese classical language as a compulsory subject in school. My husband taught Old Testament Survey at the Tokyo Theological Seminary, and in one class the students, university graduates, could not tell whether a certain passage of Scripture was positive or negative. Some claimed it was one, and others the opposite! Mr. Goto wonders whether there is any Japanese person who can read the books of Leviticus, Numbers and Job without the help of the syllabic symbols. The result has been that many pastors have avoided the Old Testament and few Japanese seem to know much about it. Missionaries were perhaps equally responsible for its neglect. Most felt that it was a waste of precious time to bother learning all the Chinese characters. Dr. Hepburn had invented a Romanized system of writing Japanese, and the New Testament was published in this *romaji* as it was called. By means of this, missionaries could comparatively early read the Scriptures fluently (even more so than many Japanese), and this greatly facilitated an earlier preaching of the Gospel than would have been possible if they had had to learn thousands of Chinese characters.

This neglect of the Old Testament is perhaps one of the reasons why there has been so much compromise on the shrine issue and idolatry in Japan. It is only through the Old Testament that we get a glimpse of the concept of a "jealous God", and see the devastating effect of the influence of "other gods" in the lives and hearts of His people. It was only after long and bitter experience that the Jews finally learned their lesson. In the New Testament letters one has to look carefully to find teaching on this subject, so it is no wonder that this aspect of truth has been missed by the average Japanese Christian.

It was a surprise to us at first to find many Japanese using an

ICM

English Bible for their private devotions, but they explained that it was much easier for them to understand than the Japanese! Not only are there Chinese characters which they cannot find in their Japanese dictionaries, but there are of course many Christian concepts and terms which would be unfamiliar to any heathen reader, Western or Oriental, and it is usually easier to understand these in an English dictionary— apart from the fact that an English dictionary is usually much lighter in weight to carry around.

Incidentally it is not only the English Bible which the Japanese find easier to understand than their own language at times. One of the faculty members at the Seminary—a brilliant young man with a higher degree from one of the best Japanese universities—told me on one occasion of the great blessing he was receiving from reading one of Ruth Paxson's books. I suggested therefore that it might be good to translate it into Japanese. He told me that had already been done, and he had read it first in Japanese, but had not got the point of it then. He has never been abroad, so is not a really fluent English speaker, and yet he could get more spiritual help from a foreign book than one written in his own language. If highly educated Japanese, with some knowledge of English find the latter easier to understand than their own language, we begin to realize how difficult it must be for those with only high school education to understand the Japanese Bible.

Some of the missionaries in the early Meiji Era did produce a colloquial version of Matthew's Gospel, but apparently it did not meet with much acceptance. Mitsuzo Goto, however, claims that it was so well done that it is hard to believe it was written eighty-two years ago, and that if all the Bible had been written in that translation he thinks Christianity might have spread far more widely than it has done, instead of being confined, as it is, mainly to the middle, and a few upper-class Japanese.

Unfortunately most of his fellow Japanese Christians did not appear to agree with Mitsuzo Goto, for the majority did not want a colloquial Bible. Several individuals in recent years have attempted colloquial versions of some of the books of the New

Testament; but all the Japanese we consulted on our arrival said these were suitable only for primary school children, and that older people would be insulted if offered literature of that low standard. Those who had painfully learned many verses by heart naturally did not wish to change. They preferred beauty of language even though its meaning was obscure, and felt that the colloquial was tantamount to sacrilege. Their feelings were no doubt akin to those English people who have painfully learned the correct way to spell "through the night", and are filled with horror when Americans for the sake of their millions of citizens of non-British ancestry change it to the simpler "thru the nite"! The Chinese had felt much the same about their classical language. The Chinese were fortunate that they were able to obtain a good translation of the Bible in modern colloquial as early as 1919, thanks largely to the vision and persistence of F. W. Baller of the C.I.M., who insisted that the translation must be understandable by the man in the street.

Finally, however, the Japan Bible Society after the war undertook the translation of a complete colloquial version to which seven scholars gave their full time and forty others acted as assistant advisers. This was eagerly awaited, at least by the new missionaries, and finally was completed in 1954, becoming a best-seller throughout Japan the following year.

It has taken some time to make a fair judgment of this latest version, and many do not have enough language to be qualified to do so. One had the pleasant experience of showing a Christian young man the Lord's Prayer in it, and seeing comprehension suddenly dawn on his face. "Is *that* what it means?" he exclaimed. This version is now generally in use among C.I.M. groups, and most seem to find it easy to understand.

Japanese pastors have not accepted it wholeheartedly, however, nor many evangelical missionaries who have a real grasp of the language. Some use it for Gospel meetings, but not for worship services. A reviewer in one of the leading Tokyo evening papers likened it to "Japanese as spoken by a foreigner whose vocabulary was scant"—a strange result when all the translators were Japanese. However, many non-Christians seem to have taken a real interest in the new version, and many copies have been sold through ordinary bookstores to people without any connection with the church, and the hope of the translators was that it would become the standard for modern colloquial writing.

However, among conservative evangelical Christians the general opinion is that the translation is "weak", and lacking in dignity in its terminology for Christ and the Holy Spirit. With centuries of use of a "respect" language in which the highest honorifics have been accorded to man, I get the impression that it does not seem appropriate to the Japanese to apply these honorifics to God only, and have the rest of the text simple and plain—either everything has to be honorific, or everything in plain style. Perhaps they have no conception yet of the time when "the loftiness of man shall be bowed down, and the haughtiness of men shall be made low, and the Lord alone shall be exalted in that day", nor that they can help prepare the way for it.

The criticism of "weakness" is perhaps the most serious. For example, the future tense in modern Japanese is expressed by the verb ending "*de aro*" or its more polite equivalents. But both Japanese and Western scholars state this is not a true future. The famous Japanese grammar book, Vaccari's, states in its lesson on this verb form "The future tense in Japanese is used only when the future action is not decidedly certain, or when we wish to express probability. . . ."

Dr. W. A. McIllwaine, probably the greatest Japanese scholar among living missionaries, says, "There is no distinctively present or future tense in Japanese, but only a certainty tense and a probability tense." In a scholarly article in the *Bible Translator* (July 1954), he pleaded for the change of tense to be made before the complete colloquial Bible was published.

Unfortunately his appeal was not heeded by the Japan Bible Society, the opinion of the Japanese translators no doubt having more weight. It is interesting therefore to consider the reasons for this peculiarity of Japanese thought with regard to the future tense. "Buddhist belief, that everything was subject to change", says Mr. J. M. L. Young, "could not but affect their

concept of truth, with the result that dogmatic, positive statements on matters concerning principle or truth were considered illogical, and anyone making them did not conform to
the standard of what was considered proper, and was therefore
impolite."

The majority of the Japanese pastors of great scholarship
have been trained in liberal theology, so do not share our
views of the infallibility of the Scriptures, and are not likely
therefore to feel so concerned about the watering down effect
of the "probable" tense on Bible prophecies and promises in
the new version; in fact it would probably appear a truer
reflection of their own uncertain views. Dr. Saijo of Kyoto
(who is an authority on the Greek New Testament and who has
recently completed his own translation of the New Testament
using the literary style but with modern characters), in an
article on the weakness of the new version reveals his knowledge of his race when he attempts to answer his own question
as to why the Japanese conservative evangelicals are meekly
keeping silent. "Do they think it wiser not to touch the hot
chestnuts that are in the fire? Or is it because the Bible Society
professes to be clear and transparent, and to publish only the
Word of God? Is it that first-class scholars were in charge, and
have officially named it the church translation? Or is it
because Prince Mikasa and Premier Hatoyama were at the
presentation ceremony and gave it authority? Could it be that
because of the above factors they have jumped to the conclusion that they must accept it with gratitude?"

Now, however, we are glad to hear that the Bible Society has
invited the Evangelical Revision Committee to collect all their
criticisms and noted errors, and present them to the society for
serious consideration.

One interesting and useful fact appeared from all the discussion of the new version, which was that the classical revision
of 1917 also contained the same inference of probability in its
future tense. Very few missionaries had been aware of this
connotation in the classical language, but evidently had read
into it their own certainty of the promises of God. No doubt this
is the reason behind the remark of a Buddhist priest who had

read all three versions and said that of the three, the first one sounded as if the men who translated it really believed it. Dr. Saijo, just quoted, also says that he himself uses this original version, buying copies in second-hand bookstores whenever he can.

Perhaps it was this strong tone of certainty in the early translation, together with a hungry heart, which caused the young man mentioned in the chapter on the fear of death to believe in God without any human teaching. The number who have done so in recent years appear to be few, however, and we look for the day when any Japanese can pick up a copy of the Bible and know with clearness and certainty of the One of whom it speaks.

For those with really hungry, seeking hearts, however, the Bible has been the means of revealing the truth even though in places it has seemed to be obscured by man. The full story of one of these is told in a film produced by the C.I.M. entitled *Miracle at Mori*, but a few details here will show how the devil's efforts to keep the sword blunt and sheathed were defeated in this case.

This girl, Miss Homma, was brought up in a home in a little fishing town on the Hokkaido coast to which three workers went in 1952. She had been trained as a hairdresser and after completing her apprenticeship with distinction she went for a special course in Tokyo. While there she developed severe tuberculosis and a telegram was sent to her home, where lived her old mother and her elder sister and her husband and children. Her brother-in-law set off on the long train journey to the capital, and while he was gone the elder sister, greatly troubled, went to consult one of the fortune-tellers in the town about her sister's illness. "Your sister's illness is a very serious one, it goes up and up", was the somewhat enigmatic answer she received in return for a high fee.

The girl was lovingly cared for by her sister after her return home, but she grew weaker and was in constant pain. She considered suicide, but knew she had no strength to walk up the rough face of the active volcano that towered above their little town. Throwing oneself into the crater of a volcano is one popular method of suicide in Japan. Then when one day she crawled out of bed to make the attempt the thought of the coldness of the deep waters caused her courage to fail and she collapsed. The doctor obviously thought she was dying, and her sister in great concern fell on her knees and cried, "Oh God, if there is a true God anywhere, heal my sister!"

The old mother, however, turned to the only gods she had known, and sent for the priest from the nearest Buddhist temple. He advised the girl to recite the name of Amida whenever she was in pain, but she found no relief in this.

The family had given her a radio to help pass the time, and one day she happened to turn it on to some Christian music, so different with its joyous major key from the more usual minor strains of traditional Japanese songs. As she lay and listened she felt strangely comforted. She knew little about Christianity—only that there was such a religion—and she began to wonder what it was like.

She asked the nurse who came to help care for her if she knew anything about it, and she exclaimed: "Christianity! Why, that is most difficult to understand! You have to study difficult books most diligently, and then pass an examination before you can enter Christianity."

This was very discouraging, of course, but she thought she would enquire about it again when the priest came.

"Christianity! You could never be a Christian. Did not the teacher Kagawa himself say that a Christian father and mother had a Christian son, and so on? You have to be born of Christian parents to be a Christian. Your parents are Buddhists. You must make a vow to Amida that you will never become a Christian." Too weak to resist, she followed the priest in a vow not to become a Christian, and he then left, after telling her he would call to see her on the 29th of every month.

Just at that time the Pocket Testament League, in response to an appeal by General MacArthur, Supreme Commander of the Occupation Forces, was seeking to get a portion of the Scriptures into every home in Japan. One day, as she glanced through a newspaper Miss Homma saw an announcement that a copy of a "Holy Book" would be sent to all who wrote to the office of the Pocket Testament League asking for one. She had no idea what the "Holy Book" was, but guessed it might have something to do with Christianity, and after hesitating a while in view of her vow, she decided there would be no harm in applying for a copy.

She waited in great excitement for more than a month, fearing at last that there must be no more copies left, but finally it came on the 29th December—just a few minutes before the arrival of the priest, so she had to hide the precious package under the bedclothes, unable to open it until he had gone.

Then she found that her book was called the Gospel of John. She began to read it, but was disappointed at the incomprehensibility of the first verse—"In the beginning was the word, and the word was with God, and the word was God." Surely the nurse had been right, and this was too difficult for an ordinary person like her. Yet she continued to read on. "God is a spirit, and they that worship him must worship him in spirit and in truth." It was the truth she wanted. Here she felt was a religion she could rely on. Eagerly she read on until she reached chapter 8 verse 12, when the words seemed to jump right out at her. "Then spake Jesus unto them saying, 'I am the light of the world: he that followeth me shall not walk in darkness, but shall have the light of life.'" Buddha was supposed to be the light of Asia, but she knew she had been walking in darkness. These words had the ring of truth. She read on and the word of life brought peace to her soul and rest to her tired aching body, and finally she began to pray to the One about whom the book spoke.

Soon afterwards she was surprised to receive another Holy Book, the New Testament, and found on reading it that her first was only a part of this. She decided to write and ask how much more there was, and if there was anyone near her town who could teach this Book. Unknown to her a Presbyterian pastor did visit a few believers there once a month, and he (with some of them) came to call on her one day. Her sister also believed at that time.

Miss Homma's strength gradually returned, and when three C.I.M. missionaries went to live there not long after, she got up and went out on the street to see them arrive, and finally took a very active part in visitation and open-air witness. The local people were amazed, some having thought she had died long ago. A friend who had not visited them for a long time came one day and remarked how strong the girl seemed. "I suppose you are getting lots of medicine from America and here and there?" she added.

"Oh yes, we're getting lots," agreed the sister with a twinkle in her eyes.

"What do you call it?"

"It's called *seisho* (holy book)," she replied laughing.

"Do you drink it or get it by injections?"

The sister laughed again and said, "Oh it is wonderful, if you take it you will go on living for ever!" Then she went to the cupboard, took out her Bible, and began to witness to their friend of the Saviour whom they had discovered in that Book.

Chapter XII

BLACK LILY OF RESENTMENT

NOT far from Karuizawa, where many of us lived during our first period of language study, there can be seen distant glimpses of the Japanese Alps. During the long winter these are snow-covered; but in early summer, among other flowers of beauty and fragrance, grows a short-stalked, unpleasant smelling purple flower known as the black lily.

There is a legend that long ago in Owari Province lived a feudal lord named Sasaki who was wilful, heartless and fickle. He had a wife who was beautiful and gentle, and trusted him completely; but one day, for some very trivial matter, he brutally killed her. As death was approaching she said: "If the black lily grows on Mount Tate, let it be regarded as the symbol of my resentment. This resentment is in the black lily eternally, and Sasaki will perish where the black lily (that is my resentment) grows."

These words were uttered with her last breath. Before long the lilies filled with her resentment grew profusely over the high mountains, and soon her husband was dead.

To us this expression of resentment sounds quite natural from one who suffered so unjustly, though of a very gentle character by nature. There are other instances of this harbouring of resentment in Japanese history, which, however, we do not find so easy to understand. For example, a feudal lord once asked three of his samurai who was the maker of a certain valuable sword. Only one gave the right answer. The other two took this as an insult, and killed him for it. This seems rather an incomprehensible mental process to us, and yet these two themes, revenge for an injury or slur received, and revenge upon someone who has been right when you were wrong, are commonplace in the best known literature and historical tales of Japan.

It is not merely a popular literary theme, however, but it is very much a part of their daily life. Children from about the age of ten are taught to be watchful for insults. Resentment is considered a virtue rather than a vice. "The world tips," they say, "as long as an insult is not requited"; and a good man therefore is one who restores the balance. Dr. Nitobe has written: "Our sense of revenge is as exact as our mathematical faculty, and until both sides of the equation are satisfied we cannot get over the sense of something left undone."

This sounds rather like the Old Testament principle of an eye for an eye, and a tooth for a tooth, but in fact it works out very differently. To us it seems as if sometimes they go much further than restoring the balance. For example the newspaper recently reported the case of a clerk who gave a Christmas cake, decorated with icing mixed with rat poison, to his employer. The latter, his wife and two sons all required hospital treatment after eating it. The clerk explained to the police that he did it out of revenge, because he had been scolded recently.

When visiting the old capital of Kyoto last year I saw a famous historic temple which had just been rebuilt. One of the underpriests had had a grudge against the head priest, and instead of taking action against him personally, had taken his revenge by destroying this national treasure.

To emphasize further the prevalence of this characteristic we can take an illustration from a book by the famous Japanese novelist Soseki, and another from a short story which recently received great acclaim.

The first is from the novel *Kokoro* which purports to be written by a student who has a tremendous admiration for a "teacher" or scholar who is really the hero of the book. Although he is given the title of "teacher" he never appears to do any work, but spends all his time brooding on the past, and waiting for an opportune moment in life to commit suicide. This man's parents had died when he was in his teens, and an aunt and uncle had become his guardians. These two gradually cheated him of his inheritance, and the effect this had on him was to influence his whole life. In his own words, "When I left my native place the idea that human beings can never be relied upon seemed to have penetrated the marrow of my bones. I began to regard my uncle and aunt, whom I held as my enemies, as the representatives of humanity. Even in the train I began furtively to watch my neighbours. . . . In the (boarding) house I sat at my desk in silence watching the behaviour of those in the house as carefully as a cat watches a mouse. . . . I was betrayed by my blood relatives. I can never forget that. I have been burdened with the humiliation and loss that they have caused me ever since my boyhood. But I have not yet taken revenge upon them. Yet I think I am having what is more than a revenge on individuals. I not only hate them, but have learned to detest the whole human race which they represent."

This is a reaction which is not unknown in the West, and is probably very familiar to psychiatrists. The difference is that in the West most people are unconscious of this result in their minds and would be ashamed to admit it, whereas this scholar is proud of it, and the student obviously admired him.

The last example is from a short story called *The Hateful Age*. This has become so famous that the title is now a common term for the period of old age. It is the story of a senile old woman who has outlived her husband and daughter and has to be cared for by married granddaughters to whom she is a great trial. One of the chief difficulties is that she cannot understand the fact of wartime food-rationing, and thinks the grand-daughters are trying to starve her. Once, though never able to walk out of the house normally, after being particularly offended with one of the granddaughters she went out to the street gate and pretended to begin to commit suicide, in order to get the sympathy of the neighbours. In desperation the kinder of the two granddaughters finally bursts out: "What a hateful old woman you really are. The one emotion you haven't forgotten in all these years is—is spite."

"Was it that these people (old women in the village) had ended by rejecting the finer feelings of life, or did the feelings themselves finally abandon people when they become too old?", wondered the husband of one of the granddaughters.

As I thought about this question I realized that probably both answers were partly true. Modern science is teaching us more about the decay of the physical body and its effect upon the mind; but perhaps part of this extreme deterioration was the result of a life lived without God. This was one of the first things Uchimura noticed when he went to the United States as a student (1895). "Why is it that heathen go into decay so soon, but Christians in general knew no decay, hope even in death itself? We (Japanese) count men above forty among the old: while in Christendom no man below fifty is considered fit for positions of responsibility. We think of rest and retirement as soon as our children come of age, and backed by the teaching of filial piety, feel we are entitled to lazy idleness, to be cared for and caressed by the young generation."

It is easy from this last remark to understand how much resentment is likely to arise within a Japanese family; and how, in spite of the closeness of the family unit, there is often much more resentment than love in the hearts of its members.

The above illustrations are enough to show us that the practice of nurturing resentment does play an important part in the life of the ordinary Japanese. It is not confined to the individual either; the nation as a whole particularly since the militarists came into power, is also taught to be alert for instances of being "minimized" by outside powers. Uchimura in speaking of the cause of the Russo-Japanese War puts it down to Russia's discourteous manner in treating Japan. "You must not expect a highly sensitive nation to remain in torpid indifference when treated as of no importance." Many Japanese too, sincerely believed that America was responsible for the outbreak of the Pacific war since the passing of the Exclusion Act was an insult of such magnitude that nothing short of war could restore the balance. Britain's unequal trade treaties were also a contributing cause of hostilities.

It will be obvious therefore to anyone with imagination that this nurturing of resentment will produce many difficulties in church life, and may indeed be one of the reasons why churches do not grow very big, or why so many members are lost to particular churches. The harbouring of resentment of course has caused tragedy in many a church in the West. It seems as if the victory over this temptation is one of the hardest to learn, even for Christians who have always been aware of the New Testament teaching on the subject. How much more difficult therefore for those who have been consistently taught that resentment is a virtue. In the Japan Christian Year book for 1956 some Japanese pastors are quoted as saying one of the main reasons for the dropping off of church attendance is that the church service has degenerated into a forum of small talk and vicious criticism, where more is torn down than built up.

Because of this stress on resentment, and the need to clear one's name from slurs, the Japanese have contrived an etiquette which will remove as far as possible the likelihood of this being necessary. The main instrument in this is the "go-between", familiar in other oriental countries too, who arranges everything from marriages and job appointments to much smaller things which might still give cause for loss of face. The foreigner with his direct approach is often therefore the unwitting means of a very great deal of misunderstanding and loss of face. One missionary who has been a long time in Japan told me she considered it impossible for a missionary to carry on successfully without the help of a Japanese co-worker. She said that these misunderstandings and resentments were bound to occur. Christians would stay away from church and the simple foreigner would have no clues as to what was wrong unless a Japanese friend took the trouble to explain. The only way for the matter ever to be put right again would be for the missionary to go and apologize very humbly, though he had been quite without any thought of offending. The fact that the insult was unintentional in no way lessens it. In fact, if you have been in Japan any length of time it seems to be more reprehensible if unintentional. For the first year or so they willingly make allowance for the ignorant foreigner, but after that you are expected to know how to behave, just as they read tremendously hard about a foreign country before they visit it.

As our Mission's new indigenous policy does not allow the employment by the C.I.M. of nationals in its work we have been at a disadvantage in this respect, though in one or two places there have been Christians willing to give advice when needed. In one city where two women missionaries were helping an already established church, the Pastor came to their aid in discharging their very unsatisfactory daily helper in the house, who was causing difficulties with some of the church people. The missionaries would only have been able to tell the girl they were not satisfied with her services, but the Pastor came along and suggested it was very cold now and the girl would probably be more comfortable at home. She understood this perfectly, but did not lose face in that way. However, it takes a long time for a missionary to get used to this way of doing things. Once you do grasp the fact that there may be a double meaning to everything that you say, or that is said to you, it can give rise to anxiety in all intercourse with the Japanese. One is almost afraid to say anything for fear of offending. So we need to pray continually for the peace and wisdom of the Lord.

An instance which occurred in one of our centres not long ago will illustrate how these misunderstandings can arise. A new missionary was transferred to this place where there had already been a small group of Christians for over a year. As it was near the season for tent campaigns she enquired if the Christians could be responsible for the travel expenses of the visiting evangelist, and asked one of the Christians, who had had a great deal of contact with the former missionary, if the visitor could sleep at her house. Both this woman and the other Christians answered "Yes" to these requests, but subsequently it transpired that they had only agreed because it was a direct question. They should have been approached by a "go-between", so that they could give their real answer of "No" without offending their sense of etiquette. This caused a great deal of ill-feeling among the Christians and lack of interest in the tent campaign and still seems to be rankling in the minds of some.

To us, of course, it would seem natural that after a year of Christian life and intercourse with foreigners one might talk straightforwardly about such a seemingly simple matter. Praise God there have been some who will make great allowances for the ignorance of the foreigner; but one cannot take anything for granted. Perhaps one of the hardest things for the missionary in Japan is to find that at first the Japanese are friendly and welcoming; but the longer they know a person the more critical they seem to become. In China it often appeared to be the opposite, antagonism and insults in the beginning, where the missionary was more or less prepared for such treatment, but later yielding a greater appreciation of their purpose as this became better known. A home representative of one society was in Japan on a visit and, after talking to some of the Japanese connected with it, told a missionary rather bluntly he did not seem to have the confidence of the Japanese. Another missionary who was present and whose work brought him in contact with different groups of Japanese said rather ruefully, "No foreigner ever does." While this may not be universally true it is very understandable when one knows their background of training in resentment, and remembers how our conduct must appear to them when we in all ignorance trample so clumsily on their centuries-old etiquette, which to them has all the sanction of a moral code. Other oriental countries notably China, use go-betweens too, and stress the importance of face, yet there does not seem to be quite the same nourishing of resentment in their culture. Here in Japan a missionary can easily reach a state of mind where he is almost afraid to say or do anything for fear of offending.

Though it does not make corporate church life any easier, it is perhaps some consolation to know that Japanese are just as exacting and as critical of each other as they are of the missionary. Praise God we do know of cases, however, where He has been able to remove that feeling of resentment from the hearts of some of His children. A young man from one of our centres, in his testimony at a Christian camp, told how he had felt so frustrated and resentful at the hard experiences in his life that he had decided he must kill somebody in order to get relief. But fortunately just at that time he had wandered into one of our tent meetings and had accepted Christ, and peace gradually came into his heart.

Kanzo Uchimura speaks of how difficult it is to forgive sins committed against us, and says man is so constituted that he

Leaving the Buddhist Temple at Nagoya. Notice the lanterns
which light the way to the temple.

Shintoists pray to the dead, Buddhists pray for the dead, at a Japanese Memorial Day celebration. But is there no way of life? asks young Japan.

cannot forgive unless he is first forgiven by his Creator. He gives us the following personal testimony, written in 1917:

"I had a man whom I hated. I desired to forgive him, but I could not; and I was unhappy. Then I remembered the Saviour's words: Love your enemies and pray for them which persecute you. I went at once to prayer, and prayed that God's richest blessings might rest with the one whom I called my enemy. And behold a great change came over me, and I began to love him from the bottom of my heart. I became happy too, and felt largeness and freedom such as I never felt before."

Dr. Ormiston (now Mrs. David Hayman) of the C.I.M. tells of another convincing proof of Christ's power to free from this bondage of resentment which she saw while helping for a time in a medical clinic run by the Conservative Baptist Mission. At a meeting one night she sat next to a woman whose quiet serenity of expression struck her. So often out here, as she says, you are painfully conscious that the sweetness of the women is only on the surface, but this woman's looked so thoroughly genuine that she felt she wanted to know her story. The woman told her later that she was from a well-to-do family, and was married to a factory owner. Her serenity, however, was not at all due to her material security, for she had previously been a discontented and bitter woman, frequently lying awake at night, her heart full of resentment, as she thought over all the unkind things people had said and done, and planned how she might get revenge.

One rainy day, this woman was travelling in a train with her little girl when a foreigner, sitting opposite, began to talk to the child, who had her nose pressed against the window watching the rain drops. He asked her in simple Japanese if she knew where the rain came from, and then told her it was sent by the one true God who loves us. The child was too shy to answer or even look around; but the mother remembered these words, and as she went home, she hoped that one day she might have an opportunity to hear more about this God.

Some time later she saw in the newspaper an advertisement of a series of Christian meetings which were soon to be held in her town, in other words a tent campaign. When at last the tent arrived she was there the very first night and who should the speaker be but the Baptist missionary she had seen in the train. Hungrily she listened to everything he said, and realized that this was what she needed. Afterwards she went up and told him so, and he asked her if she would accept Christ. She answered that she wanted to, but that she must ask her husband first.

The missionaries were afraid this might mean she would not return, but her husband's answer was, "All right, so long as you don't make a fool of yourself". So the next day she came and entered into new life and freedom in Christ. She testifies that as God worked in her heart all bitterness went and even though the persecution she has received since believing is worse than the criticism she met with before, she feels no resentment now. Her face and her actions prove this to be true, and have made a considerable impression, not only on outsiders but on her husband too. He once remarked, "The thing that impresses me is the way my wife sleeps since she has become a Christian—I lie awake and worry." Here is a woman who has been freed not only from the penalty of sin, but freed also from a mental bondage which some Western Christians have not yet escaped. Recently there has come the good news that her husband too, has become a Christian.

Just recently I read the testimony of a Japanese girl who, though born in America and never having been in Japan, yet evidently still had many traces of Japanese thought patterns in her life. She was converted in hospital when very ill with meningitis, which left her deaf and lame.

She tells us: "The Holy Spirit made me see that being ashamed of my handicaps, being easily hurt, having self-pity, false pride, resentment, prejudices, were sins in the sight of God. I had thought only murderers, thieves, etc., were sinners . . . but in the Bible God puts my wrong heart-feelings and attitudes in the same category. When I realized how terrible my feelings and attitudes were, I wanted to get rid of them . . . I claimed 1 John 1 : 9 for my own, 'If we confess our sins He is faithful and just to forgive us our sins, and to cleanse us from all unrighteousness'. I simply took God at His word. . . . Like a miracle, my burden rolled away. . . . I had thought my life would become restricted if I surrendered my will to God: it is just the opposite. He has given me His unexpected freedom instead; He has given me freedom from my inner bondage. . . . I believe now that it is not our circumstances which determine our happiness or misery, but our attitude towards them. In Proverbs 23: 7 we read 'For as he thinketh in his heart, so is he'."

This girl has discovered a great secret, and a great freedom, and we look for the day when many others of her race will rejoice in this freedom in the land of Japan.

Chapter XIII

MEETING OF EAST AND WEST

(a) THE JAPANESE IN WESTERN EYES

THE preceding chapters have given some idea of the great differences in background and ideas between the Japanese people and those with long Christian traditions; and also how these things constitute major difficulties in the way of an individual Japanese accepting Christianity as his own faith. In addition to these, however, there are many other smaller differences which may cause strained relations between these races if they are not properly understood.

Many Westerners are familiar with the idea that the Orient does things "the opposite way", so it may not cause much concern to find that a carpenter's saws and planes are pulled in when used, while in the West they are pushed out; that boats are rowed forwards instead of backwards; that addresses on envelopes begin with the country or town, and end with the person's name; or that Japanese rooms are dusted first and swept afterwards. One of the first things that does confuse a foreigner, however, is the difference in the meaning of a smile or laugh in Japan. For instance a subordinate or servant may often smile when reprimanded by a superior, a custom which the uninitiated foreigner may regard as insolence, or a failure to take the rebuke seriously. A death in the family will also be reported with a smile or even a giggle, and this has led foreigners with only a superficial knowledge of the country to assume that the Japanese have little feeling. The idea behind this is very understandable, however, once it is known, the purpose being that no guest or superior should be made uncomfortable by signs of sorrow. On the other hand we are rather bewildered to find it is quite permissible for a men's football or other sports team to dissolve into tears if they lose a game. A wedding, too, may be an appropriate occasion for weeping. It is interesting therefore to hear the reaction of a Japanese lady who witnessed the wedding of a Canadian missionary couple, and wrote a letter to the paper about it. After commenting on the fact that the ceremony began at the time stated, she describes the surprising bride. "Her face was brimming with smiles and she had no special make-up on her face, giving one a sense of cleanliness. My idea that a bride should be painted up like a doll, and should look down and be demure, was dashed to the ground. Inwardly I was a bit surprised, but her smile was so natural that while looking at her I began to feel warm and cheerful myself." A laugh in Japan is often used as a technique for covering up embarrassment or regaining poise, especially when feeling sad. When happy it is usually considered better not to show any emotion, nor to show affection in public.

Another phenomenon puzzling to the foreigner is the many apparent contradictions in the Japanese character. Ichiro Kawasaki, a prominent Japanese diplomat, in his interesting book states, "Every generalization, whether in favour of Japan or against it, can be disproved by an overwhelming mass of contradictory evidence. One can find evidence that the Japanese are industrious, lazy, efficient, incompetent, kind, cruel, peaceful or warlike."[1] Ruth Benedict conveys the same idea by saying that they may be described as "unprecedentedly polite . . . but also insolent and over bearing, . . . incomparably rigid in their behaviour, . . . but also adapt themselves readily to extreme innovations, . . . submissive . . . but not easily amenable to control from above. . . ."[2] Someone else has said the Japanese are "extremely conservative, and yet impelled onward in an eager quest for the ideal", or are always looking for something new in the way of thought. In fact with many of them their ideas change with every book they read. Some of the Seminary students have said they are nearest in character to the Galatians, and one wrote in an exam that the Japanese are like snakes, always wanting to change their skins!

[1] *The Japanese are Like That,* Ichiro Kawasaki.
[2] *The Chrysanthemum and the Sword.*

Ichiro Kawasaki gives as his reason for these seeming contradictions the great differences between different classes of people, rural and urban, and official and unofficial Japan. The farmers can perform wonderfully systematic work in the fields while the office worker has no idea how to keep orderly files; traditional Japanese style houses are kept with an almost ceremonial cleanliness while in modern Western buildings it rarely occurs to them to clean the glass windows or take proper care of floors. Oligarchical "official" Japan, which gets the best brains of the country, is comparatively efficient and outwardly governed by the same code as other governments, while the rest of Japan is still feudalistic. Trains, banks and schools are usually extremely punctual, yet in keeping business and social appointments Ichiro Kawasaki says the Japanese do not even think of apologizing if they are twenty minutes late.

The latter characteristic seems strange to the foreigner since the Japanese apologize so profusely for many other things which to us do not need an apology. Every foreigner remarks about the extreme politeness of the Japanese, and it is hard for us to believe that it is not all it appears to be. One Japanese friend told us, however, that it is usually entirely egocentric, a kind of showing off that you know the correct way to behave, and a vying with each other as to who can be the most polite —just as in China there would be endless argument and manœuvre as to who should go through a door or gate first. Ichiro Kawasaki says their traditional politeness "is often a veneer . . . aloof and pompous, and does not comprise thoughtful consideration of others, the basis of good manners in the West".[1]

However, most of us have been the recipients of so many kindnesses from the Japanese it is hard to believe that some of them did not come from the heart.

It is interesting too, to see the reaction of a Chinese girl to life in Japan. Writing a prize-winning essay at a foreign school on "The Benefits of Living in Japan", she says:

"I spent fifteen years in China. . . . All through the years in high school we studied about the Japanese invasions . . . an indelible impression of the Japanese was imprinted on my

[1] *The Japanese are Like That.*

mind . . . it seemed to me (they) were the most savage and cruel
people in the whole world. . . .

"But I found what an illusion it was after I came to Japan and
actually met them face to face. I could hardly believe that these
courteous people I saw in department stores or in the streets
were the monsters I used to see in my nightmares. They are so
different from what I thought. The courteous conductors on
trains and buses, and pedestrians who always patiently answer
my enquiries have made a deep impression on me. . . . I was
impressed to see considerate mothers taking off their children's
shoes on buses in case they might soil the velvet seats. In many
other ways I have found they are very thoughtful to others,
and often made me ashamed of myself. . . ."

Yet the other picture had also been true, at least in certain
parts of China during the war period. While Ichiro Kawasaki's
explanation accounts for many of the more superficial contradictions, probably the fundamental cause behind some of the
contradictions is that there is no absolute standard for all
occasions. Part of the explanation too, may be found in the
remark of one Japanese Christian, "My thinking is Buddhist,
my actions Confucian and my heart Christian." That they
are not so universally polite as foreigners at first believe
is revealed by one student writing in her college English newspaper under the title "Bit of Bitterness". The bus between the
station and her college was late one morning, leaving only a few
minutes before classes were due to start. "Once the students get
in a bus they will not move toward the back but insist on staying
near the door. Though the bus girl raised her voice to ask the
passengers to move towards the back the students looked un-
concerned and paid no attention to her, as if they were all deaf.

"The bus started, leaving many students behind. They could
have ridden on it if those who stopped near the door had
moved a little to the back." Those near the door dashed in to
class just in time, but she had moved to the back and could not
get out so quickly, so was late.

I was rather amused to read of a missionary in 1913 excusing
Japanese thoughtlessness on trains and buses on the ground
that these were new; but over forty years later conditions

generally are much the same, though one always meets a few polite and considerate people. I once saw a young man get up to let a pregnant woman sit down, but before she could get into the seat a middle-aged man ducked beneath her and secured it first! Another favourite trick of people travelling in long distance trains is to lie down on two seats and cover their faces with a handkerchief. Although the trains are always crowded with people standing, courtesy or timidity (I am not sure which) prevents most people from ever disturbing those reclining in two seats if they appear to be asleep.

Another of these contradictions in character mentioned is their arrogance and timidity. As a race the feeling of their superiority still persists, and also their stoic bravery in the face of some dangers. Yet they can get very nervously excited over an earthquake, and as individuals they are timid because they have been brought up in such fear of public opinion, and can rarely feel sure of themselves in unfamiliar circumstances.

In a very interesting post-war novel by Jiro Osaragi called *Homecoming*,[1] a cosmopolitan former Japanese naval officer who had had to leave the country because of a scandal before the war, comes back and has some very penetrating observations to make. In talking to a former friend in the navy, who has retired to his home, he says that when he had to leave Japan "to live entirely on my own resources I was amazed to find I didn't have to be afraid of anyone any more. That's how Japan has always been, the whole country, not only soldiers. We've all lived in constant fear of someone or something, hesitant and frightened and subservient. Everyone wastes his life justifying himself to something. . . . You pride yourself on your stubbornness, but stubbornness is the weakling's weapon. You're just curling up small inside your shell, too frightened to look outside. You sulk and wish you were dead, but that only proves you don't feel capable of living."

Another character in the story has interesting comments as he sees the after effects of war and defeat. "We're no nation of gods. . . . The idea that Japanese are different is still rooted in my head. But we're not, are we? We're a people who can do

[1] *Homecoming*, Jiro Osaragi.

nothing to save ourselves unless some outside force moves in to change our lives. We can't overcome our tendency to follow the leader. We're too proud of our borrowed plumage to have opinions of our own. A whole people rushed into the national uniform when the war started, and into aloha shirts when it was over—and hardly noticed the difference." That last sentence is probably not true of the majority of the Christians and many of the intellectuals—(certainly they have not taken to aloha shirts!)—but nevertheless a foreign observer is inclined to agree with much of this opinion.

He cannot but be struck also by the difference in psychology between the Japanese and Westerner. A sad note is preferred to a happy one; and this is common in all their literature, though not so strong in post-war days as formerly. However, even in a newsheet of the Volunteer Lay Visitation Evangelism Movement we see it. This is an organization to promote greater participation by church members in evangelism, and a number of volunteers in different churches have been responsible for winning most encouraging numbers of contacts to Christ. One newsheet gives details of a radio drama to be used both to encourage others to take part in this work, and also in institutional evangelism. If a Westerner had been producing such a drama it would probably have been about someone gloriously saved as the result of lay personal work, but not so the Japanese. This is not a success story, and the Volunteer fails to win his Prospect to Christ. The latter was one of a teenage gangster crowd, and he finally attended church and appeared to be converted and requested baptism. But the "pull" of his crowd was too much, and he began to backslide, and ran away with a girl. The Volunteer then comes in utter disappointment to his pastor, who reminds him that even Jesus washed the feet of Judas along with the other disciples. He urges the Volunteer to pray on, for sooner or later Christ will confront the Prospect again. So the Volunteer goes out to take up the battle again. The recommendation of the story is that it "underscores the tremendous barriers these lay visitation volunteers are facing in Japan, and the remarkable spirit in which they continue this work for Christ".

Fighting against great odds is a theme which has a tremendous appeal to the Japanese. The symbol of bravery is the carp whose form is so much in evidence at the annual Boys' Festival. Its characteristics are that it swims upstream, and also does not wriggle under the knife when it meets with death. When the Emperor decorated the Japanese team which recently climbed the Himalayas he referred to them as having "overcome all obstacles". The high approval with which this type of behaviour is regarded is perhaps responsible for the great emphasis on problems and difficulties in Japan. When I had been in the country only about two weeks one of our teachers told me she had a *mondai* (problem). I did not know what this meant, and I do not believe the word ever came in our study book, but she smiled as she showed it to me in the dictionary, saying it was a word the Japanese used a great deal. Probably that and *soodan* (discussion) are the two words which cause the foreign missionary more inward groans than any others in the language, for they represent the consumption of untold hours of precious time. Many of the problems, too, are of an extremely difficult nature, especially as they often involve personalities, or conflict with national culture, or family. Not all are of this nature, however. When my husband first attended committee meetings he would listen to all the details and ramifications of some difficult situation, and then, having a gift for distinguishing the wood from the trees, would say with the idea of being helpful, 'The problem really boils down to this . . . doesn't it?" But at once he would be conscious of something wrong—a kind of feeling of deflation in the group—and gradually came to surmise that they really enjoy making things appear difficult, presumably for the satisfaction of overcoming the difficulties. Another of our teachers later told us straight out that the Japanese do not like having some of their problems solved— they would feel lost without one. In this I believe they are very like the French who are also full of *le problème*, and whose situations become *très délicat* as easily as those of the Japanese become *muzukashii* (difficult). Politically too, now that they have a democratic system, they are like the French, each Party being split into warring factions, for like the French they have a strong national solidarity, yet a strange inability to work together. Japanese pastors, too, like to think of their country as "certainly the most difficult in the world" from the point of view of doing Christian work. Dr. Stanley Jones in one of his frequent visits has assured them, however, that India is more difficult, and I imagine any Muslim country must also present a bigger problem.

The Japanese have always been taught the importance of outward conformity. From the time they are babies on their mothers' backs they are trained to go through the motions of bowing when meeting people. They are taught to conform externally regardless of their inner feelings, and even resentment and anger against the gods is not thought to be wrong—so long as it is not shown in outward behaviour. The time of the persecution of the Roman Catholics gives us a picture of the importance with which externals were regarded, for there are still in existence today numerous relics showing how the hidden believers insisted on having the cross, or some other Christian symbol, to aid their worship. There are Buddhist images which have a cross concealed in some place, or sundials with crosses carved on the base which is buried in the earth, or on a side where shadow would always fall. An image of the god of wealth, who always carries a sack on his back, was made so that the sack opened to reveal a crucifix. To us this seems a strange compromise, but the importance of having these outward symbols was very real to the Japanese for they knew that both the craftsman and the possessor of such things would be executed if they were discovered.

One of the greatest problems for any Christian, and particularly a Japanese, is to know how much the church may be coloured by local conditions and customs, and how much the latter must be altered or ignored in order to live a consistent Christian life. In the past, the general tendency in Japan has been to adopt the externals of Western church life, the form of building, the clerical dress, the denominational organization (though for the first few years the churches were non-denominational), the theological textbooks, and even the music and words of Western hymns; while the message of the Gospel, the heart of Christianity, was apt to be changed to suit the Japanese way of life, or the current Western theological fashion. The blame for this latter, of course, must lie squarely on the foreigner. The faith of the early Japanese Christians was simple —"They accepted Christianity not because of its rationality or profound theology, but because they believed in its power to save them and the nation. . . . But a great change came in the 1890s. With Western civilization came materialism and liberal theology. Many completely changed their faith, and many Japanese Christians were influenced by their writings."[1] Another Christian, a professor at Sapporo wrote, "The Christians in Japan, both native and missionary, seem to have rushed after empty names rather than things real and substantial. Better sell your mission schools to money-making corporations if you cannot win souls for Christ in your magnificent halls of brick and stone."

However, the fact that there was an inherent weakness in doctrine is revealed by another Christian leader, who tells us (is it with a touch of pride?): "One element of Japanese Christianity is its indifference to matters of doctrine which are vehemently contested in the West. Such doctrines as the virgin birth, the substitutionary theory of atonement, the resurrection of the body, the second coming of Christ, verbal inspiration of the Bible, the supernatural regeneration of man, the theory of evolution, are not points of controversy . . . today theological disputes are rare." While we have no wish for needless disputes about unessentials, such important subjects as these do require to be clearly understood and believed and taught if Christianity is to remain virile and true to the New Testament pattern, but few Japanese seem to realize this. Ichiro Kawasaki says, "Along with uniformity, the unrealism of the Japanese people is something which the student of the Japanese people should always bear in mind. They tend to accept and apparently be satisfied with a nominal state of affairs, which may be quite different from actual conditions. The theoretical solution of a question is accepted without reference to the real facts. As a result, the Japanese are often

[1] *Japan Speaks for Herself.*

unable, or at least refuse to distinguish between theory and fact, or between phantasy and reality."[1] Because of the great absence of privacy in their lives they have created a kind of fictional one by the philosophy of "if we will not look we will see nothing". Thus people may change their clothes or breast feed a baby in the train; or if a guest calls and finds his host not properly clothed he will wait, even if the changing has to be done in his presence, until everything is in order before saying any word of greeting. Our superintendent was once travelling with a Japanese teacher and though they slept in the same room and shaved side by side in the hotel washroom, it was not until the latter was completely dressed that he knelt down and said an official "good morning".

Another difficulty for the foreigner is that he may be led astray by English words used by the Japanese with a different connotation from that with which we are familiar. Mention has already been made of the Japanese idea of "self-respect"—so different from ours. Sometimes one may see a heading in the newspaper such as "Morals Crisis" and imagine it may be something to do with the 150,000 licensed prostitutes, only to find it is about the rather unsportsmanlike attitude of the spectators at an international table tennis tournament held in Japan; or the fact that people are carelessly crossing their legs in public vehicles and thus putting mud on their neighbour's clothes.

"Sincerity" is another very puzzling word when used by the Japanese. The Japanese word *makoto* which has been translated "sincerity" has none of the meaning of "genuineness" which the word implies to us; but its basic meaning is "the zeal to follow the road mapped out by the Japanese code and Japanese Spirit",[2] Ruth Benedict tells us. It may be used to praise a person who is not self-seeking, or of one who is free of passion, or of someone "who never verges on the danger of insulting a person he does not mean to provoke to aggression, for man is responsible for the marginal consequences of his acts as well as for the act itself".[3] A newspaper carried the story of three children who all died as the result of heart operations conducted

[1] *The Japanese are Like That.*   [2] *The Chrysanthemum and the Sword.*   [3] Ibid.

in a hospital following a mass heart check-up in the schools of the area. The bereaved parents were planning to sue the hospital charging that the "doctors showed no sincerity regarding the operations. They said the doctors expressed no apologies on the death of the children, though they had recommended the operations." The most alarming example that Ruth Benedict gives is that of a penniless youth, who was acting as janitor in a mission school in order to get his education, and announced one day to the missionaries concerned that he was planning eventually to go to the United States. They had apparently replied, "What! *You* go to America?" He never forgave this "insincerity" on their part, and years later, when a successful artist, he wrote about it saying, "One cannot sneer at innocent people without intentional insincerity", and he regarded this as worse than murder—for in his opinion "a murderer is one who assassinates human flesh, but a sneerer assassinates another *soul*".

The Westerner therefore may not only be confused by the use of English words, but he is usually quite unaware of the force with which apparently light remarks strike a Japanese. Both Kanzo Uchimura and Etsu Sugimoto show the depth of impression which (to us) very light rebukes make upon them. While Uchimura was still a very young Christian he and another student during a vacation visited a Japanese pastor in Tokyo, and he invited them both to a meal. They picked up their chopsticks to eat, but the pastor gravely said, "Do you not pray before you eat? Let us pray." Though the two young men had never even heard of this practice before, they were filled with "terrible shame and confusion" and writing of it years later he says that in the embarrassment of the moment he "remembers to this day every marking on the fish" on the plate before him. Etsu Sugimoto tells us how one day, when she was a young child, during her two-hour lesson in which they were supposed to sit absolutely motionless on the floor, her body swayed slightly, allowing her knee to slip a trifle from the proper angle. A faint shade of surprise came on her teacher's face and very quietly he closed his book. "Little miss, it is evident your mental attitude today is not suited for study.

You should retire to your room and meditate." She continues, "My little heart was almost killed with shame. The memory of that moment hurts like a bruise to this very day." She also tells of a rebuke from her mother, and its effect upon her, when she had once walked rather fast towards the house, and had therefore been unladylike. "She met me with her usual bow, and then said with a gentle smile, 'You are growing to be very like your honourable father'." Then she records how her "cheeks went hot at the reproof". We would not even know that a reproof had been meant with these words, so we can imagine how crude, and with what sledge-hammer force, some of the remarks or reproofs of a Westerner may strike those to whom they are addressed, and how many hurts we may unconsciously cause.

While the foreigner may be completely unaware of some of these differences he does become conscious of the strange fact that sometimes in Japan vices condemned by Christian teaching appear as virtues to the Japanese, not because of mere ignorance, but because they are deliberately taught as "good" behaviour in their system of morals. Examples of this include showing "respect to persons" which James so roundly condemns in his epistle; and "be not men-pleasers", "let your yea be yea and your nay, nay", "forgive your enemies". Murder even may be highly thought of if it is to get rid of some government official who is not considered worthy of the Emperor. I was surprised to learn recently that one of the assassins of a prime minister in the 1930s is still at large, and vociferous! Or a wife or daughter may be praised for going into a life of prostitution if it is for the purpose of saving the family from financial ruin. Space forbids the giving of any more examples of these differences which the foreigner will find in Japan, but enough has been said to indicate the difficulties a missionary may face in understanding the people and working harmoniously with them.

(b) THE MISSIONARY IN THE EYES OF THE JAPANESE

If the Westerner finds the Japanese hard to understand it is obvious that they will find the foreigner the same or even more incomprehensible. To them also Christian virtues may appear as vices. Plain speaking can be one of the worst crimes, and individualism is the height of selfishness. One man who later became Japan's first Methodist bishop was so shocked at hearing Christ's words regarding leaving father and mother for the sake of the Gospel that it was months before he could bring himself to go back to the Bible class. They do not admire the stress and strain of competitive life in the West, nor the terrible impatience of the Westerner, and when they do visit our countries they find the evil in them usually more noticeable than practical Christianity. To Uchimura for instance, who had imagined America peopled with puritans like the missionaries he had known, it was a very great shock to find the reality. Now that nine out of ten of the advertisements for American films on any Japanese railway station show men with guns and scantily clothed women, they think they know what America is like, and no doubt feel comfortably superior. Some cannot understand such concepts as "the pursuit of happiness" being seriously considered as a fundamental right of man. Others find American efforts to win friends abroad very puzzling. They say that to Asians this appears unseemly. "What you should seek is respect, not love." The Western philosophy that right ultimately will prevail "infuriates some critics and confuses others. That a basically religious philosophy should be left to dominate a nation's policies is almost unthinkable in Asia." To these people religion is just a matter of personal taste, somewhat like a person's preference in music or art which we would consider completely irrelevant to state policies. While the young missionary in a foreign country is usually not conscious of any responsibility for his country's policies, in the eyes of the people to whom he goes he represents his country whose statesmen's names and acts fill their newspapers. The reactions of those who hear the Gospel for the first time are usually coloured largely by their conception of the country from which the preacher comes.

In view of all these possible misunderstandings, and the fact that the Gospel has been preached in Japan for nearly 100 years, we may wonder whether there is really still a need for the foreign missionary in Japan. Since the literacy rate is almost

100 per cent, and Japan has always been a sovereign nation managing her own affairs, it became obvious fairly early that Christian leadership should be in the hands of the Japanese. Missionary societies were therefore prepared to hand over control earlier in Japan than in most other countries. I only happen to have come across the dates for two societies, but in 1917 the Japan Holiness Church, the fruit of the Oriental Missionary Society's work, was completely self-governing, though not entirely self-supporting financially until 1928. The society representing the Congregational Church handed over control to the Japanese in 1921 in the following admirable words. "So far as our evangelistic work is concerned we are ready to commit everything to you—our churches, our money, ourselves, all that we have, all that we are, for you to administer in any way that may seem best to you. We demand nothing, we ask nothing, we make no conditions. We believe in you, and we believe in your good judgment. We entrust the enterprise to you. Our one desire henceforth is to be your helpers in the fulfilment of the great programme." It was unfortunate that at the same time the Japanese churches inherited a great deal of unorthodox doctrine from some of the older denominational churches which naturally had a very weakening effect on the vitality of the church; and we cannot therefore assess clearly the effectiveness of Japanese leadership.

Even then there was much discussion as to whether missionaries were still needed. The missionaries of the Meiji Era were usually respected for their strength of character. The Jesuits' strict self-discipline too, had appealed strongly to the Japanese centuries before. But as conditions on the mission fields of the world grew easier physically, and the changes in theological outlook took the sense of urgency out of preaching the Gospel to lost sinners, there came a generation of "sight-seeing" missionaries whose presence was not very welcome in some quarters. Uchimura said, "We can appreciate *Pilgrim's Progress*, but the happy, happy honeymoon style religion, we know not what it is—it is not the Christianity of the Crucified One." And again, "Missionaries' Christianity has not yet passed through the fire in this country. On the contrary it has studiously avoided fire; hence its weakness, worldliness and (to the spiritually minded) despicableness."

Other Japanese, while not objecting on these grounds, had other reasons for complaint. In a questionnaire sent to Japanese Christian workers asking their opinion on this question in the early twenties, a small proportion said foreign missionaries were no longer needed. They found their "boss-like" attitude very offensive. "In my forty-five years experience I never had such an unpleasant feeling as I had when I received my monthly salary from the missionary", wrote one pastor. Others have complained more recently that young workers come out full of enthusiasm, sacrificial feelings and love for the people, but after two years when they find the Japanese are not becoming Christians very readily, they think they are stiff-necked or dishonest, and that they must be on their guard against them— pastors included. Another complaint is that at first the missionary is very humble, but later gets proud and wants to do everything, just as he did it at home. Sometimes they imply in their preaching that they have given up so much in coming out to Japan, and that therefore the people ought to listen to them. The Japanese find this particularly offensive for they already feel their obligations acutely. Obligations incurred from strangers are the hardest to bear and cause the most resentment. They do not like even to be offered a cigarette by a stranger. We have noticed when travelling by train as a family, if we give out tracts the recipients usually try to give candy or fruit to our children in return.

Missionaries who have had no experience of any other country than their own often naïvely suppose that their own country's customs and manners are "natural", and that if only the Japanese would give up their elaborate manners and be "natural" they would behave like us. We of course are all trained in social behaviour even though it may be largely unconscious. The only "natural" way is having no manners, like animals, and some Japanese occasionally behave in this way thinking that is what the missionary wants, and then are considered very rude. Again the missionary is also not always clear as to what Western customs are due to Christian influence and what are merely national characteristics. Some give the impression of believing there is something essentially Christian and Scriptural about democracy.

The missionary always expects the Japanese to change his age-long customs where they conflict with Christian principles, of course; and occasionally even when they just conflict with Western practice, yet he himself finds it very difficult to change some of his own customs. In Japan this year at a meeting of the representatives of nearly all the evangelical missionary societies it was claimed that we were "united in recognition of the Bible as the only authoritative source of our beliefs, and *the only guide for our lives*". Yet how far from the truth that latter point is. Each of us is guided by national customs far more than we realize. So there are many ways in which East and West do not see eye to eye, and in which it is possible for misunderstandings to occur, and each of us of course can see the weaknesses of the other more than his own.

In the 1920s, however, the majority of the Japanese still felt they could not do without the help of the foreign missionary. The most obvious need was still in the rural areas, and it was not possible, economically, for many Japanese to work there. Christians were too few to be able to support a pastor, and since most farmers could barely feed their own families there was little scope for a Christian worker to be self-supporting. In the cities, missionaries could still do useful work as assistants to Japanese pastors, both by holding English Bible classes which always proved attractive to some, and by evangelism, for the missionary's message often seems to bring forth decisions to become Christian. Then there was always scope in teaching and training Christian workers. Most of course felt that Japanese workers were preferable because "they understand the psychology of the people, speak the same language and easily comprehend the intricate and complicated family and social systems". However, they do not always know what will be successful, under God's hand. For instance when Mr. Gurney Binford suggested the use of a tent for evangelism Japanese Christians prophesied that it would not be successful, that people would just come on the first night out of curiosity. Yet this has proved the most successful of all methods of evangelism in Japan. In the same way well meaning Christians in England did not think the ministry of such men as D. L. Moody or Billy Graham would prove successful in that country. Occasionally an outsider may have a clearer vision than the people within a country.

One Japanese leader rather surprisingly thought that missionaries were still needed in administrative positions. He wrote, "The Japanese workers have some organizing ability, but as executors they do not yet rank with foreign workers. They work long and hard without adequate results. The fruit of their labour does not seem commensurate with the labour itself. They certainly are not businesslike—a defect they share with the Japanese people as a whole." Many foreigners might be inclined to agree with this view after a few years experience in Japan. The many hours spent in "discussions" no doubt account partly for the long hours of work without adequate results. Yet on second thoughts one remembers the tremendous organizing genius of the Tokugawas; or later of the Ministry of Education, or the five great business empires of Japan known as the Zaibatsu; or even the Tenrikyo with its carefully planned campaign for the conversion of the world. Why is this administrative genius not visible in the Christian Church? Is it that the others have only been achieved through the feudalistic system of unquestioning obedience of all the followers to the acknowledged leader? Perhaps it is of some significance that the Anglican church is the largest single group in Japan, and that two Holiness groups formed since the war under the leadership of a single head, with all the functions of a bishop, have made great strides in membership.

What were the qualities desired in the missionary going to Japan at that time (the nineteen-twenties)? One is almost amused at the qualifications suggested, for such men are rare even in the churches at home: "a man of pre-eminent learning, a scientist, psychologist and theologian with a strong and winning personality"; or "of strong Christian character, personality, learning and ability, a student of scientific research and completely Japanese in his attitude—the missionary in the past knew only colloquial Japanese, and did not understand the ideas of the people. The missionary of the future should know the pantheistic and Confucian thought of Japan and should have general knowledge of the past and present literature of the country to influence the people—Conversation and social intercourse alone do not make one acquainted with Japan and its people."[1] The last sentence is certainly very true, and Uchimura, too, was very critical of those who knew nothing of the history and religions of Japan, dismissing it as "just heathenism". After residing in the United States and seeing how comparatively easy it was to accept Christ there he said, "You Christians who were brought up in Christian homes and are constantly breathing Christian atmosphere can hardly imagine what a violent process it is to try to bring heathen souls to the conception of the Risen Saviour."

Some people still feel it is a waste of time to bother with the details of heathenism, or that too detailed a sociological study might paralyse their faith that God can save the Japanese. A more subtle danger is that one can almost come to the place of feeling that it is doing the Japanese an unkindness to persuade them to become Christians; it looses such a hornets' nest of problems about their heads. This I believe is one of Satan's most effective weapons. How easily he can blind us to the fact that without hope and without Christ they are in a far more miserable condition. That a real knowledge of their beliefs and background is valuable for the missionary was illustrated in a helpful article published recently in the *Japan Harvest* (Summer 1957) by B. R. Buss, a pre-war missionary to Japan. In it he tells of an interview with an elderly widow who was seeking baptism and who states, "For two years now I've hesitated to be baptized, because I didn't want to throw my husband away." I do not know how she came to have this idea. Perhaps some missionary had once used the wrong word, or perhaps knowing nothing of the background of family god shelves had thought of them all as idols, and just said everything must be destroyed before anyone could be baptized. I am told that the Japanese do not think of their ancestor worship as idolatry

[1] *Japan Speaks for Herself.*

because in Japanese the word idolatry means literally the worship of an idol or image. The Japanese mind seems to find it so hard to distinguish between fantasy and fact, between human and divine, and the physical and spiritual, that many must regard something of the essential spirit of their ancestors or relatives to be residing still in the ancestral tablets. This lady's questions revealed her confusion of thought on this issue. She had first asked if she could keep her husband's picture, and received the answer yes, so long as she did not worship it—all Christians keep pictures of their dead loved ones. Then she asked if she "must sever all connections with my ancestors?" The missionary told her that the Bible tells us to honour our parents, and that we do not give up our love for our ancestors when they are dead, but a Christian must not *worship* them. No doubt the whole imaginary conception of the functions and powers of the spirits of the ancestors must be cleared up before a new believer can "sever connections" with them with a clear conscience; he must realize that the offerings of food and drink, etc., cannot benefit the spirits in any way.

One of the qualifications Uchimura suggested for the missionary was "with your Christianity sifted from your -isms, and common sense sharpened with devils fought out in your own soul"—in other words those with a real experience of Christ in their own lives were needed.

The Japanese whom our mission survey team consulted stressed the need for men of humility and spirituality too. With only 270,000 Protestant Christians in a rapidly expanding population of over 90 million, the need for labourers is still great, but they must be labourers who are prepared by God. They must have love and grace as they proclaim the Gospel, and as they help in the training of Japanese leaders. Perhaps their most important function is to help them to take unto themselves the whole armour of God, and in particular to have their "loins girt about with truth". Above all, they must be those who have confidence that God will fulfil His Word that the captives of the mighty shall be released.

Part Two

THE PREACHING OF RELEASE

Chapter XIV

WITH LONG PATIENCE

IN recent years two main methods have been used in opening up new work in Japan. Some Christian leaders, both missionary and Japanese, have felt that the ideal way is to send a tent team in as a spearhead. Then when some have professed conversion a Japanese or missionary worker should take up residence in that area, teach the nucleus of new believers, with the purpose of establishing a local church, and when numbers warrant it, encourage them to secure a church-building.

Others, mainly missionary societies with funds at their disposal, decide on a strategic location in a city, build a church building, announce a schedule of services and meetings, and gradually gather a group together. They feel the establishing of a central church base is essential, and that other evangelistic efforts should work out from there. As one missionary has expressed it, "Pure surroundings are necessary for the learning of God's Word. Idolatry's counterattack seems strong enough to overthrow most evangelism which meets in homes and rented halls defiled with idolatry. There are few Christian homes where the head of the family is a believer and so the idols remain untouched. Bringing God's ark into Dagon's house spells trouble for both camps." Further it is said that in Japan as long as a meeting place is temporary the people of the community tend to think of the whole work as temporary. Leading city men, the heads of households, usually avoid tent meetings and dirty public halls, yet these are the people most needed in the forming of a stable church.

God seems to have blessed both these methods and we cannot answer with any authority as to which is the better in the long run. During the war those which had no building or government recognition were not allowed to meet, while those which were registered were all placed in one organization controlled by the government. The majority of individual members from every group compromised by outwardly conforming to State Shinto worship.

When the C.I.M. began to work in Japan in 1951 the Mission's newly developed indigenous policy formulated on withdrawal from China, did not allow the paying of any national Christian to do evangelistic work, nor the building or renting of any premises for the purpose of holding meetings. We tried to find towns where there was no Christian witness, and where at the same time there were small cheap houses to rent—an exceedingly difficult undertaking in a country which had so recently lost such a large proportion of its houses through bombing raids. However, many people were surprisingly friendly. God did finally lead to available houses here and there on the island of Hokkaido, and later in Aomori prefecture in northern Honshu, Japan's main island. Since Aomori is one of the few places with a difficult dialect it has been largely neglected by both foreigners and Japanese Christian workers.

Four C.I.M. women missionaries were able to share in the work of already existing Presbyterian churches, but the rest of the workers, with no Christian Japanese helper, without any known contacts, and with little more than a year's study of this country's difficult language and even less knowledge of its customs, had to begin pioneer work in various small country towns and villages where the "web society" is usually at its strongest.

One of our young men who went to such a place in Aomori wrote something of his feelings at the time, in a letter home. "Most of our time is taken up with language study. At present we still feel quite unable to do anything much. It's hard to have been in Japan almost two years and not be able to read one paragraph of the Bible with any fluency or without making a number of mistakes. I can't write a letter in simple Japanese yet, nor can I read an eight-year-old's school reader." (Changes have since been made in our study course which give us some Bible work a little earlier.) "Any talks I give I go through with the teacher first, and he corrects all the grammar, etc. Then I write it all out in romanised letters and read it; if I take my eyes off the paper, I am lost. As for the hymns I can sing the sounds, but don't know what the words mean. We always have one of the Japanese read the Bible, and we try to follow in the English version: they read too fast for us to follow the Japanese. I usually write the prayer out or memorize it, and then pray. So, as you can imagine, any meeting we take is a strain from beginning to end, and we realize it is only the work of the Holy Spirit which brings any people along more than once."

Fortunately they were not entirely limited in their work and witness to the stumbling little sermons they were able to read in Japanese to the handful of people who were courageous enough to climb to their upstairs rooms to listen. One thing that even the least experienced can do is give out tracts, and this was done frequently when travelling, and also in systematic house to house visitation in the neighbourhood. There is an organization in Japan called the Every Home Crusade whose aim is to place a series of tracts in every home in the country. Over 13 million, more than two-thirds of the nation's homes, have so far received at least one tract; and 17,000 people have enrolled in a follow-up Bible correspondence course as a result of this work, though some did not continue for long.

Perhaps it will be of interest to follow the missionary Stephen Metcalf, whose early letter I have just quoted. Six months later he tells more of their patient sowing and tending of the seed through the long northern winter.

"It started to snow shortly before Christmas, and didn't let up till the end of March. Living on the plain as we do, the snow used to be blown in great drifts; we saw it slowly heaping up till all our downstairs windows were filled in. Every time we went out it was a struggle all the way, putting on layers of thick clothes and walking in the constantly blowing snow.

"As our district is predominantly a farming one, the long cold winters give us a wonderful opportunity of reaching these people in their homes, and we spend a lot of time going from door to door selling Scripture portions and distributing tracts. We have so far only managed to cover this town (population

8,000) and about three nearby villages of 3,000-6,000 people each. We introduce ourselves and tell the people very simply what we are there for, and if any seem interested we speak for a short time about the Gospel. But in spite of all the homes visited, with the exception of a girl of twenty, no one has come to our meetings as a result of all this house to house visitation. I am of the opinion that unless we are able to visit many times, little will be achieved by this kind of work.

"One week we had a letter from the principal of a country school asking us to visit him and his family, and a few days later he came for a talk. His main purpose was to get the best he could for his family and he wanted his fifteen-year-old son to learn English from us. He explained that the gods of Japan were defeated during the war, so they were left without a faith, and he wanted his children to adopt Christianity rather than turn to materialistic philosophy which could not improve the moral structure of the nation.

"We promised to visit him the following week-end and had to go a long cross-country journey by train. All the trains were late because of the snow storms and we had to shelter behind walls from the blowing snow while waiting (some stations have no waiting rooms). The trains were so late that when we arrived at this man's nearest station there were no horse sleighs to meet the train and we had to set out to walk the last five miles across the plain in the raging blizzard. For the last mile or so we caught up with a farmer's sleigh and crouched in the back of it while the snow piled in on us and we got colder and colder.

"When we arrived we were very hospitably received and had a good opportunity to talk with the family. . . . The son has been coming over to our Bible class ever since, but so far there seems no true seeking after God. At first some people feel they want a religion, and like the Christian teaching, but they do not want the Cross to become a personal issue."

So much physical, mental and spiritual effort, and yet so little apparent result. Truly our workers had to wait with long patience to see the precious fruit of their sowing. But at last Metcalf was able to write of the first green shoot appearing from the hard ground, the conversion of the nineteen-year-old son of the next-door neighbour.

Another missionary, now Mrs. Olga Abrahams, wrote of her systematic tract distribution in an inland city of Hokkaido during her second year in Japan.

"Two weeks later we returned to the same houses with the next tract of the series, and were greeted with less fear, and at the third visit we were greeted by: 'Every time! Thank you very much. . . .'

"A tradesman received the first tracts, and asked for more teaching, but was too busy over New Year, and we have heard no more.

"Mrs. Y. received them eagerly, but was leaving the district. Would we send on the tracts if she left her address? But she never did.

"One grey-haired man always encouraged us with his gracious manner. . . . One day he had a request, the tracts were in a series, but two were missing. Would they let him have nos. 44 and 45?

"A barber, brought to the Lord through the Salvation Army ten years ago, was moved on receiving the tracts to return to the church. He came one night, and has come no more."

Much work was done, and much patience needed, but now four years later, we can add to the stories of this early tract distribution. The old man who wanted to complete the series of tracts was later visited by a Bible Society colporteur, and bought some gospel portions and attended the church that night to hear this man speak. He continued to attend church and eventually became language teacher for one of the missionaries.

One day they were studying a story about three blind men trying to describe an elephant. He suddenly said he was like the blind men, and could not understand Christianity. Thelma Brown turned to the Bible and showed him 1 John 1: 9 ("If we confess our sins, He is faithful and just to forgive us our sins, and to cleanse us from all unrighteousness"), and he broke down and prayed for salvation. He had had an important position in the city Electricity Department before his retirement, but used to drink himself to sleep every night. Now he has two desks, one for Bible study and one for ordinary work. His greatest difficulty is getting a quiet time, for as soon as he stirs in the morning all the women of the household, in true Japanese style, are there to wait on him hand and foot with his clothes and breakfast.

Another man to whom Olga Abrahams had first given tracts in hospital is also a very different person now from when she first knew him. Just before that he had an unsuccessful operation for tuberculosis which meant he would probably be in hospital for life. He read the New Testament through and many other books on Christianity and gradually came to a saving faith in Christ. Now he reads the whole Bible. Because it is too heavy for him in his very weak condition he has had a special frame made to hold it. Other patients in the ward, seeing his real enjoyment in reading this Book have asked to be able to read it too. His doctor was so surprised at the change in him that both he and his wife have begun attending meetings. They asked the missionaries to visit a friend of theirs who also had tuberculosis, hoping she would be changed just like Mr. Tamiya. He says he is glad now that the operation was unsuccessful, otherwise he might never have heard the Gospel. Nor is this the end of the sequence of events since that original visit with a tract. For the doctor's friend also became a Christian and his wife proved to be a backslider now restored. The doctor himself was converted in Tokyo when Margrit Bahler, from that same Hokkaido city, visited him.

These latter converts are all the result of the last two years of work when language has come more easily and the ways of the people are beginning to be understood. What goes through the minds of these people when they first meet the missionaries? What is the process which brings them eventually to the place where they feel a desire to worship the unknown God about whom they hear in the halting language of the strange and awkward foreigner?

I was fortunate to be able to learn something of this from the daughter of the landlord of two C.I.M. missionaries living in a small seaside town in Hokkaido. She, through prolonged contact with Lucille Hall and Winnifred Medhurst (now Mrs. Don Morris) and the help of a Christian friend, came to put her trust in Christ. Single women missionaries cannot live as public a life as the men, and are more limited in the scope of their work. But it is good to know that fruit is borne by lives quietly lived for the glory of Christ as well as by the preaching of the Gospel. I give this account as nearly as possible in the girl's words.

"It is about two years now since I was saved. From my childhood I had always had all the material things I needed or desired, but sometimes I felt that something was lacking.

"Just after the war I entered the district senior high school which was two hours journey by train from my house. Often we older girls would talk about the great difficulties of travelling to school. About that time I started praying at night; but, as I look back now, I realize it was to a god I had conjured up in my own mind. As post-war conditions improved, however, I forgot about this experience." (I had a taste of these "improved" conditions during my visit to Hokkaido when I travelled on that same train which is still crowded with students. It was so tightly packed that I had bruises at the back of both legs from pressure against the framework of the train.)

"In May 1953 God sent missionaries to our town and their home was close to my house. There they held a Bible Class, and my brother suggested I go to this on Sunday evenings, but I didn't feel like going at all. At that time I went away for a year to a sewing school in Sapporo. Then the teacher asked me to stay and do another year of more advanced work, but as my brother was getting married I went home for the summer vacation intending to go back to Sapporo. After the wedding I decided I would go over to the missionaries' house. So on 11th July, 1954, I heard the Gospel for the first time. I don't remember anything that was said, but I enjoyed the atmosphere and the hymn singing.

"The second time I went Miss Medhurst asked me if I could teach her Japanese for a month, and I finally decided I would. After that I was asked for a second month, and then Miss Hall lost her teacher, so I taught them both. Often I wished I knew more English so I could be of more help to them. Through teaching them I heard a lot about Jesus Christ, and read the Bible with them, but it didn't have much meaning for me. Many times a missionary would pray that people might believe in Christ, and I wondered very much why foreigners had to take all the trouble to come to Japan to tell people about Jesus. I often heard that all people are sinners and about the only true and living God; and I wondered why the Christian's God was the only one qualified for these adjectives!

"I began to be aware of the truth that all men are sinners, that the wages of sin is death, but that there is life in Christ. I learned that Jesus died on the Cross in place of sinners, but I myself never thought of receiving Him into my own heart.

"I also began to realize a lot of the inconveniences which would arise if I became a Christian. But in coming to know the missionaries better, and the way in which they lived, I would compare myself with them and feel really ashamed.

"Once one of them said, 'Believe on the Lord Jesus, for those who don't are against Him.' In my diary that night I wrote that I didn't think I could ever become a Christian unless I experienced some real problem or shock in my life. I looked around and saw that other people were living without God. Why shouldn't I?

"I continued going to meetings, however. At that time Miss Medhurst was sick and had to go away for some months. In October Miss Hall was away too. One day I received a letter from the one who was sick, saying that though she couldn't speak freely because of lack of language, she wanted me to know that salvation was a gift from God, because of what Christ had done on the Cross, and all I had to do was receive it. I was very touched at her troubling to write, since I had only known her a short time, and I was also glad to know receiving Christ was such a wonderful thing. I began to feel I must speak with other Christians, so I wrote to a former high school class mate of mine who was a Christian and lived two hours journey away.

"My friend wrote giving her testimony, and said God was

knocking at my heart, quoting Rev. 3: 20. On 25th October I visited this friend's home. The whole family were Christians and welcomed me very much and told me many new things. Then I believed that God who made the earth and all things was the only true God. I talked with them long into the night, and next morning joined them in family worship, then came home full of praise that God had had mercy on me and brought me to Himself. I wrote to Miss Medhurst and was glad to receive the testimonies of two of her teachers in Karuizawa. I realized how silly my former fears had been, and that no man can serve two masters.

"Then Miss Hall came back and I rejoiced with her, and felt I must tell others about Christ. So on 1st December I was able to give my testimony at the service. The desk in my room which formerly was used only for writing letters and my diary now became a place for fellowship with the Lord and His Word. I realized why foreigners came to Japan to do evangelistic work, and began to realize what a great responsibility it was to help them in their language studies. I also began to teach in the Sunday School.

"On 17th July I was baptized . . . and in the following January went to the first Christian Conference held in Sapporo and received much blessing there. I realized in a new way the greatness of the Lord's love, and gave myself completely to Him. Now I am praying for my family to be saved. There are many things I don't know yet, and I do stumble sometimes; but I rejoice that the Lord is helping me."

As our workers after long patient sowing and watering hear words like these their hearts rejoice, although at the same time crying out that the work of release begun for these people may be permanent. The January Conference mentioned above was a time when the Hokkaido workers could see something of the fruit of the Spirit's working, as forty Christians gathered from the different centres, and experienced, for the first time in their lives, the fellowship of other Christians and heard two experienced Japanese workers give messages. Some who were there have since fallen away—Satan has them caught again in his bonds. The girl who has told us her experiences so graphically has had to leave home for refusing a non-Christian marriage and is helping Mrs. Morris (formerly Miss Medhurst) with the housework in Sapporo while trying to find another job. Others too, are continuing in the faith, still rejoicing in what they learnt at the Conference.

Chapter XV

TENT EVANGELISM

AS far as he knows, Gurney Binford, the Quaker missionary, was the first to use a tent as a means of evangelism in Japan, in 1915. Gradually others adopted the idea and now it is probably the most widely used method in the country. I do not know why this is so. Perhaps one reason is that the weather is uncertain in Japan, and it is a cheap and convenient way of providing a public auditorium in whatever place one wishes. Perhaps part of the reason is that open-air speaking is "distasteful" to the average Japanese, and Dr. J. Natori tells us in Japan "such proceedings are eyed with suspicion".[1] In China one had no difficulty in getting a hearing anywhere in the market-place—the foreigner had only to show his face and a crowd would immediately gather. Public story-tellers also were a common sight in the open tea-shops, and they too would easily draw a crowd. In Japan, however, only the *kamishibai* (paper play) man usually operates in the open air, and his audience is limited to small children. He goes around one or two streets beating a gong or banging two sticks together. Then ten or fifteen children will come running and pay their coppers to receive some gaudy coloured candy which entitles them to watch the paper play. A wooden framework is usually fixed on the front or back of the man's bicycle, and large picture cards perhaps a foot square are slipped through the frame in sequence as the story proceeds. Some people have produced Bible and other Christian stories on these *kamishibai* cards, feeling it is an excellent way of reaching the children. Others believe that presented in this way the children think of the stories merely as fiction, just like their own Japanese stories.

Apart from these *kamishibai* men there is little personal public

[1] *Historical Stories of Christianity in Japan.*

speaking in the streets. There is, however, a very great deal of speaking and advertising by means of loudspeakers. Politicians in the numerous election campaigns will speak from the seclusion of cars, and stores will often advertise from vans and trucks until a neighbourhood is deafened. Communists have not been slow to use this method, but I have no means of knowing if they have found it successful or not. Some Christians who did open-air work at some of the busy railway stations soon after the war have told me there were no lasting results from it. Kagawa wrote in the 1920s, "Though for sixteen years I never gave up preaching by the wayside twice every week, yet I can reckon but few men who became Christians as a result of the method. Most of those whom I was able to lead to Christ were led by personal contact and friendship."[1]

The harvest from tent campaigns is one of the most encouraging aspects of evangelism in Japan, however. The Japan Evangelistic Band has used this method for some time and find there are always some permanent results from each campaign, the cost of which is only about $50 for a week or ten days of meetings. The Oriental Missionary Society and The Evangelical Alliance Mission of North America also have well trained Japanese teams who specialize in this work. These are not only the means of forming churches for their own Japanese church organizations, but willingly accept invitations from other churches or missionaries to help evangelize their areas. The Oriental Missionary Society has teams of one or two missionaries and several Japanese who stay four or five weeks in one area having evangelistic meetings the first three weeks, then meetings for those who have professed conversion for two weeks. These numbers vary from a dozen to 100 people, and often a church is formed, with a graduate from their Bible school coming to take charge. Many churches have been formed in this way, and they plan to cover every prefecture of Japan by means of tent evangelism.

Just recently I have heard of the encouraging example of a young man brought to Christ through a tent campaign, run by a team consisting of a young missionary and experienced

[1] *Japan Speaks for Herself.*

Japanese workers, in a village some distance out from Tokyo. The missionary was to speak by interpretation, and a young farmer decided to cycle over from a village five miles away, so that he could hear some English. He went on a number of occasions, sometimes taking his crippled mother on the back of his bicycle, and finally at one of the meetings he decided to become a Christian. There was no church group in his own village, and he did not show signs of being a very strong Christian. A little later at a Youth for Christ rally in Tokyo, however, he surrendered his life to Christ, and felt called to become a preacher of the Gospel. But being the only son in a farming family, it was not very easy for him to leave home. His eldest sister had committed suicide some time before, and his father had taken to drink, selling some of the family possessions in order to buy liquor. It seemed as if his place should be in the home, yet he went and helped in several tent missions run by the Oriental Missionary Society and was much used by the Lord there. On the day he returned home from one of these campaigns he spent much time pleading with his mother to accept Christ, and finally around midnight she believed. His father had angrily gone off to bed when he started speaking of the Gospel, but when he heard their voices raised in prayer and praise after the mother was converted, he got up and, with tears, fell on his knees and accepted the Lord.

On the son's next visit home he found the *kamidana* and *butsudan* (god shelves) both taken out of the home, though he had not mentioned this subject to them, and there was no one else to give them any Christian teaching. They told him they had just realized in their hearts that it was wrong to have them. They experienced a good deal of opposition in their community at first; but now their neighbours are beginning to be impressed with the reality of their religion. Seventy children are meeting in their home for Sunday School, and just a year after the son's conversion seven members of that family had become Christian. The son himself is now a student in Bible School.

Three teams, trained under the auspices of the Evangelical Alliance Mission, were working in some C.I.M. centres last summer, and I received a number of letters telling of some of the results, and the methods of work.

In one mining area in Hokkaido they were not granted permission to set up a tent, but were allowed to use the little assembly halls provided by the mining company for their workers in the various settlements. These halls were packed tight, 500 at a time, for the children's meeting. One of the chief difficulties in tent work is to keep the children out of the adult meetings. However, older people did attend; and, at one of the places, 1,500 people gathered in the open air for the showing of a film and an hour's preaching. This is the largest crowd ever to gather so far in any of our meetings.

Decision cards are handed out after most tent meetings to those who ask for them; but one C.I.M. worker has suggested it would be more accurate to call them interest cards. It is probably true that few oriental people realize fully to what they are giving their assent when they put up their hands or sign their names on decision cards. Often it is more a gesture of politeness, thinking they are doing a small action to please the speaker. Sometimes perhaps, they regard it as signing up to undertake a course of study. As we saw in our chapters on the religions of Japan there is little to prepare them there for the great moral issues involved in becoming a Christian. A former missionary of the Japan Evangelistic Band once told us that in their preaching hall in a particularly notorious section of Kobe eighty per cent. of those who say they want to believe, and who are talked to, and prayed with by a trained Japanese personal worker, are discovered during the "follow-up" to have given false addresses. However, the other twenty per cent. prove a harvest infinitely worth while, and a score of churches in the surrounding areas have resulted from this Kobe Gospel Hall work alone.

In another centre where Arthur and Joy Reynolds of the C.I.M. have been working, and where there was previously no permanent witness for Christ, it was discovered that a tent campaign had been held there some years before by a Japanese Holiness Church group and nearly 100 had professed conversion, many of them children. The only fruit still visible in the town is one young woman and her brother, who are now helping in the Sunday School which has been organized. One reason may be the movement of population, especially young people, towards the cities, and this was an evacuation area from Tokyo during the war, and has since emptied again. But even if all the rest of the harvest was lost except for these two, the campaign we believe was still worth while; for there is joy in heaven over one sinner repenting and turning to Christ, and becoming a glimmer of light in this spiritually dark corner of Satan's stronghold.

To return to our Hokkaido mining area, there have been about 400 cards signed and handed in, over half of them being from eleven to fourteen year olds. Some of these addresses have already been visited in follow-up work, and the reception accorded has varied from cold, to very warm-hearted by some of the adults who, our worker says, really seem to be "carrying faith". While time will tell which really entered into newness of life, it seems as if there may be about a dozen adults. Meanwhile it is good to have a pretext for visiting many homes to speak further of Christ. It is encouraging also to know that in some cases we are reaping the fruit of others' sowing. Some of these people had attended Sunday School in other places during their childhood; some had already been influenced towards Christ by hearing the "Lutheran Hour" radio programme. So even if the work of these particular campaigns may have been largely that of sowing we can look forward to a day when those who are still bound, but have been made aware of their chains, may realize they can indeed be made free by the power of Christ, and will knowingly take that step of faith.

Another of these tent teams went to Hachinohe, a city of about 160,000, which is a big commercial centre in Aomori prefecture. Here, where more sophisticated entertainment is always available, numbers attending were much smaller than in the more remote mining settlements of Hokkaido. Here again, however, the Holy Spirit was at work delivering some of the captives. In the adult meetings eighty to 100 people would usually stay and listen throughout the meetings, and about thirty signed cards. Five attended the Sunday service the following week, and so here again we trust a nucleus will remain to form a church in this area to which one C.I.M. couple, Mr. and Mrs. Lea Little, have recently moved.

As you can imagine, this type of campaign is hard work, but in these cold northern areas there are only about three months in which such meetings can be held, so Japanese and missionaries keep at it, foregoing the pleasure of a needed vacation at the time when it is most pleasant to take one. Perhaps you would like to hear how most of the days are spent, so that you can enter more fully into the labours of these for whom you pray. David Hayman, the C.I.M. missionary in the mining district, writes that the members of the team, who all stayed in his house, seemed pretty well worn out, having preached with all their might in various parts of Japan in almost continuous meetings since the beginning of April. (It was mid-July when they came to him.) "Their day time was spent in rest, doing their laundry, or lying on their tummies reading the Scriptures or going over their messages for the night. At about 3 p.m. they would go out announcing the children's meeting which lasted from 4 to 5 p.m. Back for a clean up, *obento* (a kind of picnic style supper usually consisting of cold rice balls and hot green tea), then out on the streets for three-quarters of an hour with the portable loudspeaker, announcing the evening meeting which lasted from 7.30 to 9 p.m. Personal work usually occupied them from 9.0 to 10.0 p.m., and one of the team particularly was quick to dart from the front at the end of the meeting to sit beside some older person and speak to them personally of Christ. Others would gather four or five people around them. Eventually we would stow the gear, then home for a slice of water melon or cup of milk, pull out our *futon* (mattress and bedding) and flop into bed." (Bed of course being the floor.) As these particular meetings were not in a tent they were spared the necessity of acting as watchmen there.

Mr. Gurney Binford who originated tent campaigns had an even more ambitious programme. He usually went with a team of Japanese specialists to a place where there was already an existing work, and had several daily meetings for the Christians in addition.

As well as the exacting programme one has to remember the total absence of privacy during these campaigns, which is an additional strain on most Westerners. I was interested to see in Gurney Binford's book,[1] and also in Amy Carmichael's letters from Japan, that their meetings in the evening were usually later than those our workers arrange. Miss Carmichael writes, "long past midnight, but nobody seems inclined to go. The children have fallen asleep on the mats or in their mothers' arms, and the elder ones press closer together. We cannot send them away, and the meeting begins again." When I was able to visit some of our tent meetings later it seemed that many people were not free till after eight o'clock. Yet constant late meetings are a heavy strain physically, and it is not surprising that many of the earlier workers suffered breakdowns in health.

Apart from the trained teams of tent evangelists who serve all over the country, local churches also own tents and organize campaigns as special evangelistic efforts near at home, using their own personnel, and possibly a visiting speaker. Some of these I was privileged to see during my visit to Hokkaido and Aomori, and I shall write of them later. To me one of the most encouraging things about these was that nearly all the Japanese speakers I heard had themselves been converted in tent meetings.

Some churches hold campaigns at the sites of big local festivals, such as cherry viewing. Some C.I.M. workers are living in the historic city of Hirosaki where hundreds of thousands of people come each year to see the giant cherry trees which are planted around the remains of the 350-year-old feudal castle. It is a most entrancing sight, especially when the trees are illuminated at night. There is a special verb in the Japanese language for going to view their famous cherry trees, and bulletins are issued beforehand as to the exact day when the petals will begin to open at every well-known site. These are the scenes of family picnics and organizational outings, but for a Christian foreigner the whole thing is spoilt by the inevitable huge two-quart bottles of *sake*, and litter of lunch boxes, which

[1] *Forty Years in Japan.*

accompany the viewing. Possibly this is the result of post-war changes in outlook and custom, for Amy Carmichael gives us a very different picture of this event towards the end of the last century. "These people have the most delicate sense of enjoyment conceivable, and they express it as delicately . . . they come in little companies, and wander among the trees, staying where the view is fairest to lovingly admire. Sometimes they bring lunches in little lacquer boxes tied up in coloured handkerchiefs, so that they may spend all day in gentle pleasuring. There is nothing rude here, no boisterous display. They accord to their flowers far more reverence than many a Christian bestows upon his Christ."

Now, however, the picture is rather different, but whatever the conditions it is a time when people have some leisure. This year therefore, C.I.M. workers, who are beginning to be able to speak more freely, were able to organize some tent meetings there, with the help of other missionaries and experienced Japanese Christians from the city of Aomori. They had no loudspeaker, so were handicapped in competing against the commercial ones advertising many products and amusements, ranging from the harmless to the definitely obscene. Nearly half a million tracts were given out and very eagerly received; and it was encouraging to see that very few of these were thrown away. Various small open-air meetings were held, but with no loudspeaker it was impossible for most voices to carry more than a few yards. The tent, however, was pitched in a quieter spot below, near the moat of the castle, and in the evenings the film *God of Creation* was shown. As soon as the tent became dark people seemed willing to enter, and many stayed on to listen to the Gospel message. Most of the people were at least partially drunk by that time. One who was in pretty bad condition came in and sat down, only to be taken out again by his friends. He came in again, but his friends once more dragged him out, calling as he went, "I want to believe in Christ. I want to believe." Whether it was the cry of his heart, or mere intoxication we do not know, but at least his opportunity for deliverance then was denied him.

To our workers it seemed remarkable that well dressed,

important looking men of all ages were among the crowds, in the same state as everyone else. Teachers in charge of school parties were drunk too, and people staggered and fell with babies on their backs. One man lay across the top of the steep slope from the castle ruins, and only a friend hanging on to him prevented him rolling down into the moat. This was obviously one of the occasions when all could escape for a few hours from "the web" and its obligations, and were free from public censure and criticism of any kind, whatever they did. Someone has said that no people so desperately want to get drunk as the Japanese. A writer, Kimpei Sheba, says that many Japanese actually feign drunkenness because they are afraid to act naturally otherwise, they are bound by so many artificial restraints in everyday life. But what sort of freedom is this obtained through intoxication? Merely an exchange from one form of Satan's bondage to another. During the war the officers of the Japanese Army occasionally gave their men freedom to do just as they liked in some of the foreign countries they invaded, and the result was the horrible outbreaks of rape and cruelty which have not been forgotten in parts of China, Hongkong and Manila. These things prove that the Japanese are like all other human beings; in spite of all their painfully-learned, strong, cultural habits, their heart is not changed by these habits. For out of the heart of man proceedeth adulteries, murders, etc. Freedom from their cultural restraints for a few moments may be a tremendous relief, but the cost is heavy— the little children trying to lead their drunken parents home, the prostitute's bills the longsuffering wife has to pay for her husband, the money wasted on drink which should go into nourishing food for the family. Perhaps worst of all is the fact that none of these things are regarded as wrong, in their place, and at the proper time. The god of this world has blinded their eyes and they cannot know freedom in its true sense until they have found Christ. "If the Son shall make you free ye shall be free indeed."

Some, even at such a time of sensuality as cherry viewing, have found this freedom. Twelve people signed decision cards during those meetings, and from that time a break really came in the little group which had been meeting in the missionaries' home, after months of discouragement.

One of the most interesting converts was a young man who was apprenticed to the Tsugaru lacquer craft—a type of lacquer ware peculiar to that area. He had to work from very early in the morning to late at night, but one day he decided to walk home through the park since the cherries were in blossom. There he heard the Gospel, and later came to the house to make further enquiries. One of the younger workers, Thelma Brown, was the only one at home and she talked to him as best she could, but did not feel sure if she had made herself understood or not, when he said he believed all she had told him. Later she asked one of the more experienced T.E.A.M. missionaries to speak to him and he was obviously quite clear about his salvation. Because of his work he can only come late at night, but is now attending regularly on Friday and Sunday nights for Bible study.

So God has spoken many times through His servants as they have proclaimed the message of salvation under canvas throughout the length of the Japanese islands; and perhaps more have been born again, sitting on narrow backless benches or kneeling on coarse straw mats beneath a tent, than in any other type of meeting place. Many new churches too, have come into being as the result of a tent campaign.

Chapter XVI

THE NORTHERN ISLAND

HAVING prayed about the places and people of Hokkaido ever since the first two C.I.M. workers had felt called to begin work there three years before, I was very glad of an opportunity last summer to see for myself the missionaries at work. But most of all I rejoiced to meet some of the Japanese up there who have become followers of Christ. My heart instinctively warmed to this austere, cold, yet beautiful country, and the hardy people who have only comparatively recently begun to populate it.

It was the end of June when I arrived, and the short but warm summer was just beginning, making everything a rich green beneath the clear blue sky and the mountains still occasionally snow-clad. But I know from experience in Canada what it would be like in the long winter with the whole land blanketed under several feet of snow. In most places I visited, the missionaries too, were enjoying the early summer of their spiritual harvest; there were the green shoots, and even blossom and fruit visible after a year or more of Christian experience in the lives of some who are now bearing open testimony to their faith.

There were some, however, who the previous year had accepted Christ, but whose spiritual life is now invisible, as if a soft smothering blanket of snow had fallen on it. The constant opposition of their families and social culture, rarely violent, but patient, gentle, persevering, like the falling of snow flakes day after day, had finally obscured their faith, and caused them to stop their fellowship with other Christians, and even their reading of the Bible. Nothing remains visible to the human eye of their profession of faith save perhaps a signed decision card after one of the tent campaigns. God alone knows if these were really born again. But it may be that some are fertile seeds, hidden now for a time, it is true, by the winter snow yet which one day will be released from their cold prison to blossom to the glory of God. To this end we continually pray.

The industries of Hokkaido are mainly timber, pulp and fishing, with dairy farming taking an increasing place now that butter, cheese and powdered milk are finding a place in the national diet, and mining.

I arrived at the first place I visited just after lunch to find our missionary David Hayman, in the midst of an ordinarily busy schedule plus extra calls on his time and hospitality just then. He had already had his regular nurses' meeting in the morning at the hospital, where twenty to thirty came to study the Bible. Three Japanese guests were staying in his small house. One was a Mr. Koyama, the advance contact man of The Evangelical Alliance Mission tent teams, who visited places beforehand making all the arrangements for the evangelistic campaigns which were to follow in a few weeks.

At three o'clock six young people came in for a Japanese Bible class. Mr. Koyama spoke to them very well on John 3: 16. As soon as that ended at 4 p.m. the English Bible class started which I was able to take. Twenty-two were finally sitting round the floor for this. Most left soon after five o'clock, but four who were Christians remained in one corner looking at tracts while the rest of us ate some supper. Afterwards Mr. Koyama spoke to them until 7 p.m. about the coming tent campaign, and how they could help there.

Then we had to leave for a meeting in a home in a mining settlement about twenty-five minutes walk away. The settlement was built and owned by the mining company, and seemed to be well run, with hospital, school and Shinto and Buddhist shrines provided for the people. The house we entered consisted of two tatami-covered rooms and a wood floored kitchen. As most of the paper doors dividing them had been removed there was plenty of room for ten of us who had gathered to sit on the floor. No one took any notice when the two children of the house were undressed and put to bed during the talk, which once again was given by Mr. Koyama, and lasted until 9 p.m.

Then an elderly woman who was present began to ask questions, talking very much about her "feelings". She was told that our feelings are always changing, but the Bible is always the same, and Christ is the same, He changes not. She became more explicit then, but I could not follow all she said and could only watch and pray as Mr. Koyama and the missionary tried to lead her to put her faith in Christ. The lower part of her body remained motionless, her legs neatly folded under her, in Japanese fashion, for two hours. Only a slight heaving of her bosom under the over-wrapping kimono, an occasional flicker of her eyelids, and a small tract which she ceaselessly wrapped and unwrapped around her pencil betrayed the strong emotion she was experiencing as she listened to the claims of the Gospel. At last she gave a final twist to the tract and put down the pencil with an air of finality, saying she could not understand.

Was this another victory for the devil? Here was a middle-aged woman not afraid to be the first to speak in a gathering—a valuable person to have in the starting of a new work, if only she belonged to Christ. The man of the house, who was a church member from another place, told her to keep on coming and she would gradually understand. By this time it was 10.30 p.m. and we had to prepare to leave. She finally arranged that she would go and have another talk with the missionary two evenings later. I have since learned, however, that she decided in the end that she was too old to give up her ancestral gods. She felt they were watching her and disapproving as she read her Bible, so she handed back her New Testament and said she would come to the meetings no more. After that she had to take a journey and during it had a dream of the crucified Christ. She admitted she was very impressed by it, but still has not come back to any meetings.

On our way to this meeting we had stopped for a moment at the beauty parlour which in fact was the other half of the house in which the missionaries lived. There I was introduced to the proprietor of the business, an intelligent looking, attractive woman of early middle age. With her two apprentices she continued rapidly fixing the little papers and curlers for the permanent wave she was giving a client. When I was introduced she merely remarked that it must be cold there after Tokyo. I politely disagreed, but as she made no move to come over to us we regretfully turned away. We were indeed aware that the blanket of snow had fallen on one of the choicest souls yet encountered in our few years of missionary work in Japan.

This lady had been converted very shortly after two of our missionaries moved into that mining area. It was a miracle which caused the owner of that property to rent half of it to unknown foreigners when he had already refused it to this lady who naturally would have preferred her living quarters next to her business. Strangely enough she had shown no sign of resentment whatever and proved most helpful, coming in to paste new paper over the torn windows and in other ways assisting the undomesticated bachelors. In return for this help they presented her with a copy of the New Testament. After reading Mark's Gospel she came in to see them one evening conscious of sin and her need of a Saviour.

She gave evidence of being truly born again, and was soon full of eagerness to witness to others. At this time David Hayman received a letter from a woman to whom he had given a tract, asking for further information. She lived in a village some distance away, and the missionary was not able to go out there immediately. But he told this lady about the letter and asked if she would go with him to visit the writer later on. Instead, she went at once by herself, anxious to do something for her new Master. This is an unusual step for a Japanese to take so early in the Christian life, for normally they make no effort to be friendly with those outside their immediate circle. As one Japanese writer has said about his own people, "They are sociable in the sense that they are kind and polite to relatives, friends and acquaintances; but in the past they have taken very little interest in people outside these circles. This attitude of mind is not confined to foreigners, but is manifested towards their own people."

This lady attended the church conference in Sapporo and was much blessed there, like the girl in the previous chapter.

She came back shining with joy in the Lord and the first working day of the New Year gave all her takings to the Lord. She put texts up in her shop, and felt that she had to be honest with her income tax though others in her guild according to Japanese custom had "fixed" the amount of profit they should all declare. So in many ways she had demonstrated clearly that she was a new creation in Christ. Much prayer was made for her husband, who at first was very opposed, but then began to show some interest in the Gospel.

A short time before my visit, however, the change had begun. She showed loss of interest in the woman contacted through the tract, and whom she had visited several times. The "glory" disappeared from her face and she was indignant when it was suggested she close her shop on Sunday partly for her own health's sake. She was not at all well, suffering from high blood pressure at this time, but she said it would be very selfish to her customers to close on her busiest day, just for the sake of her health, and that she was in no way bound by Old Testament regulations. So a coldness developed which nothing the missionary could think of doing seemed able to dispel. She would take no part in the tent campaigns, and wrote to one of the Japanese leaders in another town that she knew her present condition was wrong, but she could not get out of it. Much of this may be due to her weakened physical condition and those who know her hold on in faith believing the Lord will yet perfect that which concerns her. But the heart-break of seeing those who have run well losing their joy and coming into bondage again is much more painful to bear than any physical hardship in missionary life.

A few days later I visited the town where lives the young Christian leader to whom this lady wrote. It was easy to see why she had confidence in writing to him, having met him earlier at the Sapporo conference. He is still very young, yet one who gave promise of being a man after God's own heart. As I heard something of his present circumstance I felt like privately naming him Mr. Greatheart. He was one who apparently had experienced most of his doubts first, and now had a steady confidence in God.

N<small>CM</small>

Though bearing one of the oldest names in Japan, and therefore of aristocratic stock probably, since no others were allowed
surnames until the Meiji Restoration, this boy came from a
very poor family, the father not being very strong either in
character or physique. The boy finished middle school but was
too poor to go on to high school. Just before his graduation his
father opened a laundry. The son was well aware he must help
his father or he would never make a success of the new business,
but he did it with an ill grace, hating it every day. Then his
father had an affair with another woman, making their home
life very unhappy. The father was very abusive, until at last the
son made plans to run away from home. He had his few
possessions ready in a bundle, and at night when everyone was
asleep he crept to the door, hoping to escape unnoticed. He
made a slight sound, however, and his father heard him. He
was shocked to hear how unhappy his son was, and after that
tried to improve a little, but without any permanent success.
A short time later, in 1953, a Mr. MacLeod of the United
Church of Canada visited the town to hold tent meetings and
the young man went every night. It was the first time he had
ever heard the Gospel, and he had many doubts in his heart.

Soon after this two of our workers took up residence there,
and Mr. MacLeod suggested he go along to their meetings.
Apparently he never doubted that the Bible was true, but his
problem was how to get the life of which the Bible spoke.
He tried to live this in his own strength. The following New
Year, when all the shops close for a few days he went away with
his Bible and hymnbook in the hope of finding peace for his
soul but came back much the same as he left. He had various
talks with the missionaries, but still felt no assurance in his
heart.

When tent meetings were arranged in his town in 1955 he
agreed to give his testimony, but did not really have one to
give. A student from the Tokyo Theological Seminary was
helping in this campaign. Afterwards at a follow-up meeting in
the house he could see that this young fellow was miserable and
asked: "What is it you are doubting, is it the word of God?"
Being assured it was not that, he somehow got it across to him

that if he from the heart believed what the Bible said, then he was saved. The young man went home to think this over and has been different ever since. He was ready at once to be baptized the next time a service was arranged.

Eventually the two men missionaries moved on to open new work, and two women workers came to live in this town. The young man then assumed that the main responsibility of the work was now his, and took over the superintendency of the Sunday School, which at that time had fifty to sixty children and three teachers. He arranged with his parents that he would work extra hard on Saturdays so that the laundry might close on Sundays. He has made some mistakes, such as a funeral in a partly Christian home where he arranged that the Christian service and Buddhist rites should go on simultaneously. But he had glimpsed the possibility of a life lived in and through the power of Christ, in which the old self is dead, and was following on to know the Lord.

At the time I was there he was a character in a real life drama which was essentially Japanese, and yet through which Christian faith shone out strongly and truly. The drama concerned him and a Christian girl and another fellow. It all started when a Christian farmer from another of our centres wrote the girl a letter proposing marriage. He is twenty-eight, and constantly being urged by his mother to get married. Yet there are no Christian girls of suitable age in his area. He had attended the Sapporo Conference and had seen this girl there and thought her suitable in every way. Not only is she very attractive to look at, but she also is a farm girl, and therefore used to the life she would have to live with him. Furthermore she had the reputation of being the best Christian in her group. She was one of the few Japanese whom the missionary had never so far seen "down" spiritually, and her story is certainly an interesting one.

She too had only been able to finish middle school because she was needed at home to work on the farm, but she had longed to have a high school education. She did not get on well with her mother, and was always quarrelling with her. One day she heard some words on the radio which made a real impression on her, "Come unto me, all ye that labour and are heavy laden, and I will give you rest. Take my yoke upon you, and learn of me." She had no idea what this programme was, but the words stuck in her mind. She had had no contact with any Christians up to this time, though she had seen a Bible and knew it was a book about God.

Meanwhile at home things grew more and more difficult, and she finally decided to commit suicide. So she started off for the river. As she walked along the bank wondering where to jump in, she began thinking of the past and the troublesomeness of life. Suddenly the words came back to her, "Come unto me, and I will give you rest". Then she knew there was hope for her, and she turned back to go home. She had no idea where the programme she had heard before had come from; but, after experimenting for a few days, she discovered it was the "Lutheran Hour". She heard them announce a Bible Correspondence course, so she wrote to Tokyo for it. She did not find the course very interesting, however, and stopped once, but finally started again. Her address was sent to the nearest Lutheran pastor in Hokkaido, who was some distance away in another town. One December day in the midst of a snow storm the pastor walked four miles from the station to her farm home in the country. It took him half a day to walk the distance, the snow was so deep. She was very moved at such concern for her, and put her trust in Christ that very day, and a month later was baptized.

Soon after that she found that missionaries had moved into her own town. So now after her long day's work in the fields she cycles the four miles in to the services in the summer, and walks that distance in winter. She is a good teacher in the Sunday School and her relationship with her mother is much improved. She admits that the fault was all on her side. She just did not want to work at home before.

It is obvious therefore why the Christian farmer from Hidaka should feel she would make him a good wife. His letter of proposal had arrived on the Thursday of the week preceding my visit. On the next day, Friday, she received a letter from the local Christian leader, the laundry man, asking her to marry him! She had already begun to answer this last one, favourably, when on the Saturday she developed acute appendicitis and had to be taken to the hospital and operated on immediately.

Young Mr. Greatheart visited her every day, and she seemed very glad to see him, until the following Sunday when he dropped in on his way to church, and she just covered her face with the bedclothes and would not speak to him. Much distressed and puzzled by this he had to go off and take a little village meeting in the afternoon, still not knowing the reason for the girl's behaviour! However, one of the other Christian girls met him at the station on his return and explained what had happened.

The missionaries hold a weekly service in the hospital and a student from a Teachers Training College who was a T.B. patient in there had attended the meetings and professed conversion two months before. This man had now also written the girl a letter asking her to marry him, and furthermore had threatened to give up Christianity and go back to a life of sin if she did not accept him. The girl was very troubled about this; but finally in true Japanese fashion, decided she must sacrifice her own feelings in the matter. Mr. Greatheart she believed was a strong Christian and would overcome his disappointment by prayer and faith, while the other man was still a very weak Christian. She could not bear to think of him being lost, and felt she must do all she could to save him. That night she could not sleep at all and her temperature jumped suddenly, much to the bewilderment of the doctor, since the operation had been quite successful.

Mr. Greatheart also did not sleep on Sunday night, and looked so worn out the next morning that his mother suggested he take a day off. But he refused. He prayed as he worked away starching and ironing shirts, till at last he could truly say the Lord had taken all the bitterness out of his heart, and given him real peace and the power to pray for the other two, that God would bless them both.

During the lunch hour he went up to the hospital to say a "good-bye" to the girl, but first said he must just ask two questions. Was she sure it was the will of God? Did she really feel she could save the other man? Then they prayed together and sang their favourite hymn, "When I survey the wondrous Cross". When he left her Mr. Greatheart also visited the student in his ward and read the Bible and prayed with him, not mentioning anything about his letter to the girl. That night he was able to sleep peacefully.

The next day he heard that the man with T.B. had sent a letter of repentance to the girl confessing his sin of lust and selfishness. He said he had been separated from the Lord when he wrote it, and now he released her from any obligation to him. So Mr. Greatheart visited the hospital again that evening and together they thanked the Lord for His goodness and for this opportunity to prove in a new way that He can give peace and undertake for us in all our problems.

This was the story up to the day I arrived. That afternoon I had the privilege of going to the hospital with the missionaries. We met the girl outside in the grounds, taking her first walk since the operation. She certainly is attractive, slim and graceful, with a good complexion. It was hard to imagine her doing farm work all day. It was not at all surprising she had received so many proposals, though it is rare in Japan still for them to be made direct, and not through a middle man.

We left her talking to a visitor, and went along to the T.B. wards. The student was in the kitchen cooking something so we could not talk to him privately there, and went into the women's ward intending to visit his room later. Eva Glass had a special friend there, an elderly lady with very few teeth. She kept laughing and telling us about her shoulder which ached so much with lying in bed. I found it hard to understand much she said, but as she lay there seemingly joking I began to think what a relief it must be to the thousands of T.B. patients in Japan to get into hospital for a while, away from their hard, crowded lives and the constant strain of things. Great was my surprise later to learn that what she had said with laughter was that she was so miserable with the pain she had been considering asking someone to bring her in some poison to end her life. The missionary started telling her again of Christ. Then, although everyone's supper of fish and rice had been brought in and placed beside the beds, someone suggested they should sing some hymns, although it was not the regular day for the service. The student who had wandered in went and got the hymn books, the Christian girl came in and sat on the old lady's bed, and soon quite a little group were singing of Christ. At last, when the fish must have been stone cold, we were escorted to the entrance by all who could walk.

The next morning on my way to the station we called in at the laundry for a few minutes. Mr. Greatheart looked very tired and admitted something was troubling him, but could not speak then as other customers came in. I have learnt since that the girl still thinks she should marry the student riddled with T.B. because he may need her help more. To the missionary it would seem ideal to have the two strongest Christians united in marriage and setting up a Christian home which might be an inspiration and help to all in that place. But Japanese thought is so different from ours we hesitate to interfere in matters of marriage, except to stress a Christian should not marry a non-Christian. We rest in the knowledge there is One who ever lives to make intercession for His children, and is able to transform men's minds so that they may know what is the good and perfect will of God.

Chapter XVII

NORTH GLORY CHURCH

SAPPORO has been called the Edinburgh of Japan, but as I have only spent one day in each of these famous cities I am not sure of what the comparison consists, beyond the fact that Edinburgh is the capital of the northern section of the British Isles, and Sapporo of the most northern of the Japanese islands, also they each have a well-known medical school in their university.

Because the climate of Hokkaido is cold and unsuited to Japanese tropical style housing the island was left largely to the Ainu until about 100 years ago. In 1877 an agricultural college was opened at Sapporo, Dr. W. S. Clark, principal of the Massachusetts School of Agriculture, being invited by the Governor of Hokkaido to come out and initiate this work. His influence is still everywhere visible—in the crops grown (corn, winter wheat, potatoes), dairy farms, New England style barns and silos; houses that are built to withstand the cold—and the fact that the Japanese farmers even say "whoa" to their horses!

However, Clark's influence went far deeper than these externals. As one Japanese editorial, written this year when Hokkaido University paid special honour to its first president, puts it: "He stuck to the principle of whole-character education based on the Puritan spirit—His methods are obsolete in many respects, but he accomplished something far beyond the achievements of the mechanical education system of today. He transcended racial boundaries, sought to enlighten men, set examples of what he preached. . . ." He lived in Japan only eight months and yet produced a little group of Christians which has been the means of leading nearly 100,000 people to adopt the Christian faith. Since, as a consequence of his coming, a higher proportion of the population of Sapporo attends church than of any other city of Japan, it is worth considering this man in more detail. How could he achieve so much when the efforts of the present day young missionary after even five years seem so puny?

On the human level it was probably because he was a man of intellectual and social stature in the eyes of the Japanese. He was forty-one years old, and the principal of an American college, so they were prepared to listen to him. Also no doubt he was a man of very strong personality and convictions, and the Japanese are hero worshippers. According to the newspaper editorial, "He insisted on teaching Christian ethics, which are strictly forbidden in Japanese government schools. By the force of his personality, he got away with it, and each student was given a Bible and thorough indoctrination in Christianity." The modern missionary, of course, is not free to act quite in this way! The details which account for his spiritual success, as I have heard them, are that on his way to Japan he stopped at Hawaii where his wife's parents were missionaries, and there entered into a vital experience of Christ. The Buddhist Governor of Hokkaido met him when he docked in Japan, and then took him, with sixteen picked students who had been chosen out of many applicants, in a small coastal ship up to Hokkaido. On the way these students spent all their time drinking and gambling, to such an extent that even the Governor was disgusted, and told Clark that when they landed these would be dismissed and the next sixteen on the list taken as students.

Clark replied that what they needed was the transforming power of Christ in their lives, and insisted that he should be allowed to teach them the Bible. The Buddhist Governor was very much opposed to this, but finally consented to the students having fifteen minutes of ethics daily, from 8.0 to 8.15 a.m. with the Bible as text-book. Japanese records give the number of first-year students as twenty-four, so some were probably local men, but out of these, according to Kanzo Uchimura, fifteen signed with Clark the "Covenant of Believers in Jesus" which stated in English:

"The undersigned members of Sapporo Agricultural College,

desiring to confess Christ according to His command and to perform with true fidelity every Christian duty in order to show our love and gratitude to that blessed Saviour who has made atonement for our sins by His death on the Cross, and earnestly wishing to advance His kingdom among men, for the promotion of His glory and salvation of those for whom He died, do solemnly covenant with God and with each other from this time forth to be His faithful disciples, and to live in strict compliance with the letter and spirit of His teachings; and, whenever a suitable opportunity offers, to promise to present ourselves for examination, baptism and admission to some evangelical church." (Sapporo then only had about 3,000 residents and no missionaries.)

Then followed a statement of faith, beginning with the heartening words, "We believe the Bible to be the only direct revelation in language from God to man, and the only perfect and infallible guide to a glorious future life." For a non-professional theologian Clark certainly made an excellent job of this statement of faith, and it seems a tragedy he could not have stayed longer to implant it more deeply.

When he finally left at the end of the academic year, his students rode with him on horseback for twelve miles. As his parting words he said, "Boys, be ambitious for Jesus Christ." These words have been greatly publicized and unfortunately shortened to "Boys, be ambitious". It is for these only that he is famous today. The Agricultural College developed into Hokkaido University with eleven departments, and today has 4,500 students. The University coat-of-arms bears the letters B.B.A., after Dr. Clark's parting words.

True to their covenant, that first group of Christians with great zeal sought to win the freshmen to Christ. Among those freshmen from Tokyo was Kanzo Uchimura. It is rather amusing to read of his unwilling conversion. In his diary he writes: "I early learned to honour my nation above all others, and to worship my nation's gods. I thought I could not be forced even by death itself to bow my allegiance to any other gods." He even dreamed of re-converting the Christian seniors, but "The public opinion of the college was too strong

against me. (All the seniors had been converted by this time).
I alone was left a 'heathen', the much detested idolator. I well
remember the extremity and loneliness to which I was reduced.
I finally yielded and signed the covenant against my will."
This statement should help us to realize the terrible strength of
public opinion in Japan, either for good or bad. Many may
think that such a person as this would not make a strong
Christian, but Uchimura is recognized as the strongest Christian individualist in Japan. It is estimated there are today
50,000 to 70,000 of his followers in the *Mukyokai* (Non-church
group) which has neither organization nor sacraments, but
concentrates on the study of the Bible. I have heard that his
many volumes of Bible commentary are found on more
Japanese pastors' shelves than any other books. Opinions
differ as to whether it would have been good if the Emperor
had become even a nominal Christian after the war. At least
it would have removed tremendous barriers which at present
keep most Japanese from becoming Christian. Some people
feel that then many would just be nominal Christians, and
it is better to have a few real ones. Yet if conditions were
exactly the same in Japan as they are in nominally Christian
England, I believe Japan would have far better Christians
than the average Western ones. The real danger is that if
Christianity were to become the national Japanese religion,
it might somehow become contaminated with old Shinto
ideas.

I wish I had more space to tell of these early student meetings
in Sapporo which Uchimura describes so graphically in his
diary. They had no help at all except some English Christian
books, though a missionary of the Methodist church did visit
once or twice a year to administer the rite of baptism. They were
full of zeal, though some of it seems to have been in the energy
of human strength, and with a strange lack of love. In their
final meeting (I think it was), at graduation, one said: "As I
think of the heavy responsibility I have to bear, how I must
go among the sons of Satan (the world) I feel how strong
should my faith become", and another, "Let us disperse
heathen as we do street dogs, and conquer men, devils and all

with our united force and courage". Others, even today, have found a similar, or "scolding" attitude among Japanese as they try to get others to become Christians. However, Uchimura did take a great deal of trouble to get his father converted. He did very well in his graduation examinations, and earned a money prize, so he used this, after praying about it, to buy his father the five volumes of the Chinese edition of Faber's commentary on Mark's Gospel. His father was a great Confucian scholar and he thought the difficulty of reading this might whet his father's intellectual appetite! However, his father threw all five volumes on the rubbish heap. Fortunately, his son rescued them, and, after much weeping in secret, put just Volume I on his father's table. Again it was thrown out. Again it was replaced, and finally his father read it. When he reached the end he had stopped scoffing at Christianity. By the time he had finished Volume II he began to speak favourably about it. As he read Volume III there began to be a change in his manners—he drank less wine and was more affectionate to his wife and children. After completing Volume IV he became a Christian, and his mother, brothers and sister, a cousin, and an uncle, all became Christians eventually.

When these young Christians graduated it was their dream to have a real church. They nearly all stayed on a few years in Hokkaido to work on Government agricultural projects, and "before we thought of having homes or making money we thought of building a church". They contributed to this at tremendous personal sacrifice, and returned money which had been sent by a denominational group because they wished to be independent. This gave rise to hurt feelings on both sides, which unfortunately never seem to have been completely erased. Many missionaries never understood Uchimura, and he was driven unduly far from any form of organized Christianity. Today, even among his followers, liberalism has crept in and each local group is largely coloured by the theological shade of thought of its particular leader.

This seems a very long introduction to the C.I.M. work in Sapporo, but it is important because Uchimura's stature has grown considerably since his death. He is now one of Hokkaido University's most famous sons. Many of the traditions of that early group live on, unfortunately without the sound theological basis that they first had.

Sapporo is now a city with a population of 250,000. The church with the largest membership is Presbyterian. Mr. G. Chapman, a missionary who worked with them, was due for furlough at the time some C.I.M. workers were ready to leave Language School. He therefore suggested they should take over his house and carry on his English Bible classes and two Evening Bible School classes in a Student Centre he had started. These classes were all interpreted, by a Christian medical student, so that our workers were able to get across all that they wished to say. Encouragements came more rapidly there than at other places where C.I.M. workers could only use their very limited Japanese at the beginning of their ministry.

Several special times of fruitfulness seem to have been experienced there, interspersed with periods when only a few have professed conversion and others seem to have fallen away. The first break came at the close of an English Bible class when a university freshman said, "Until today I had never heard anything about the Christian faith, but I want the salvation you have spoken about. Will you please instruct me?" Knowing how far from the truth the Japanese concept of God usually is, the missionary began to tell him something about God as Creator, the Living God, but the student interrupted, "I will believe whatever you show me from this Book, which you tell me is God's Word for man. But can that not wait? Please tell me first how I may receive forgiveness of my sins." Maureen Flowers who wrote an account of this said, "It is not often that a man is saved upon the first hearing of the Gospel, but it happened that day, and this young student went away filled with the joy of the Lord." This was the firstfruits after several months of work and prayer and was also a great encouragement to the Christians attending the classes. Five other students were saved within the next six weeks.

At last the time came when the Presbyterian house was

needed again, and our workers moved out to a suburb of 10,000 people where there was no church witness of any kind. The Field Superintendent, his wife, secretary and one of the Mission doctors had been the workers there up to that time. But then it was decided to move the C.I.M. field headquarters to Aomori on the main island of Honshu. Shortage of workers meant that Mary Milner, who for the past year had had to spend more time in secretarial work than language study, was left alone in this strategic place where the need for establishing a local Christian witness seemed imperative. The management of the Student Centre had been taken over by a different organization, however, and some of the members of the English Bible class decided they would like to help Mary Milner in forming a new group, although it meant a journey of more than an hour for most of them.

An older missionary, Elizabeth Wimer, was able to go and help there before long, and soon she was writing of another period of joyous reaping, which began one week-end. "One of the civil engineering students had the joy of leading one of his sister's classmates to the Lord on Saturday, 12th. This girl, with two other friends, attended the meeting the following day, and in personal conversations with some of the Christian girls and myself afterwards, both accepted Christ as their Saviour. While this was going on in one room, Mr. Maruyama, the medical student interpreter who was one of the leaders of the group, was in earnest conversation with some boys in the dining-room. When the girls had left he asked me to join in their discussion, and after a little time of prayer we sought together to show the non-Christians the way of salvation from the Word of God. One of these, Mr. Murayama, a medical student in Mr. Maruyama's class, accepted Christ in a very simple way—he was like a little child more than a fifth-year university student." (This is the way Christ said it must be done, and events since have proved him to be one of the most promising Christians.) "We were on the point of giving him some other Scriptures on which to rest his new-found faith when another man said he also had decided to become a Christian. It is little wonder that at the end Mr.

Maruyama said, 'What a wonderful day!' But the end was not then, for on Tuesday afternoon another young man came to see me. He had heard of what happened on Sunday, and he too now wanted to believe."

Some who professed conversion at that time have not continued to come to meetings, and the civil engineering student who led his sister's friend to Christ has unfortunately lost his faith and says now he was being a hypocrite before. His sister, however, is full of zeal, and the medical student has gone on steadily, all except for the few days after his baptism when he did not put in an appearance. He came back beaming, however, and admitted that he had had a *su-ra-mu-pu* (the nearest Japanese can get to "slump"), but he knew this was the work of Satan and now he had the victory.

There is another student in whom the Lord seems to be doing a lasting work. He is one who has lost his father, and has often testified to the wonderful joy of being able to call God "Father". He has a real concern for personal work, and at the New Year conference had the joy of winning to the Lord someone contacted through a tract. This man lives over two hours' journey from Sapporo, but the student goes out to visit him and sometimes brings him to church. An extract from a letter he once wrote Mary Milner, while she was away, reveals something of his sense of responsibility in this direction: "As there were other people in the room I could not talk clearly and earnestly with him. Though he came that day he went out while the speaker was speaking. He did not come on 10th or 17th, so I will call on him again. It is now 3 a.m., so I must stop."

The group of Christians in Sapporo now averages about thirty, most of whom are still students. Though visitation has been done in the neighbourhood the number of local people attending is small. The fact that most are students makes the ordinary older person disinclined to join them, for there seems a distinct barrier existing between the young and older age groups in Japan. When some of these students had been Christians for some time the question of baptism naturally arose. A good many converted through the English Bible class find a home in some of the other churches of Sapporo, but some felt they wanted to have their own church in this needy area. So a missionary from another place was asked to come and baptize those who were ready. A committee of three was finally elected to take responsibility for the group which they decided to call the North Glory Church.

The Sunday I spent with them was very wet, but numbers were good in spite of this. Because many come a long distance they have planned a series of meetings straight after each other on Sunday, which may seem an odd and tiring arrangement to us, but appears to work well enough with them. During the week there is the English Bible class on Wednesday evening, and a prayer meeting on Saturday since the group became organized. On Sunday from 1.0 to 2.0 p.m. the Sunday School is in session, and at the same time a preparation class for those wishing to be baptized. From 2 to 2.15 p.m. there is a short prayer meeting, then the main service from 2.30 to 3.30 p.m. The day I was there an independent Japanese pastor, Mr. Noguchi, from another part of the city, was the guest preacher. From 3.30 p.m. to 4.30 p.m. there was a less formal service arranged by the Christians. That day it mainly took the form of special singing numbers with appropriate Scripture readings, and any newcomers were asked to introduce themselves.

It was the period after this which I found the most interesting and inspiring. Sitting on the floor all round the room were different groups each busy in discussion of some kind, all except a small group of three who were sitting on the edge of the *tokonoma*. (Raised alcove where the flower arrangement and an object of art are placed in a Japanese room.) This consisted of two students who took turns reading passages of Scripture to a blind man. I learned afterwards that he was a teacher at a school for the blind. Just a few weeks later came the good news that he had testified to receiving Christ as his Saviour.

In two other groups there were older Christians with open Bibles answering questions earnestly put to them by seekers or those still young in the faith. Those who had attended the

baptism preparation class earlier were in another group dis-
cussing something which had arisen there. The guest preacher
joined another group where a young student seemed to be trying
to make himself the centre of attention and aroused repeated
laughter from the group of girls who gathered admiringly
round. I felt rather concerned as I watched this, but Mr.
Noguchi with skill and grace gradually had them consulting
their Bibles and a deeper seriousness settled over them as they
began to ask vital questions such as whether or not a Christian
should worship at the family *butsudan*.

Then one of the fellows came up and squatting beside me asked
if he might ask a question. He turned to Matthew 27: 52 and 53,
and asked who the saints were whose bodies rose, and what was
the holy city. I did not know who he was, and wondered for a
moment if he were just trying to be smart, but soon found it was
genuine interest, as well it would be for someone reading those
words for the first time. Gradually I discovered he was the
fifth-year medical student who had accepted Christ so simply.
He had recently been one of the three elected to the church
committee, and he was feeling full of zeal and a sense of
responsibility for the church. He asked if I had ever seen a
church like this at home. Feeling a bit fearful that the Scripture
injunction not to make a novice an overseer of the church
might have been disregarded, for he had only been baptized
three months before, I explained that I had not seen one like
it: that to me it seemed more like a student group in a university, and that a well-balanced church should normally include
all age groups. At home no student had the full burden of
responsibility for a church, but were backed up by their church
in their main work of witness on the campus. Here they were in
a peculiar situation and had a very heavy responsibility,
especially in the year of their final medical examinations.
Then he asked if I thought the Holy Spirit could teach them,
and I could only reply that He certainly would if they sought
wisdom from Him. My heart went out to this group so full of
zeal and earnestness and life. Yet there was the shadow of fear
that the devil, coveting them back within his kingdom, would
use those things, coupled with their lack of Christian experience

CM

and knowledge of the Bible, to bring heartache out of this brave young church. This boy spoke of Kanzo Uchimura with great pride. It was only after I had read his diary that I realized that to a considerable extent they were developing their group after the pattern of the early Sapporo Christians.

Fortunately the real leader of the group is the medical student who had done the interpreting for so long. He was the fruit of earlier Presbyterian work. He has known the Lord for five years, and is a mature Christian of spiritual insight. He realizes the weaknesses of his own people, and refuses to use the artificial polite phrases with which the Japanese language abounds but which a Christian cannot truthfully use. He has the rare quality of not wanting to win followers for himself. From fear of having them lean on him too much he pushes the young Christians forward, and gives them responsibilities which we would hesitate to put on those so young in the faith. At first he felt he could in personal work deal only with students, but gradually the Lord has led him occasionally to a wider ministry among others. He has already thought out what he will do in that most difficult of all situations for a Japanese Christian— his father's funeral. His father is medical superintendent of the city hospital and an active Buddhist. He tells his friends he is surprised at the way his son has stuck to Christianity so long, but he knows that it will not last once he gets out into the world. The son's ideals are high, and rather than go into a Christian hospital like St. Luke's for his hospital residence, as he first thought of doing, he now wants to prove that it is possible to be a Christian in ordinary society. Accordingly he has just entered his father's hospital to do some particular research work while in residence, and this has meant he will not be free for any church responsibilities for the next year.

His friend who graduated at the same time had a less exact- ing job as a hospital resident. But just this week has come news that he has had to return to his native city, so two of the church leaders are gone. Mary Milner has been transferred again to take up secretarial duties. As she had been with them through all the stages of the establishing of the church this was felt very much by the Christians; but most of them seem to be standing by the married couple who have taken over there. They have been able to contact a few more local people, so perhaps the work will gradually become more balanced and may continue to bring increasing glory to the Lord in that northern suburb.

Chapter XVIII

HIDAKA COAST

I HAD planned my visit along the Hidaka coast so that I could see at first hand what was involved in the preparation for a tent campaign, and how it was conducted by local Christians.

The two women missionaries in the little town of Tomikawa had long been praying for a tent campaign, which would make known to the people there the real purpose of their coming to that place a few months before. They and the few girls who had already been won to Christ invited Pastor Noguchi (who had been the guest speaker at Sapporo on the Sunday), to come as their main speaker in the campaign.

I had the privilege of travelling in the train with Pastor Noguchi, and it was encouraging to learn that he himself had been brought to Christ at a tent meeting down in the south about five years before. He had been brought up in China, where his father had been working for one of the big Japanese shipping companies, and he was a university student in Peking when the Communists took control of the country and he had had to return to Japan with his family. They were then in very reduced circumstances, and he developed tuberculosis, so was unable to continue his studies. Finally, after his conversion he went to a Bible School, and in rather a remarkable way felt called to go and work in distant Hokkaido. He had become familiar with the story of Hudson Taylor, and was inspired by this to go in faith, without support from any organization. He soon found a Christian wife up there, and did a little private teaching to support himself and his wife and baby; but he has gathered together a little group of converts who meet on Sundays, and he is always very willing to help other Christian groups if invited. He is a man of vision, and has ideas of developing some kind of Christian business, so that those who are turned out of their homes because of their faith in Christ may have some means of livelihood, and he also hopes to start a Bible School in Hokkaido some time, since there is nothing there for the training of Christians. He is a wonderful example of what a Japanese who has not been brought up in the "web society" of Japan can become when his life is yielded fully to God, and provides good reason why the devil has been at such pains to preserve that web through all the changes of Japanese history.

We arrived at Tomikawa to find most of the preparations for the campaign were completed. Tracts, together with a notice about the meetings, had been delivered to every house in the town. The tent had been put up that morning by Douglas Abrahams and Don Morris, who had come from other centres along the Hidaka coast, together with several Japanese Christian men who had also come to help through the first night of the meetings. All that remained to be done after lunch was the sticking up of directions to the tent site, the arranging of books and Bibles for sale, and the preparation of a few more hymn sheets written in large characters.

One of the problems in these campaigns when there are few local Christians, is that of hospitality for the visiting helpers. Most of the C.I.M. workers have been single men or single women, living in very small houses, and to feed all the helpers would take up much time, which was needed for doing personal work and other things in the tent. It was therefore arranged that each evening we should all go to a little eating place along the street for a bowl of noodles (whenever each could conveniently fit in the time to eat), instead of preparing supper at home. In most places some of the men, at least, sleep in the tent, but here it was really cold at night in spite of being July—a cold spell which was to mean a disastrous failure of crops throughout Hokkaido that summer. It had rained for almost a week before the time for the tent's erection, so the ground was still very damp; but fortunately the parents of one of the Christian girls, whose house was next to the tent site, offered the use of one of their rooms.

Later in the afternoon the men went out with the portable

loudspeaker, and at strategic spots around the town announced the meetings and also preached the Gospel briefly. The rest of us spread the long straw mats, on which the audience was to sit, over the damp ground in the tent.

A children's meeting was to be held first, followed by the main meeting at 7.30 p.m. Only about forty or fifty children came the first night; for no children's meetings had been held in the town before, and most seemed a little scared to venture into this strange place. Mr. Noguchi was very skilful, however. First of all he had them singing one of their familiar kinder-garten songs, and they soon joined in heartily. Then he went on to a song or two taught in the Christian Japanese kinder-gartens, and they could easily grasp the meaning of these. One was about what we must do if the hands are dirty; and from there he could very naturally go to the question of what to do if the heart is unclean.

As the time for the adult meeting drew near we were much in prayer that the Spirit of God would cause many to come along and hear and believe. It was encouraging to see the six Christian girls there in good time, singing a few hymns together before-hand, and also a middle school boy who had recently believed, his face alight with joy. About 100 people were in the tent for some part of the meeting, though some did not wait, even for the talk. As I watched carefully I noticed that there were always some who went out when the name of Jesus was mentioned, and others again at the mention of the Bible or the Cross.

There was quite a sprinkling of elderly men and women, a group for whose salvation we often pray as there are so few among our Christians. Some stayed to the end of the meeting, but we did not see them again. They, like many others, seem to have decided that Christianity is not for them, although Mr. Noguchi had spoken very plainly of the uncertainty of life and the reality of judgment to come.

One young man, a primary school teacher, who had stayed right through, spoke to Mr. Noguchi afterwards and seemed to be thinking very seriously, but would not make a decision then. So finally we gathered up all the straw mats off the floor, moved them and the organ and bookstall, etc., into the house next door, and went home, a little sad that none had professed belief in Christ, but thankful that the Gospel had been clearly preached in that place.

Next morning I had to go on further round the coast to visit two other places, but early on Thursday afternoon I was able to return. At the Mombetsu stop one of the Christian men I had met on Monday boarded the train and informed me that both Pastor Noguchi and Douglas Abrahams had lost their voices, and he was having to do the preaching that night!

When I arrived at the house I found that things had gathered a little momentum, and several had professed faith in Christ at the meetings. One of the Christian girls had persuaded her father to allow a meeting to be held in one of the plywood factories that afternoon, too. I was able to go along there and saw about twenty adults and the same number of children seated on the stacked piles of lumber outside, listening in the open air while Pastor Noguchi somehow made his lost voice heard by means of the portable loudspeaker, and it was amazing how full a view of the Gospel he was able to give in a comparatively short time—a rare gift among the Japanese.

Afterwards, this Christian girl invited us to her home for a cup of tea, but none of her relatives appeared during the visit. Then it was time to do more loudspeaker work on the street, before the time for our bowl of noodles and the children's meeting. I had been especially looking forward to this children's meeting because the girl whose testimony is given in chapter 14 was coming over that evening to be the speaker. When we entered the tent we saw about 200 children crowded in. She had them completely in control as she just taught them a few choruses, and then gave them the story of Zacchaeus by means of flannelgraph. How I praised God in my heart for this product of His grace and power, and prayed that her life might continue to be at His disposal.

The evening meeting also was an inspiring one, in that the two speakers were men who only a year before had become Christians during tent meetings held in their own towns. The first, who gave quite a long testimony, had been converted in a tent campaign held by a Swedish missionary in Tomakomai.

He mentioned among other things his slavery to drink, and that he had tried to give it up before he became a Christian, but could not. After he had accepted Christ as his Saviour, however, he found he had the victory over drink.

Then the young man I had met in the train that morning got up to speak. He had gone into the tent in Mombetsu the previous year for the purpose of getting some fun out of hearing a foreigner try and speak Japanese, but a Chinese Christian who had gone up to help our missionaries with the meetings had been used of God to bring him to Christ. He had at first tried to persuade this young man to become a Christian, but when he just argued back the Chinese gave up talking to him and instead prayed for him aloud, right in front of the young man, that God would show him his need. So, as he said later, what else *could* he do but accept Christ!

He is one of the rare upright, good-living, *healthy*, hard-working and respected young men in Japan who have become Christians. He sells fish from his own little three-wheel truck, and is now saving up his money to build a house of his own in which the church can meet. This is not perhaps in the ultimate best interests of the church, but he is full of zeal and has assumed the leadership of the Christians both in Mombetsu and Tomikawa, and has been even further afield in the Lord's work. The testimony of one of the other Christians is that this young man "puts his job second, after the Lord".

He gave what has been described as the "Genesis to Revelation" type of message, yet it filled in many gaps which the missionary is apt to leave, in his messages, taking for granted a knowledge of some things of which people who have never known God are really ignorant. One man was converted that night who had already heard the witness of a Christian friend in another city, and a man who had professed conversion the previous night came again, bringing a friend. I had to leave early the next morning but heard later that two young men, two slightly older women and a teen-aged boy who had made decisions were all attending meetings. Two other young men and a high school boy who had made a profession in the tent had not been since. One final joy at the end of the week was that

Mr. Noguchi was able to baptize two of the girls who had previously believed, the one who had arranged the meeting in the factory, and the one whose house was next to the tent.

My next stop, after two more hours round the coast in the train, was Shizunai. I found this an interesting and encouraging place, though it has the reputation of being the most wicked spot in that part of the country. The maid had once told Mrs. Abrahams, when she had made enquiries about eating out, that there was not a single "pure" restaurant in the place, meaning that all of them catered to every fleshly appetite of man. It is the biggest centre on the Hidaka coast, and with its growing population will soon reach the status of a city. There is a district senior high school located there, and a teachers' training college. In addition to our little group of Christians there is a small Seventh Day Adventist meeting, and the Roman Catholics are planning to build a church there within the next three years.

We are fortunate in having a married couple in this place; for humanly speaking this makes it easier to get a more balanced group of Christians to form a church. The Japanese are inclined to view single men as not yet worthy of much respect, and one missionary said how conscious he was that his stock had risen in the eyes of the community after his marriage. Single women of course can expect even less respect than the men, and single women above a certain age are very rare in Japan, since a family's prime objective always seems to be to get their daughters married off.

Douglas Abrahams was still away at the tent in Tomikawa but Olga Abrahams was able to show me much of interest in my brief stay. First we visited the pleasant little home of a married couple who both teach English in the high school. They were originally in the S.D.A. group, and had received some instruction in the S.D.A. training college near Tokyo; but they now seem to be clearly saved and give quite strong support to the Christian work in Shizunai. Though as a teacher in a government school, the man is not free to teach religious doctrine, he has given his testimony in the open air, and has also invited Douglas Abrahams to the school to teach one period of English, so that he can have an opportunity to get to know the students and even suggested that next term they might study Dickens' *Life of Christ* as an English text book, so that there might be some opportunity to introduce the Gospel. When this couple were living in rented rooms before obtaining their present house in the school grounds, their landlady once remarked to the wife, "What a wonderful religion yours must be! You and your husband never quarrel."

There are still quite a number of Ainu tribespeople, the original inhabitants of Japan, left in Hokkaido, and many of them are in villages surrounding Shizunai. Our next visit, therefore, was to an old Ainu man, formerly an evangelist, who lives in a small house opposite the very handsome new town office building. Most of the full-blooded Ainu are very different in physical appearance from the Japanese, and this man had beetling eyebrows and an almost ape-like body. However, he was intelligent and very interesting to talk to, and very free and natural in manner compared with the average Japanese on first acquaintance.

This area had been the scene of a disastrous flood the previous year when many houses were washed away, and the man pointed out the watermarks showing how high the flood had reached in his house. He also brought out an old photograph album stained by the flood waters, which proved most interesting. He had had considerable contact with foreigners in the past, chiefly Mr. Bachelor of the Anglican Church, and also former workers of the Oriental Missionary Society, and had had some training in their Bible School. He had even gone as far as Korea to attend their conventions. Mr. Bachelor had specialized in Ainu work and had reduced the language to writing, so this man produced his old Ainu hymn-book and sang to us "What a Friend we have in Jesus", and "Bringing in the sheaves". Now, however, nearly all Ainu people under fifty years of age can speak Japanese, and it seems as if the Ainu language will soon die out.

During the war this man, like many other pastors, gave up his Christian work. He took a job in the town ward office writing letters and interpreting for Ainu who could not speak

Japanese. He is the only Christian worker any of our missionaries have ever heard express any repentance for his actions
during the war. He never took on evangelistic work again, but
he has now started attending our services and is very willing
to give of the little he has.

We came away with a feeling of sadness in our hearts
because from all the work which had been put into this area
in the past there is now scarcely a trace left. This may be partly
due to the constant move of the young people towards the cities,
but there was one village Olga Abrahams knew which had had
the reputation of being a "Christian village" in the past, yet
now there is no trace of any Christianity in it. It seems that
those earlier parents never passed on their beliefs to their
children. This old Ainu pastor's children too, do not seem to
make any Christian profession. One daughter was considering
opening one of the typical restaurants of the town, with
inferior geisha in attendance, and a son is a drunkard living in
another town where we have missionaries. Once more the
devil has been successful in his efforts to ensnare again those
who were within reach of freedom. We cannot assume that the
quality of the missionary is any better today than in former
years. Perhaps it was that the earlier turning to Christianity
seemed to come easily and friends at home were not made
aware of the great battle in the heavenlies which must be
fought if these people are to remain free. So as you read of
some here in this place who have believed will you join in the
battle and pray that these and their children and children's
children may remain free, unentangled again with the yoke of
bondage, until the Lord shall come?

There is another married couple among the group of Christians in that place, as well as the high school English teachers.
This couple own a small business for the repairing of saws,
quite important in an area where lumber is the chief industry,
and this man was among the other Christians I had met who
had come to help in the preparations for the tent campaign
at Tomikawa. He is a man who early turned the god shelves out
of his home after believing, and he witnesses to all who come
into his shop, and has a real concern for those who work for

him in the business. In view of the fact that there are several of these small business men among the Hokkaido Christians it is very interesting to note what Kanzo Uchimura had to say about such men, "From my own experience I am scarcely able to count up how many of those who had been converted through my preaching have since given up their faith. This is particularly the case with the educated, high class, and wealthy, who mostly lapse after five, ten, or fifteen years. Those who remain steadfast twenty, thirty, fifty years in the face of many persecutions, are the farmers, merchants, manufacturers, bankers." This was written long before the war, but we pray that it may still remain true of these classes of people among whom much of our work is done.

A little weekly meeting was held in the missionaries' home the evening I was there, arranged primarily for some who have to work on Sundays and therefore cannot worship with the others then. About seven came that night, including a student from the teachers' training college, who had been brought previously by a friend and who admitted that his thinking had been turned completely upside down by this new teaching.

The last man to come in was one for whom I had been waiting with much interest. He had been saved from a life of sin, and even crime, just over a year ago, and is now unmistakably transformed by the Spirit of Christ. Soon after his confession of faith he wanted to pull down the god shelves in his home, and his father finally gave him permission. His mother was terrified as she watched it being done, but her son said, "If these gods are real, then I shall be paralysed tomorrow." Nothing happened to him, however, and his mother has occasionally accompanied him to church since.

He began witnessing before he was baptized, and soon lost what friends he had when they noticed certain changes in his conduct. Most of the townspeople were not convinced any radical change had taken place in him, however, because he still had no regular work. He had a great desire to preach, but not to settle down. Even in his school days he had often gone off fishing instead of attending classes. When he was not working, however, he did a great deal of Christian reading, and he finally came to realize the Lord's will for him was to do an honest job for a while, as a testimony to the change in his life. His father persuaded a friend who owned a hardware store to take him on as an assistant, and at the end of his first month he proudly brought a tithe of his wages for the Lord's work. He was even allowed a little time off on Sunday morning so that he could attend church.

The previous autumn he had gone to help at one of the tent campaigns in another place, working the projector, helping with the children's talks and giving his testimony. So when he came into the room that evening, the first thing he did after being introduced was to ask me about the present tent campaign. As I told him what was going on he raised his clenched fists in an agony of longing to be there himself preaching, and he had to remind himself aloud that God's place for him was still in the store.

He stayed there for six months, and then applied for entrance to a free, three-month training course for Christian workers, where the emphasis was all on soul winning. This is an emphasis which is much needed in Japan, yet those who knew him felt his particular need was more for a disciplined Bible study course. However, he would not listen to any advice, and the latest word I had was that this training school had closed down before the end of the three months, and he was back, very much with the air of one who has "attained" all that is needed for Christian service. Pray that the Lord who has done so much for him already may still be able to mould his life for whatever purpose He chooses.

Chapter XIX

SAMANI—BY-PATH MEADOW

SAMANI is the small terminus of the diesel train run around the beautiful Hidaka coast, and gives the feeling of being the end of nowhere in particular. It was here, however, that the first two C.I.M. missionaries, Hubert and Mary Fisher, at last found a room which they could rent and where they could begin to witness for Christ in Hokkaido.

They had hoped to get into a larger town further back along the railway line, but nothing was available at a rent they could afford. So as a last resort they went to the end of the line and got out at Samani. Even in that beautiful but sleepy little town, which enjoys a slightly warmer climate and less snowfall than most places in Hokkaido, their Japanese middleman could find no place to rent.

After a rather disheartened meal at the little hotel, Hubert Fisher thought he would make a last trip down to the harbour, which was the only place they had not visited, and try and give away his remaining tracts. There he met a Mr. M—— in the canning business, who immediately got into conversation with him. On learning their objective he told them that a relative of his had a spare room which a teacher was vacating that very afternoon, and he would enquire if she would rent to them. He went at once, and arrangements were made for the Fishers to rent this room and share their landlady's kitchen.

The Lord had an even more wonderful provision and answer to prayer in that remote and backward little town. The Fishers, though having years of experience as missionaries in China, had had barely a year's study of the Japanese language, and were therefore not equipped to do much more than carry on a simple conversation. Mary Fisher especially had been praying that they might go to a place where there would be someone who understood some English, so that they could witness more quickly of the living Christ, and have help in the preparation of messages. They discovered that their friend Mr. M—— had a wife who was born in Hawaii, and spoke perfect American! She was willing to become their language teacher, and they soon found that she was well taught in Buddhism. Her only knowledge of Christianity was hearing a Salvation Army band sing "Onward, Christian soldiers, marching as to war", during her childhood in Hawaii, and she had sometimes wondered vaguely what "war" this was.

After three weeks of language study and reading the Bible with her, and much prayer in private that the Lord would prepare the ground for the reception of the seed, Mary Fisher one day gave her personal testimony of what Christ meant to her. Mrs. M—— after some consideration remarked that she thought Christianity and Buddhism were much the same. It was rather discouraging to find these much prayed over words of testimony seemed to have so little effect, but then Hubert Fisher had an inspiration. He explained to her that one of the biggest differences between the two religions was the empty tomb of Christianity; there were no bones left like those of Buddha (which are much venerated) and all other human beings. This seemed to make a real impression, and Mrs. M—— referred to it when giving a word of testimony at a public meeting some time later.

After a few days she came to say that she had had a dream— and that her dreams usually came true. For instance, towards the end of the war she had dreamed that the American forces would come and bombard the coast there, and though no one else thought they would in that remote area, this actually happened. In this last dream Hubert Fisher had kept calling to her, "Run, Run!" She did nothing, however. Then bombs began to fall, and she awoke.

"What does it mean?" she asked them. So they suggested that it was really God speaking to her and warning her to "flee from the wrath to come". After further explanation she finally knelt down, prayed, and accepted Christ as her Saviour. Later she had great joy in speaking to her two sons about Christ and heaven, and God seemed very real to them, she said.

When they began to hold a little Sunday service she would translate the message for the Fishers, and was a great help to them in many ways. Later when a children's meeting was started she would come and tell the story at this. There were several changes of personnel at this little place, however. The Fishers had to go on furlough since they had gone to Japan from China, and two single women took their place. Then the Fishers returned for a brief period but had to leave again to take charge of our language school, and the Morrises went there. No one knows exactly why or when, but gradually Mrs. M——'s enthusiasm cooled. Her husband never showed any sustained interest, and theirs being socially one of the most important families in the community, there were many other calls on her time and interest. She also began teaching English in the local school and finally asked to be excused from teaching the missionaries Japanese because of lack of time. On Sundays she would often just turn up at the children's meeting in time to give the talk and then not stop for the main service.

Don Morris took me to visit her home, and she just stood in the doorway and spoke briefly to us in perfect American. Such a charming person, and one who could do so much for the spread of the Gospel in that place, but at present it seems that the cares of this world are choking the seed which we cannot doubt took root earlier on.

I arrived to find Winnifred Morris confined to bed and on a very rigid diet, so here perhaps is a good place to tell what are the few physical hardships of living in rural Japan. There are no tigers, crocodiles or cannibals to add colour to life there, nor even the scourge of virulent disease; such things as small-pox, cholera and typhoid being kept in check by compulsory injections. Even the more remote parts of Japan usually have electricity, and communications are good. About the only things which do constitute a trial to the flesh, for a woman especially, are the constant ceremonial sitting on the thick, straw-matted floors, with legs folded neatly under one, and little change of movement allowed. All life is lived on the floor, eating, study, writing are done at a low table, sitting on the floor. The heavy bed quilts have to be put down and taken up morning and evening and stored in big wall cupboards, so that the room can be used for other purposes during the day. Shoes are always taken off just inside the entrance hall of a Japanese house and slippers worn on the wood-floored passages or kitchen, but these too must be removed when stepping on to the *tatami* mats which usually cover the floors of all the rooms. One of our workers had no bedding cupboard in the room she slept in, and had to put her slippers on and off eight times every night when she made her bed, and again when she put it away in the morning. Since the rooms are all-purpose rooms it is hard to get any privacy in case of sickness, for the whole floor space of most of the two- or three-roomed houses the missionaries live in is occupied by the Sunday School when it meets, sometimes seventy or eighty children packing into this small space.

Diet is another problem in the long winter in the north, where vegetables have to be bought in the autumn and stored in the ground, and the choice is limited to potatoes, carrots and onions. Even in summer the more distant places only offer a very small quantity of perishable fruits and vegetables for sale; and the only way to get these in Samani was to go along to the stores shortly after each train came in from the capital. Meat too, in the smaller places is limited to pork tasting of fish, as do also the eggs, since dried fish is used as both feed and fertilizer in Japan. In Samani the shops had not much refrigeration, and everyone's margarine had gone green at the time of my visit. Cooking is done on a charcoal brazier which has to be fanned a great deal, making a lot of ash fly, but some of the missionaries now have oil stoves.

Among all the houses rented for the missionaries in Hokkaido, only the one in the capital has the "honourable bath tub", so important a feature of Japanese life. Since the war, usually only middle and upper class houses are built with a bath; but within a few minutes' walk of every home will be found a big public bath house. Here much of the neighbourhood meets every night for a time of friendly gossip as they scrub each other's backs, and when thoroughly washed clean outside, soak and relax together in the big, steaming hot, communal pool, one for women and one for men. Here Communists and others propagate their ideas in a friendly conversational way, and this is obviously the logical place for getting to know one's neighbours and "gossiping the Gospel". A few of our men have done a little of this, but for a woman brought up in Western tradition, it is hard enough even to go for a hurried bath in such circumstances. It is not easy either to have their underwear picked up and examined with curiosity, or a finger poked in their ribs to see the depth of the foreign fat! Some have never had the courage to go, and must therefore have a rather poor reputation in their community in consequence, since everyone knows there is no bath in their houses.

I remember so well in our early days in Language School one of our teachers, a dear elderly Christian lady, telling me about Japanese bathing habits. She explained that many Japanese entered the bath every day, others only twice a week. There were even *some* (obviously very undesirable creatures) who only entered the bath once a week! I was hoping desperately during this discourse that she would not ask how often *we* bathed, since for reasons of rigid economy necessary at the time, it had been decided by those in authority that the bath water should only be heated once a week for the Mission Language School. Of course she did not ask, and I realize now she probably knew from the maids that we only entered our "honourable tub" once a week, and was trying tactfully to put across the Japanese viewpoint. Various Japanese have complained in print about the nauseating smell of the perspiring meat-eating Westerner, and maids sometimes complain at having to wash foreigners' clothes for the same reason. A sponge down with a bowl of hot water does not seem common in Japan, therefore our workers are probably not given credit for this type of cleanliness. As the only place to wash in a Japanese house is the kitchen sink, with its pump for cold water in Hokkaido, such washing has usually to be done late at night when visitors are unlikely, since in the Samani house, for instance, the front door opens into the kitchen. The Japanese also have a very poor opinion of a shower as a means of washing, in spite of the economy of such a method. The three-foot deep, very hot water in which they submerge up to the neck, is almost a ceremonial cleansing for them, and soaking in it is not only an important heating device for the Japanese in their cold houses, but I am sure has a very important function in helping them to relax after all the tensions to which they subject themselves during the day, and which no doubt are largely responsible for their having the highest incidence of stomach ulcers in the world.

One other hardship, and the only one, in fact, of which I have heard much complaint from any of our workers, is the constant deafening noise of loudspeakers advertising something, or else the sound track of the local cinema which can be heard for a wide distance in a small town. It is the same on pleasure boats at sea or lake resorts—they often play records so loudly you literally cannot carry on a conversation. Vehicles on the roads constantly use their horns, and household radios are often turned on so that they can be heard clearly by the neighbours.

After lunch at Samani, Don Morris took me out visiting again, and since Winnifred Morris had been ordered complete rest, we locked her in the house so that callers would not be too persistent. No Japanese, it seems, would ever refuse to welcome a visitor, however sick they are, and irrespective of the doctor's orders to the contrary. In fact it is still considered discourteous to shut the house during the daytime, and we were told in Tokyo we must always have someone in residence—one house we lived in for a year just had no means of locking it from the outside! However, in Hokkaido some people did lock their houses when they were out at work I was told, so we went with a clear conscience.

Our first visit was to the local hospital where I had the privilege of meeting Okabe San, a man with strong muscular shoulders and a young, intelligent-looking face which it was hard to associate with his more than forty-year-old, broken body. He had been a telegraph worker and had fallen from a pole twenty-one years ago, and had had to lie in bed ever since —"bed" being a high wooden frame with the usual thick straw mat laid on top of it, such as most Japanese sleep on.

Having no sensation in his back, he had developed terrible sores without being aware of it, and these would be dressed daily by one of the hospital staff, irrespective of whether a visitor was present or not. His old mother, who was crippled with arthritis, had shared the hospital room with him for many years, and managed to take care of most of his other needs, while other relatives did what shopping was required. One of the most noticeable differences between a heathen country and one with a strong Christian tradition is the absence of any nursing care done with a sense of vocation (in China it was the same). It is the relatives who must of necessity come and care for their own sick.

There was no appearance of self-pity about Mr. Okabe, however, and learning that I came from Tokyo, he eagerly told me about the visit of one of our former Seminary students, and how earnestly yet gently he had sought to lead him to faith in Christ. Apparently he had visited him morning and afternoon during his short stay in Samani, in his desire to see him accept the Lord; and it had been largely through his influence and Margaret Maass's interest that Mr. Okabe had become a Christian. Both he and his mother spoke very highly of the student, and the fact that he still wrote to them, and it was an encouragement to those of us who teach in the Seminary to hear such results of the witness of the students.

As we walked back we met an unusually tall, and rather scholarly looking young man who had himself been in the hospital for a year with an injured back, and had been discharged only a short time before. He had attended the little services held in Okabe San's room, and gradually had come to an understanding of the truth, and had accepted Christ. His Bible is already much studied and well marked, and he also reads all the other books on Christianity he can borrow. Soon after he left the hospital he was asked if he would give his testimony at the informal Sunday evening meeting. This he willingly did. Don Morris then asked him if he would lead the singing the following Sunday; but when the time came he not only led the singing but conducted the whole service and gave the main message! He is now considering entering a Bible

School, although he has been offered an entrance in a secular college, a highly coveted goal for thousands of Japan's youth.

I was fortunate to be at Samani the night a weekly meeting is held in the next town, the place where it would have been more logical to start a Christian work but where no housing could be found when the Fishers tried there. It is an interesting story how this opening finally came.

In the previous January a few of the Christians and missionaries from the Hidaka coast had visited this town to distribute tracts. An electrician received a tract which was stamped with the Mission address in Shizunai, and he wrote there making further enquiries. His name and address was then sent on to Don Morris, who was nearer to him, and he visited the electrician in his little shop, explained what Christianity was, and sold the man a Bible. During this visit a watchmaker from the shop next door came in and listened too. A little later two of the Japanese Christians from the Hidaka coast came back to visit the electrician and gave their testimonies. As they told of some of the implications of being a Christian, the man decided that Christianity was not for him. He therefore offered to sell his Bible to the watchmaker next door.

This man was passing through a time of trouble, for his wife had just died of cancer, leaving him with four children. Soon after he bought the Bible a friend of his went on a journey to northern Hokkaido and came back with an important question. How would he like to have a Christian wife for his motherless children?

The watchmaker considered the matter carefully and finally decided it would be a good thing. So arrangements were soon made for the wedding. The bride was a woman nearing middle age who had been converted at a Holiness mission church in the north, six years before. As soon as she was established in her new home she made enquiries about the nearest Christian church. Finding this in Samani she invited Don Morris to come and hold a meeting each week in her home, so it was to this place I was taken on Wednesday night. The young man who had been converted in the hospital came with us too, although the bus ride was extremely bumpy and his back, which was still in some kind of surgical belt, was obviously paining him.

We walked into the narrow little watch shop and were greeted very courteously by the proprietor who opened up the counter for us to go through into the back room where his buxom new wife took our coats. Then she led us up the stairs to a beautiful wide, tatami-covered room where there was ample space for the ten people who eventually gathered for this, the third meeting to be held there. Four were the children of the house, all of whom were of school age, and it was obvious their new mother had already taught them to pray. I found it a little disconcerting at first to hear them all chorus "Amen" at the end of every sentence in the prayers!

At the end of the talk the father brought out some coloured pictures one of his children had once received at a Roman Catholic church, and asked what the difference was between that religion and ours. The young man who had come with us had recently been reading a little book on the subject and at once started off on a long but pretty accurate description of the difference, and added that there were similarities between Romanism and Japanese Tenrikyo, for instance that in both you were promised a better place in heaven in proportion to the amount of money you contributed.

Some of the visitors then plucked up courage to take part in the earnest discussion as the talk moved on to the things of God, until we suddenly realized it was almost time for the last bus to leave. The hostess found to her consternation that there was not even time to serve tea, but every one agreed it was much more important to think about God than to drink a ceremonial cup of tea, and with that we had to say a hurried goodbye. It was a great joy to hear two months later that the watchmaker himself had accepted Christ and that there are now seventeen people meeting in that upper room.

A veteran missionary of wide experience told me once that during all her more than thirty years in Japan she had never heard of a fisherman accepting Christ. I had also read elsewhere of the corporate life these fishermen live, and how closely bound up with religion are all their customs and procedure as they live together in dormitories at the ports for certain times of the year. One of the most famous shrines in Japan is worshipped by fishermen, and is one of the three shrines which receive the largest offerings in all Japan, although the fishermen are among the poorest of the people. Because of this situation we had made it a special matter of prayer at our last missionary conference that some fishermen might be saved.

In Mori, Miss Homma (whose story is told in an earlier chapter) had felt a burden for the fishermen in the dormitories there, and had organized visitation work and tract distribution among them; but up to the present we do not know of any there who have received Christ, or even evinced any particular interest. From a Presbyterian missionary in the south of Japan, I heard of a young man who was converted in a city meeting and decided to train as a pastor and go back to his native fishing village to win them for Christ, but after several years' residence among them he had not succeeded in getting one to become a Christian.

It was a great joy therefore, to learn that in the next village to Samani there was a fisherman who had made an open profession of accepting Christ, and had put up Gospel posters in both the dining-room and sleeping quarters of his dormitory, as well as in the house he lived in with his wife and her sister and husband. This man had been a "bruised reed", a social reject, and for that reason no doubt it was easier for him to break with social custom and follow Christ. He had fallen from a window when a child of three, and may have received some kind of brain injury which caused strange fits of trembling. These brought him much unhappiness and teasing at school. Later he developed the habit of stealing which finally caused him to be sent to a mental hospital in Sapporo.

During the tent campaign held in Samani the previous summer it so happened that he was passing down the street earlier in the day when a small open-air meeting was being held. He stopped and talked to one of the Christians, and said he was interested and that someone had spoken to him about Christianity in the train when he had been travelling back from Sapporo.

He was afraid to come to the evening meetings, however, for

the police were always suspicious of him if he were out at night and would follow him and question him. But he started to read the Bible, and by November had gained courage to attend the Sunday meetings. There he announced one night that he now had the assurance of salvation. He began to want to give out tracts and to witness to the people with whom he works. He is usually at sea a week at a time, and life then cannot be easy for a Christian, but we believe he is experiencing the joy and keeping power of the indwelling Christ. Not long ago a bicycle was stolen from the next town, and the police came from there to question him; and for the first time in his life he was not upset or disturbed in any way by this, for he now has a conscience clear in the sight of God, and by His strength is living an honest life.

Two of our workers, Mr. and Mrs. Lea Little, lived for more than a year in a city in Aomori prefecture where nearly all their neighbourhood was inhabited by fishermen, and during all that time they did not see one soul converted. Just at the time I was in Samani, however, they had the joy of seeing two fishermen accept Christ, and at least one of these has continued to grow in the faith and recently burned his god shelves. Later came the news of his baptism.

Quite a number of people had signed decision cards at the tent campaign in Samani at which this fisherman was first contacted; but, though they were all visited afterwards and invited to services, none have remained for any length of time. One for whom they entertained great hopes was a son of the Ainu pastor I had met in Shizunai. He came to some of the meetings but is still a slave to drink, and will not accept the freedom he could have in Christ.

Don Morris had worked in both our Aomori field and Hokkaido, and I asked him what he felt was the chief difference in the people of the two areas. He replied that on the main island of Honshu the people seemed more ambitious, and took more care of their houses and their appearance. Some of this difference is perhaps due to the hard work of just keeping alive and warm through the long cold winters in Hokkaido; but many of the people give the impression of having been misfits or failures in the more rigid social life of the main islands where they formerly lived.

In the bigger cities those with ambition have found a place, and there is a general feeling of friendliness and lack of formality which is refreshing. But in the smaller places most of the people seem to have little purpose in life, and are content to keep themselves alive with a roof over their heads, and indulge in their particular weaknesses without too much fear of criticism. The missionaries knew two men in that little town of Samani who had killed themselves through drink during the past twelve months.

It is true that the people of Hokkaido on the whole are more free from some of the pressures and customs of long established small communities, and to that extent it is a little easier for them to become Christians. The number who actually listen to the Gospel is small, however, and the power of sin in their lives is as strong as anywhere else, and its presence often more evident. As my train travelled back, winding slowly along the single track through beautiful greenery which served to enhance the rich colours of the wild flowers—purple and yellow iris, roses, clover, and flame-coloured lilies—I saw on one side the wooded hills and distant mountains, and on the other the blue sea gently lapping against grey rock and lush green pasture, and felt that for many people down there it had proved to be By-path Meadow. They were people who had tried to escape from the difficulties of life; and, for the most part, were unwilling to face the testing involved in being a true child of God. "How oft would I . . . but ye would not", said the One who created the beauty of this lovely country, so instead of it being a source of praise and thanksgiving for them it serves merely to shelter them from some of the hard facts and duties of life. Although outwardly it appears in all the beauty and attractiveness of By-path Meadow, for those who have been called to fight a spiritual warfare there it has proved one of the hardest and most disappointing of all the C.I.M. centres of work.

Chapter XX

AOMORI—THE GOSPEL IN THE CAPITAL

SOME of the train journeys through Hokkaido were made interesting by the presence of parties of middle or high school students. These are a great feature of life in Japan. Further south these trips are arranged in May and October when the weather is usually clear, but in Hokkaido June and July are the best months, and several trains I had travelled on had been crowded with these parties. These excursions usually involve one or two whole nights of travel, sitting up, of course, with a day full of sightseeing at some traditional beauty spots, historical scenes or famous temples, and very few children complete their school life without an organized trip to Tokyo to see the Emperor's palace, the shrine of the war dead, and other things where the spirit of Japan, and feeling of national unity, are strongly impressed upon them.

Most Japanese are very studious, and in Hokkaido particularly, welcome an opportunity to try out their English on a foreigner. On one train I found myself in the midst of a group led by their school principal, who was an expert wrestler. He showed me a magazine with photographs of himself and his school team, and told me they were going to take part in a big sports meeting at Aomori on the main island. From there they would go to Hirosaki, one of the famous historical cities I myself planned to visit two days later.

There were two particularly nice-looking, interesting boys in this group, and one could see the sweat standing out in beads on their faces as they summed up courage to speak to me in English. However, we soon got friendly, and I was just wondering what was the best way of introducing the Gospel to them when another group boarded the train. These were evidently regular travellers to the district high school. As soon as they saw me they rushed up with some very difficult English homework—part of it a rather complicated joke in English about some dull wit saying we needed the moon to shine at night because it was dark, but there was no need for the sun in the daytime because it is light then anyway! They could not get the point of this at all, and as one of the words for "sun" in Japanese also means "day" I had a very complicated time trying to explain it to them in my limited Japanese. Soon we reached their station and I gave them a few tracts to share as they got out.

Meanwhile the other students had begun their lunch which I was interested to see, consisted of cold balls of rice and tins of fish and fruit which they shared with their neighbours. The two I had been talking to before moved over again to share some peanuts and candy with me, but I had only time to tell them of our services in Sapporo, and give them my last remaining tracts, before I had to get out at Kutchan. One of the boys especially, named Goto, remains on my heart particularly, and I prayed that these tracts might be a link in the chain which will bring him to Christ, as have many train contacts in the past.

When I boarded the train again the following afternoon, I found myself opposite a nice-looking young man of twenty-five. As soon as we were settled he pulled out of his pocket a quart whisky bottle with a familiar Scots plaid label and steadily drank cup after cup, interspersed with peanuts and a kind of Japanese cracker. He cast frequent glances in my direction and when about one-third of the bottle was empty he gained courage to address me, and announced in careful English, "I like whisky!"

I asked him why he liked it, but he looked completely at a loss, and murmured he did not know. Such a question had obviously never occurred to him! Drink is so integral a part of a happy occasion or an outing for the Japanese. On the opposite side of the train aisle there was a party of humbler looking folk, Ainu (tribespeople) judging by their appearance, who had a huge two-quart bottle of *sake* which they were joyfully, though by now rather unsteadily, passing around. This young man had probably been saving up for some time for this bottle of whisky as the appropriate accompaniment of an important journey, for he told me next, "I go to Tokyo to learn English."

I tried to keep him talking as much as possible, hoping in this way to gain longer pauses between the refilling of the little cup. I learned that he was a primary school teacher with ten days' vacation, and was going to Tokyo, where his brother was attending university, to study English with one of his brother's friends. I was interested to hear he lived in Kitami where there are three C.I.M. missionaries, and urged him to attend their English Bible classes when he returned. Then I gave him two tracts to read which took him some time, and he asked a few questions about them, though without any real understanding. However, I was thankful that the bottle was still one-third full when we arrived at Hakodate, the port where we transferred to the ferry boat which takes trains and passengers over to the main island.

It was here that the disastrous typhoon unexpectedly hit three years ago, overturning the ferry boat and causing the death of over 1,000 Japanese as well as two missionaries and a number of U.S. military personnel. September is the month of typhoons, however, and this glorious afternoon in early July the sea was peaceful and blue, and the strains of "Auld Lang Syne" coming softly over the water as the fussy little tugs pulled us away from the quay, created a pleasantly nostalgic atmosphere. The stewards had been most efficient and courteous in welcoming us on board, and as I stood on deck watching the retreating shore line I suddenly remembered the last time I had been on board a Japanese vessel of any size. (I had had to fly to Hokkaido because of teaching commitments in Tokyo.) That had been in October 1940 when I, with a number of other foreigners, had sailed from Shanghai to Tsingtao, the first stage of our long journey across occupied China, no-man's-land, and finally into the free West. On that ship we were anything but honoured guests, and were treated to certain indignities which we felt very much at the time, but have almost forgotten now. As I stood there on the deck it struck me how well the Japanese are taught to act—whether it is the rôle of conqueror or that of the gracious host, they play the part to the full. I felt thankful that this time I was in the position of guest, and as I had passed by the crowded mats on the floor of the third-class area where I would have had to kneel or lie with most of my intoxicated train companions, I was glad I had taken a second-class ticket on the ferry. It was pleasant to enjoy a few hours in the fresh air on the upper deck after the hours in crowded trains thick with the fumes of tobacco and liquor, and the luxury of the easy chairs in the second-class lounge was wonderful after days on the floor in our missionaries' simple homes.

As it grew dusk we entered Aomori harbour, probably the most important city in Northern Honshu. Walter Searle, the acting field superintendent, was at the dock to meet me and led me down through the long station platform, surely one of the longest in the world, from which the crowded express trains leave five times daily to transport the thousands of Japanese who seem to travel back and forth from Tokyo all the year round. It is always difficult getting a seat for this fourteen-hour train journey; and, for those who do the trip right through to or from Hokkaido, as our missionaries usually do, it is a very wearying business. I was fortunate in having had only nine hours travel. A short bus ride soon brought us to the Japan C.I.M. headquarters, now established in Aomori city. This is a dignified, five-roomed Japanese house where the C.I.M. superintendent and his family and secretary live, and where varied numbers of guests passing through can be accommodated for the night on the tatami floor of the living-room where Bible classes are held at various times during the week. There is a nice little garden where fresh vegetables and flowers can be grown. Also in it is a small building, originally a store-room, which is now in fact a one-bed hospital where a C.I.M. doctor and nurse, who live nearby in a small rented house, can treat any missionary needing medical care. The lady doctor is, I believe, the only foreign civilian doctor in the whole of Hokkaido and the northern half of Japan.

A full programme had been arranged for me the next day, which was Sunday. First a quick visit round the neighbourhood

after breakfast, seeing the sea beach from which some Christians were to be baptized that afternoon. We also passed the
huge sports arena to which the party I had met on the train
from Sapporo had been going, and which was already showing
signs of activity since Sunday is the great day for all extra-
curricular school events to take place in Japan. During this
walk Mrs. Searle told me of some of their most recent problems
and disappointments. One of these was a friend of their
servant's who had shown real interest in Christianity, but a
few days before had felt a cold sensation on her shoulder and
thought it was the spirits showing their disapproval of her
reading the Bible, and she therefore felt she must give this up.
Another story was about one of their teachers whose sister had
very recently tried to commit suicide and had only been stopped
by a friend calling to her just as she was about to jump into the
sea. She was still very unhappy, however, and all the church
was praying for her.

Afterwards Dr. Roslyn Ormiston (now Mrs. David Hayman)
took me to a Japanese morning service. This was a very interesting
group, meeting in a kindergarten classroom, with about thirty
adults sitting round three sides of the room at the low benches
and tables used by four and five year olds. This group of
believers has grown from the witness of two Evangelical
Alliance missionary couples who went up there three years
ago, and by means of tent campaigns in the area gradually
got a little group of Christians established. There is very
little in the way of organization yet. The missionary does most
of the Bible teaching, but otherwise everyone in the group is
equal and a spirit of love seems to prevail, and also a real
sense of responsibility for evangelism. It does not have the
disadvantage of being predominantly a student church, as are
so many in the larger cities, and the Christians are from very
ordinary occupations, thus helping to disprove the common
belief that Christianity is only for the highly educated. One of
the most prominent Christians is a Mr. Chiba whom I had met
at the station the night before when he had collected my ticket
at the barrier. At this particular service a missionary gave a
Bible reading prior to the Communion service, and only one

Christian gave a testimony, but I was told that usually the local Christians took a large share in the services, and that the prayer meetings were long and fervent gatherings, the believers really strengthening each other in the Lord.

In the afternoon I had the choice of seeing the baptism service, visiting a Sunday School just begun by some of the language school students, and visiting the local leprosarium. I had heard of this leper work previously and was anxious to see it, so the Christians, some of whom usually go once a month for a service, kindly arranged for one of their number to go with a group of us missionaries and hold an extra service, so that I might meet the lepers.

I had first heard of this leprosarium at the time of Billy Graham's visit to Japan in February. One of our language school students who had visited the place told me how much the Christians of the leprosarium were praying for Dr. Graham. They had his picture in prominent places round the compound and were praying for revival to result from his visit to the East. There are about 600 lepers there. In February ninety-six of them were Christians and they were praying very much that their number might grow to 100. I was therefore very interested to hear if this number had been reached, and learned with joy that there were now 102 Christians.

It is a government institution, and Sunday services have been conducted by various groups for some years now. There had already been the regular Protestant service that morning, and when we arrived the Roman Catholic service was in progress in the auditorium. Consequently we had to meet in a small guest room consisting of a platform for visitors, with a wooden partition between them and the rest of the *tatami*-matted room where the patients sat on the floor.

Many were resting at that time and did not even know of this extra meeting which had been very hurriedly arranged after the morning service, so only twenty-three attended, but it was a moving sight to watch them come in. They, for the most part, entered in pairs, the majority being blind, and some very seriously maimed. There were two young women, however, smartly dressed, on whom there were no outward signs of the disease; only on their faces a look of strain or shock, perhaps at the realization that one day they might be in a similar condition to those they saw around them. They had no books but seemed to know all the words, and the numbers of the hymns, and when an opportunity was given for them to choose, the title selected was "Christ is all". In the time of open prayer one followed another without pause, and it was strangely moving to hear that for the most part their prayers were ones of thanksgiving.

Afterwards we visited one of the residential blocks, to see a Christian woman who was known to some of the missionaries and who had not been at the meeting. She came from the city of Goshogawara where two C.I.M. missionaries now work. Her husband had been a prominent professing Christian in an older church there, but when she developed leprosy he divorced her and married again. She then entered the leprosarium and became one of the leaders of the Christians there.

We left the leprosarium in time to arrive at the former Language School in time for supper. This house was known as "The Farm" because it does in fact belong to and adjoins the home of a farmer, and its yard is complete with farm animals. Here twelve C.I.M. new arrivals had been living for nearly a year in very cramped quarters with little privacy possible. Six had scattered to begin work in other places and there were now only about six in residence.

A tent campaign was in progress not far away, run by some of the Christians from the group already seen that morning. The new workers who still did not have enough language to do much in the way of preaching or personal work, were helping in as many ways as possible. Daphne Kelly played the little organ at all the meetings, and Hubert Fisher took the unenviable job of being caretaker of the tent, sleeping there through the night, eating cold picnic meals there, and helping with the selling of literature, inviting people in and doing personal work.

The service that evening was led by a Mr. Osaka who is one of their finest evangelists. According to Mr. Fadel, their missionary, he "preaches with a broken heart". This man is a carpenter and had been converted about two years before. He had sought peace and rest of heart for a long time but had tried to pretend to himself that he did possess it, until he heard the Gospel. He had some dark months of seeking the truth in his own strength, but at last the words "I am crucified with Christ: nevertheless I live; yet not I, but Christ liveth in me" brought a revelation to him. In his own words, "The more I was enlightened with God's light, I found in myself pride, jealousy and unbelief, but if I cast all this on Christ I could receive the assurance that all my sinful nature was crucified with Christ, and have power to live my daily life and get victory over myself."

Two girls gave their testimonies next. One of them had been converted in the tent campaign held there the previous year. The other told in a dramatic way how she had been saved through a fear of death after hearing a little about Roman Catholicism. She is now doing office work in connection with a Bible correspondence course.

Mr. Chiba the railway worker was the main speaker, and he really held the attention of the audience. One of the things which impressed me was that he seemed so very typically Japanese. Often both in China and Japan it seems that the ones who attract the missionary, and vice versa, are a little different from the normal, perhaps a little more Western in appearance or outlook, and as such do not always receive the full approval of their fellow countrymen. But to me Mr. Chiba seemed thoroughly Japanese, and yet at the same time was one who had completely given himself to the Lord. He had only been married a few months before, and even his choice of a bride is an indication of the type of man he is. He had mentioned to Mr. Fadel some time before that he would like to get married, and of course wanted to have a Christian wife. From time to time Mr. Fadel mentioned the names of Christian girls of suitable age in the city, but he did not appear interested in any of them. One day going to church Mr. Fadel happened to mention a girl away off near Karuizawa whom he and a friend had led to the Lord when they were still language students. She had continued steadily in the Christian life for four years and, with very little help in her village and much opposition, she had carried on a Sunday School. He remarked that she was not the type to become discouraged and knew the secret of leaving her burdens with the Lord. At once Mr. Chiba was interested, and asked the missionary if he would write to her and see if she would consider marrying him. After some correspondence the girl wrote to say that at a certain time when she was praying, the Lord revealed to her that it was His will that she marry Mr. Chiba. He and his go-between therefore paid a visit to her village, twenty hours by train, and the parents agreed to the marriage.

At the end of that meeting in the tent the teacher's sister who had tried to commit suicide (whom I had heard about that morning) professed conversion, and also her husband.

When I left the house before 8 a.m. the next morning I found Mr. Chiba on the bus and about to go on duty at the station again that morning. They work twenty-four hours on and twenty-four off, and he had been on duty when I arrived Saturday evening, finishing Sunday morning early. From that time, in his twenty-four hours off, he had attended the morning service, conducted a baptism service in the afternoon, in the evening done the hard preaching to the restless, ever-changing audience of a tent meeting, and had been engaged in personal work afterwards. Then a few hours sleep and he was now off for another twenty-four hours' stretch of work at the busy railway station. Here surely is a man after God's own heart, perhaps one of the Japanese Christian leaders we have been praying for.

The latest word I have had is that Mr. Chiba has tuberculosis and the railway company has given him three months' leave, to enter a sanatorium. He at first refused to go, saying if he were going to die he wanted to spend his remaining months preaching the Gospel, but I understand that his Christian friends have persuaded him to go to the sanatorium after all. No doubt he will find a harvest field there with plenty of opportunity to witness for His Master; and his little wife will have further opportunity to practise casting her burden upon the Lord.

Chapter XXI

IN CITIES NEW AND OLD

I HAD set out from Aomori city early that morning with Eileen Singleton to guide me, on a hurried visit around four of our five centres of work in Aomori prefecture. This is mainly an agricultural area, and the most famous apple-growing district in Japan. The apple was introduced to Japan by a missionary only within the last century, but now vast acres of land both in Aomori and the island of Hokkaido are devoted to this product. I am told that every blossom is fertilized by hand. Now, as far as the eye could see as we travelled along on the train and later walked in some of the orchards, there were groups of girls everywhere thinning out the young apples and covering each good fruit with a little bag made of newspaper, to protect it from insects. This would remain on until the fruit was fully ripe, unless washed away by the heavy typhoon rains and wind in September. It is probably the apple which has brought prosperity to this formerly rather poor and isolated northern prefecture with a very distinct dialect of its own.

Our first destination was Goshogawara, a small but developing city which had been entered only a month previously by Stephen Metcalf and one of the young men from the language school, Abe Friesen. Stephen Metcalf had begun work at Kanagi, a country town at the end of a little branch line running from Goshogawara, more than a year before, and from there had developed a few contacts in the larger city, mainly in the district high school, where he had been invited to hold a weekly English Bible class.

Two weeks after they moved into the city to live they arranged to show one of the Moody *Faith and Fact* films, to be followed by an evangelistic meeting, in the town hall which holds about 1,000 people. This was packed full for the meeting, but the majority who came were children. The services of the young lady who operates the city public address system were included with the use of the hall, and afterwards she invited all those who were really interested in Christianity to remain. Nearly 200 people did so. A show of hands was asked for, to indicate how many were already Christians, and nine responded. After that just six put up their hands indicating they had already heard something about Christianity. The pastor from the only other church in the city (a member of the Kyodan) was present, and he told Stephen Metcalf afterwards he was shocked to see how few knew anything at all about Christianity, for his church had been established there seventy years ago, although it had been closed for twenty years preceding and during the war.

After speaking a little further about the Gospel, tracts were handed out and people invited to think seriously about the matter, and to attend the next meeting which would be held in the missionaries' home. From all these 200, however, only three turned up at the next meeting, and two of these had only come into the town hall right at the end and had just heard there was to be another meeting! Two of them were barber's assistants, and all these three have continued coming regularly since. Now, four months later, has come word that they and a third barber's boy have all believed and been baptized, together with a mechanic and an older woman. The latter has been a widow for fifteen years and has two daughters, one in high school and one attending university; she seems to have found real peace and joy in the Lord.

All this is the fruit of later days, however; and when we arrived there, around ten o'clock on that Monday morning, they were still feeling rather exhausted from their previous day's work.

They had begun at 8.30 a.m. with a meeting in Japanese for students, mainly the result of the high school class they had conducted while still living in Kanagi. Twenty to twenty-five had attended and some of them stayed right on until midday. The missionaries then tried to get a little lunch, but one of the boys who had been there most of the morning returned with his elder brother while they were still only halfway through the meal. This boy was a university student who had been forced to give up study temporarily through illness. His first question was, "What is the difference between Roman Catholicism and Christianity?"

After half an hour of this two more high school students came in wanting to study English, so Abe Friesen took them off to his room. Meanwhile the question in the other room had turned to the atomic bomb, and how could a Christian nation reconcile the making of these with its Christian teaching. From one o'clock to six o'clock they stayed, and the taxing work of listening hard to a foreign language and trying to make one's answers plain in it, went on. Some of the questions would be difficult enough to answer in English! So always there was a heart-prayer at the same time, that somehow some word might pierce the armour and score a victory for Christ. As they finally rose to leave the elder brother said, "I came to enjoy having an argument with you, but I didn't know what the Christian faith really is." He seemed to leave with a sincere interest and asked for a New Testament to study on his own.

After supper this elder brother returned for the evening meeting to which nine people came altogether, including four barber boys. As they parted at the door afterwards one of them suddenly said, "Do you mean to say that simply on the act of repentance and confession we can be saved?" With that they departed leaving two physically and mentally exhausted servants of the Lord, yet with spirits optimistic in the belief that God was soon going to bring new life into that place.

We spent a very pleasant morning there hearing of the beginnings of the work, and having a good Japanese meal in their little kitchen-dining-room presided over by their daily help, who already gave the impression of being an old and faithful retainer. After lunch we walked through a part of the little city which has been largely burned out twice within three years. These fires seem tragically common in the northern cities where fire-fighting apparatus is inadequate and strong winds are very frequent in the winter months.

The local Bible Society colporteur had been a great help to

them, both in finding the rooms for them to live in and also introducing them to some of the people. One of these was the manager of an accountancy business, a man of about fifty, who seemed very interested in the Gospel and who arranged to have a weekly meeting in his office to which eight or nine of the clerks came. This had been going on for some months while Stephen Metcalf was still in Kanagi. Some of these Bible Society men stay in a definite area, others gradually cover the whole of Japan, and some of our Hokkaido workers had enjoyed occasional fellowship with them. Mary Weller, writing from Yayoi, a new coal-mining area to which they had just moved, says: "Just now a Bible Society colporteur is here, selling the colloquial Bible. We go around with him and distribute tracts. It's a very good way of getting to know the people and the neighbourhood. He is very skilled in the right way to approach different folk, and seems to have the right verse of Scripture for each one. For a tired mother he will quote: "Come unto Me and I will give you rest", for an autocratic-looking father, "Honour thy father and thy mother", for a sin-marked face, "The pure in heart shall see God". There are not many folks who refuse to buy. It's quite an education to go around with him and as we go he tells everyone about our meetings. Half a day of it wears me out, but these men keep at it day in and day out, visiting one to 200 houses every day. I certainly admire them."

Another very interesting story was that of a man away up in the mountains outside the city to whom the colporteur had introduced Stephen Metcalf. He was a schoolteacher who experienced a great feeling of depression after the war. Their gods had failed them and he was wondering what more there was in life, and whether it was worthwhile to continue living. Then one day when he was down in the city he saw a second-hand copy of the Bible in a bookstore, and bought it. He took it back with him up into the mountains and read it and believed. At first he thought of going into the ministry, but other Christians, whom he found in Hirosaki, advised him to continue teaching and witnessing up in the mountain villages where there were no churches. He did this for a time, but as we have already mentioned, Japanese schools have many activities on Sundays to which teachers are compelled to give their time, so finally he resigned from his teaching post and opened a shop, so that he could control his own time. The Bible Society man had taken Stephen Metcalf up there to visit him and he found the home covered with Gospel pictures and texts, and no sign of any god shelves. Here was a man who was truly letting his light shine in a dark place, with no help from any other human source—one who had found freedom in Christ, and who was remaining free.

The story of the Japanese pastor there was also very interesting. His father had died when he was young, and his mother had opened a kind of inferior geisha restaurant in order to support her family. While the Japanese claim there is no sin in patronizing these places there does, however, seem to be some social stigma attached to those who operate them and those who work in them, though many prostitutes are widows trying to support their children, or wives with sick husbands to support. A student writing to one of the Tokyo newspapers once said, "Just as in past years, the streets of Tokyo are beginning to bustle with Christmas sales, but I wonder how the farmers in poor crop areas are going to pass the winter. I am chagrined to read and hear newspaper and radio comment making fun of these unfortunate farmers. The tragic plight of some farmers who are selling their daughters is taken up as the subject for entertainment features. No sympathy is shown, instead the plight of these people is viewed with a sneering attitude." Even just to be an orphan appears to have a stigma attached judging from another letter written by a farmer:

"Editor:
My sister who is in the third year of junior high school, returned home one day and sadly remarked, 'They told me to apply at another factory as our family background is not too good.' We both lost our parents when we were still small. They died a year before the end of the war. Fortunately we had farmland, and were raised by grandmother and my aunt and uncle. Since we had no parents, however, my elder sister,

myself and two younger sisters experienced unpleasantness when we sought employment. We tried to spend our days as cheerfully as possible by forgetting that our parents were no longer living. However, the suffering and shock I had when I went out into the world have made me distrust and harbour suspicion against society. After seeing the sad face of my sister I felt as if I had to make a strong appeal to society—Let us have no more discriminatory treatment."

These extracts will perhaps help us to understand a little of the shadow under which this young man, who later became a pastor, grew up. As long as he could remember he had never been really happy. One day, however, he heard an open-air preacher speaking about the Lord and the woman taken in adultery, and he suddenly realized with a great sense of relief that everyone else was really just as bad as his own family, although they were always pretending they were better! Fortunately he did not stop at this rather negative attitude. He was particularly impressed with Christ's words "Go and sin no more". So moved was he by this experience that he finally went into the nearest city, Hirosaki, trying to find a church. This was a great centre of missionary work at that time, both Protestant and Roman Catholic, but he had no idea of the difference between any of the churches and merely enquired when he got inside the city where there was a Christian church. The nearest, a Methodist one, was pointed out to him, and through its ministry he eventually came into a real experience of Christ as Saviour, and felt called to the ministry. A Presbyterian missionary also somehow got in touch with him, and denied himself many necessities in order to help this young man through college, generosity which made a tremendous impression upon him. When war broke out he was pastor of a church in Yokohama all the congregation of which gradually melted away as the war progressed and more and more pressure was brought to bear on the Christians. He felt afterwards that he wanted to start from scratch, and not have a congregation of "guests" who could not be relied upon to stand by the church. He therefore came to the little church in this city which had been closed for twenty years, and has gradually built it up until now there is an attendance of about forty.

I had an opportunity to visit Hirosaki the next day. It is an interesting old city, though I found the actual remains of the 350-year-old castle were much smaller than one imagined from the angle at which it is usually photographed in the famous cherry blossom pictures. In early days the lord of Hirosaki castle was a Roman Catholic, and so of course were most of his underlings. In this area therefore, Buddhism has been quite influenced by Romanist teaching and many of the people still seem to have a unique belief in a supreme god, but think they have to be Buddhists because they are Japanese.

This is the educational centre of Aomori prefecture, all the institutions of higher learning being located here. Several denominational missionary societies started schools and colleges here. These are now controlled by Japanese, but there are four missionaries all engaged in educational work. As the city has a population of 140,000, and it seemed there was little or nothing being done in the way of direct evangelism, it was decided that two of our women missionaries should live there. Largely at first through the means of student Bible classes they proclaim the message of One who can free from the penalty and power of sin.

The work was very hard going for many months. Christianity is no longer "news" in that city, and foreigners no novelty, some having been there for the last eighty years. From the roof of the main department store can be seen imposing church buildings in several directions. One very beautiful one was not far from the only house we were able to rent. When our workers gave their address to any contacts they might meet, some of these naturally went to this beautiful foreign-looking church when trying to find them.

English Bible classes were started on Saturday afternoons for middle school students and in the evening for high school students. About twenty were attending these until one day when they were asked, nine said they wished to believe in Christ—and then never attended again! On Monday evenings there was a class for university students with a much smaller number attending.

They were also given the names of seventeen radio contacts from that area who had written in to the Christian programme sponsors asking for further information. Of these only three showed any interest when visited, and only one seemed to have really believed.

For months numbers and interest seemed to grow less rather than more. It was a time of inconspicuous sowing and holding on in faith and persistent patient prayer for a harvest to come. At last came the spring and all the black, lifeless looking branches of the huge old cherry trees around the moat of the ancient castle showed their first tiny specks of life. Then our two young workers there, with the help of T.E.A.M. missionaries and Japanese Christians from Aomori city, as well as a few others who were able to visit for a day or two, prepared to bring the Word of Life to the thousands who come to see the glorious evidence of renewed life in those wonderful old cherry trees. That campaign was really the breaking point, or rather the moment of release of new spiritual life in that discouraged little centre in Hirosaki, as we saw in the chapter on tent evangelism.

Three Christians from other places have moved to Hirosaki and are now meeting with our missionaries there. About nine attend the Sunday morning worship service, and a larger number a kind of enquirers' meeting on Friday evenings when a number of the Christians are each willing to speak on a paragraph of the chapter they are studying.

Another tent campaign was held in the summer, led by one of the T.E.A.M. group, and at this a woman patient from the Tuberculosis Hospital was soundly converted and has come regularly to meetings since. She happened to see a notice about the tent campaign, and wanted to go, but was afraid to do so alone. Finally a friend who belonged to the Seichonoie sect agreed to go with her, but drew back when they got to the entrance of the tent. Someone on duty there managed to persuade her to go in alone, however; and she came every evening after that. Later when one of the missionaries was speaking of the nature of sin, and the character of Christ, she was very convicted of the "narrowness" of her heart and lack of love for others, particularly the man who lived in her room at the hospital. There, in what appears to us a very odd arrangement, they had one man and two women in a small ward. In the mornings when the women wanted to do the cleaning of the room he would lie in bed, and in the afternoons when they wished to rest he would turn on his radio loudly. Consequently the women were feeling a not unnatural resentment against their roommate. This woman and a pre-medical student, also converted in the tent, have both recently asked for baptism.

One particularly encouraging convert in the tent campaign was a carpenter who was one of the half-million people to whom a tract had been given during the Cherry Blossom festival. It was the end of the day, and he was in his working clothes, half drunk, when Mabel Fredlund offered him a tract adding, "I expect you are tired." It was these simple words which touched his heart. He went home wondering that any stranger should bother to say such words to him, and he read through the tract carefully. When he saw the advertisement of the next tent campaign he decided to go and hear, and was converted there. Now in his testimony he can say, "Before I became a Christian I did nothing but my work during the day, and then got drunk every night. But in that tent the Lord delivered me." Here is another captive freed by the power of Christ and walking in newness of life.

Chapter XXII

IN QUIET COUNTRY TOWNS

K ANAGI was the first place to be pioneered by C.I.M. workers in Aomori prefecture. Situated at the end of a little single track branch railway line, it is a rather sleepy, unprogressive little town, so it was easier there to find rooms to rent. One of the younger brothers of a former governor of the prefecture used to live there in a beautiful home which is now a hotel. He was a novelist and as soon as he had written his last book he went and committed suicide with his concubine which considerably helped to publicize the book. We were shown around this hotel during my visit there, as the present owner is also the landlord of the little sewing school over which our workers have their rooms. A weekly bath at the hotel is included in the rental agreement since there is no bath at the house! Many different kinds of beautiful ornamental wood were used in the building of this former mansion, and the house where the sewing school is also has very good woodwork, and beautiful paintings on the paper doors between the three upstairs rooms where the two C.I.M. missionaries live. This artistic beauty, however, does not quite compensate for the very small and inconvenient kitchen, the toilet shared with all the sewing school, and the deep well from which all the water has to be drawn by thick, ice-stiffened ropes in the long freezing winter.

When the C.I.M. survey team first visited this place they found there was one Christian living there, an elderly shoe-maker who had in the first place been converted through the work of the Holiness church. During the war he had stood firm, and suffered some persecution for his faith. As a result, when he sees any young Christians he wonders how long they will stand, and expects that most will fail, just as all his own con-temporaries did. He comes regularly to meetings, but his very pessimistic and critical outlook is not very helpful to new believers.

About forty people crowded into their rooms when meetings were first announced, for foreigners are rare in that district. But the two men who first went there had gone straight from language school, and they had not enough Japanese to hold the people for long, so interest soon waned until only two continued to come regularly. However, the young man living next door eventually accepted Christ and began to witness. Finally after about a year there were five young men and five young women who had believed. The five fellows then prepared for baptism, but the girls all drew back from this step owing to pressure from their families who believed that they would never get husbands if they should be baptized. (Why did not the five young men marry the five women? They were too young to think of marriage yet; most of the women were of higher social class than the boys; and there were other good Japanese reasons.)

The missionaries had often prayed specifically that a church might be raised up, and that of the early Christians each might be given one special gift of the Spirit. It was very encouraging therefore that of these five firstfruits among the men, one showed promise of being an evangelist, another seemed to have a gift for organization and leadership, another liked children's work, while another was able to explain the Bible in a way which others liked to hear. This last young man was one to whom the next-door boy had witnessed; but the latter had not had much education and his friend thought he had just become interested in some new cult. However, he read some of Kanzo Uchimura's writings and was very impressed. He worked in a bookstore from 7 a.m. until 9.30 p.m., however, and had only one day off a month. Sometimes to the dismay of the weary missionaries, he would turn up at ten o'clock at night when the meetings were finished, wanting to have some teaching. One day this young man was feeling very depressed, and happened to open his Bible at John, chapter 3, which he read; and right then he was truly converted. Because of his long hours of work, however, he never had very much time to study the Bible, and one day he came and announced, to the missionary's great surprise, that he was giving up his job and going to Bible School so that he could have time to study God's Word. He is now at a school recently started in Central Japan by two Japanese men of God, Mr. Ando and Mr. Hatori. After three months there he went home for his first vacation obviously having learned a great deal even in that short period.

His going meant the weakening of the force that remained, however, and the young man with the gift for leadership, who worked for the Forestry Department, was moved to another post up in the mountains, and can get only occasional Sundays off. Then Stephen Metcalf was transferred to Goshogawara and two women workers replaced him at Kanagi, so it has proved a time of testing in many ways. The boy next door apparently does not have too high an opinion of women, and does many things to make life difficult; sometimes speaking himself at a meeting when he knows someone else has been invited to do so; sometimes not turning up at all for a teen-age meeting for which he has the responsibility!

A tent meeting was arranged early in September at which one of the pastors connected with the Central Japan Pioneer Mission was invited to speak. His mature messages resulted in thirty-one people signing a declaration of their faith. Some of these began to attend regular services after that; but the older Christians seem to have no sense of responsibility for helping the new ones, or even giving them a welcome. This has been found to be a characteristic in many places, and perhaps partly accounts for the small number attending an average Japanese church.

Some of the young women who had refused baptism before are now showing more interest, though one, as soon as the former missionary had left, announced she would no longer be coming to services. One of the others, however, who had not been for a long time came to the house, introduced herself and said she was finding she could not do anything without the power of Christ, and wanted to come back to services.

Another girl who has brought much joy to the hearts of those who know her, Narumi San, does not live in Kanagi itself, but is the daughter of a farmer out in the country. Stephen Metcalf was once out in her village giving out tracts and selling Bibles, and visited the sewing school which she was attending to learn Japanese style dressmaking. She bought a New Testament, but, when she tried to read it, found she could not understand it. She therefore came into Kanagi to try to get help. But when she found the missionaries lived upstairs she was too shy to go up, and returned home. She came again, however, and this time plucked up courage to enter. She stayed for three or four hours, came back again the next day, and on the third day came bringing some friends. She accepted Christ as her Saviour that day. She has met with persecution since then and her Bible was taken from her for a time, but she has never backslidden. She attended the New Year Conference for Christians of the Aomori area arranged by T.E.A.M. and our own workers, which was held in Kanagi that year. Then she seemed to have a real and deep experience of repentance, and soon after was baptized, the first girl in that area who was willing to take this step. Later she came into the Kanagi Sewing School to learn Western style dressmaking. (These courses are almost compulsory in Japan for girls who are hoping to have a marriage arranged for them.) She had a wonderful opportunity to study the Bible each day with the two missionaries who had moved there. She witnessed to every one of the students in the School, and also spent a good deal of time with the teacher, who now also has professed faith in Christ.

All the contacts at the Sewing School have not been so happy, however. Some months before, when Stephen Metcalf had been away on holiday, two other missionaries went over there to take the Sunday evening service, and had to stay overnight since the train did its last trip in the early evening. As these two went up to bed, one of them saw someone walk across to the sewing rooms in the darkness, but they assumed it was the caretaker and thought no more about it. In the morning, however, the body of one of the students was found in a bedding cupboard, with a note apologizing for inconveniencing the school by using the premises to commit suicide.

She had decided to take an overdose of sleeping pills as she had embarrassed her parents by going heavily into debt, buying clothes and other luxuries. She was a girl who had attended some of the Bible classes; but evidently had not seen in the messages anything to meet her own need.

Not far away, and near the foot of beautiful Mount Iwaki, "the Fuji of northern Honshu", in the midst of the rich apple-growing district, is the comparatively wealthy little town of Itayanagi. It is close enough to Hirosaki for the people to receive a city education if they desire it, and is inclined to be a little more sophisticated than Goshogawara or Kanagi.

It was to this place I went from Kanagi, arriving just after dark. Eileen Singleton was able to point out from the train the rather barn-like structure which was my destination, and continued on her journey back to Aomori. This was the only house available to rent at the time C.I.M. workers were ready to move there, being bigger than the average Japanese family would think of having, with three rooms and a kitchen downstairs and two rooms upstairs. Also it was very noisy, being right beside the railway tracks. They learned later it was right next to the red light district of that little town, so not very desirable on that account.

I found Margaret Maass alone there for the final night of her fellow-worker's holiday absence, so she was quite glad to have some company. Since then they have found a much more desirable house at only about half the rent, which was an answer to prayer for both the missionaries and Japanese Christians, who had been sharing the prayer burden. On the very last day before they would have had to renew their year's rent for the old house, the two girls were out walking near the outskirts of the town and saw a pleasant looking little house on the edge of an apple orchard. Dorothy Cornelius remarked that it was exactly the kind of house for them. That evening one of the Christians, a Miss Yasuda, came hurrying round to say she had found another house for them—which turned out to be the very one they had noticed earlier in the day! It was almost new, the owner having built it for himself about a year before.

Now he was in need of ready cash and had planned on selling it, but was willing to rent if he could have the year's rent paid in advance.

Two of the students from the Tokyo Theological Seminary went up to Aomori two summers ago and Stephen Metcalf took them to this little town for a small evangelistic campaign in the town hall for three nights. About twenty or thirty people attended these meetings, and afterwards Stephen Metcalf continued to go there for a weekly evening meeting to which six people came with fair regularity.

When two of our women workers went there to live, this mid-week service continued as the main evangelistic effort, sometimes as many as twenty-five attending. Very few adults were free to come on Sunday mornings, but a number of girls who attended a mission middle school in Hirosaki were given points there for attending a Sunday School or church service on Sunday. They found it much easier to go to a service right in their own community instead of taking the bus journey into the city, so a class was started mainly for them on Sunday mornings. This work has been rewarding and several of these girls have now been baptized, and have volunteered to teach in the Sunday School which has recently been organized with five or six classes.

Dorothy Cornelius, who had had experience of work in Hokkaido, told me that the Aomori people seemed much more reserved and suspicious, and rarely came on their own to enquire about Christianity. At Itayanagi they were therefore especially fortunate in making a friend of the Miss Yasuda who found the new house for them. They were out on the main street handing out tracts soon after they moved into the town, and she actually crossed the street to speak to them. They felt very encouraged by this unexpected friendliness, but it was some weeks before she actually came to visit them. Once she began coming to the meetings, however, she never stopped, and furthermore usually brought some friends or relatives with her. She is a very rare person in Japan, a middle-aged spinster, but sick members of her family had been her care when she was younger and so she had never been able to marry. Now she has

much time on her hands, and knows everyone in the neighbourhood. For some time she proved a little bit of a problem as well
as a help, for she wished to take an active part in everything in
the church, and yet was not a Christian. However, when Mr.
Koyama, the contact man for the T.E.A.M. tent teams, to
whom we have referred before, came to make the preliminary
arrangements for a team to come to Itayanagi, he preached a
fine Gospel sermon at the mid-week meeting and afterwards
asked those who wanted to become Christians to put up their
hands. Several did so and among them were Miss Yasuda, and
also the missionaries' daily helper who had been hesitating a
long time about taking this step.

When the tent campaign finally took place, soon after my
visit, over fifty decision cards were signed. But the missionaries
had to be away immediately afterwards, and when they
returned most of the people were very busy harvesting and
very few have come to any of the regular meetings. However,
the campaign did much for the Christians in strengthening
their faith and giving them opportunities to witness. One at
least who came to know Christ at that time made the campaign
definitely worthwhile. He is a boy in his last year in middle
school, rather older than usual and quite mature. As soon as he
believed he was ready at once to witness on the street. After
three months he was baptized and possessed a very well-read
Bible. One day he was reading in 2 Corinthians and was rather
puzzled over the verse "He died for all, that they which live
should not henceforth live unto themselves, but unto Him".
"What actually does it mean to 'live unto Him'?" he asked the
missionary. His father has an electrical appliance business and
it had always been assumed that he would be going into the
business. So the missionary suggested it meant that if you were
an electrician you did your work honestly and to the best of
your ability seeking to please God; if you were a farmer you did
the same. But the boy was not satisfied. "I don't think you quite
understand my question," he said, and went on to explain how
his father wanted him to be an electrician and how his school
principal was advising him to go on to a technical school and
study more about electricity—then he would get a bride easily,

could enter his father's business, and be comfortable for life.

"But what does a Christian want with a comfortable life?" he asked. "Is that really living unto Him?" Then he said he felt now that he should go to high school—perhaps the mission school in Hirosaki, and take a general course instead. But he was meeting with much opposition from his father, elder brother and teacher. The missionaries wondered if he were feeling a call to full-time Christian work and began to pray very much about his future. He is now a good Sunday School teacher and is taking more and more a leading part in the little group of Christians among whom there are no strong men as yet. This of course has its dangers for one so young in years and the faith as he is. Of the few men who do associate with them at present one is a shoemaker who professes to be a Christian of long standing, but does not give much support to the work. Another is a very bashful young apple farmer who has little to say, but who has finally obtained a grudging consent from his family to receive baptism—quite a step for the eldest son of a farming family to take. They usually do not mind so much what the younger sons do, but the eldest is generally responsible for the main duties of ancestor worship.

One girl, a conductress whom Stephen Metcalf first met in a bus when he was on the survey trip to Aomori and to whom he gave a tract, really seemed to believe. She came regularly to meetings but, when she wanted to be baptized, her family was very opposed and even made her leave her job with the bus company so that she would not be able to attend meetings. Recently I have heard a very encouraging account of another bus conductress from Aomori city who graduated from high school last spring and began service in one of the sightseeing bus companies operating out of Aomori city to one of the most famous scenic areas in Japan. Regulations require these guide-conductresses to wear lipstick but when she objected they finally decided she looked attractive enough anyway and waived the regulation in her case. Some of the parties she conducted this summer were schools, and to help pass the long hours happily she taught the children such songs as *Jesus loves me* and *What a Friend we have in Jesus*—in spite of frowns from some of the accompanying teachers! The bus company specially gave her these assignments as she had had experience in Sunday School teaching and so was used to handling children.

There is another girl in Itayanagi in whom the Lord has produced a decided change in character. She is a primary school teacher who was very troubled at heart because she lost her temper frequently in front of the children. When the missionaries went to live there she began to feel she might find the answer to her problem in Christianity. So one evening she went to their house, having already counted the cost, and made up her mind to become a Christian. She has not looked back since that day, but gone steadily on. Deeply aware of her need, she has found in Christ the One who is able to bring victory into defeated lives.

The most encouraging recent news is that a middle-aged coal and coke merchant who professed belief some months ago has now been baptized and has decided to devote his Sundays to the Lord. He has made his three-wheel truck available for village evangelism on Sunday afternoons, so for the last month the missionaries and Christians have been able to preach the Gospel in a number of surrounding villages. These are the hardest of any places to reap a spiritual harvest, and history has usually revealed that after decades of Christian work in these places not more than a handful are ever won for Christ, or if they are won, they cannot remain in the villages. I learned just recently from Charles W. Inglehart's interesting book *Cross and Crisis in Japan* that in the early days of Christianity a number of rural churches began. "They often centred in a man or family of means and responsibility—who could do as he wished, even to accepting the Christian faith. He tended to look upon himself as a benefactor, and if the church members were also his tenants, the church ran the danger of being a kind of adjunct to the agricultural situation.—As the generations followed these rural family churches have almost disappeared. Second or third generation sons, tiring of the constant tension created by holding a different faith, have cooled in zeal, or have moved away. Today genuinely rooted churches made up of the non-movable classes in the villages are very few."[1] In a village not far from Itayanagi a formerly wealthy farmer, who has been unable to work much on account of a stroke, accepted Christ not long ago, and has just been baptized. Now regular meetings are being held in his home. Let us pray that these may not go the way of so many other rural groups in Japan in earlier years.

[1] *Cross and Crisis in Japan*, Charles W. Inglehart.

Chapter XXIII

THIRST FOR KNOWLEDGE

ONE of the most marked characteristics of the Japanese is their thirst for knowledge. Japanese students are "emotional, idealistic and fanatic in their pursuit of new classroom theories",[1] although for those who do not enter a definitely scholastic career this characteristic seems to be lost soon after they begin to undertake the support and responsibility of a family. For those who are still of student status, however, there seems no limit to the effort they will put forth to acquire a little more learning.

Some of this appears to us a bit misdirected at times, and of no real value. For example it is common with many middle and high school students to learn endless lists of words from an English dictionary, and yet not be able to understand very simple English sentences! I have heard that any Japanese middle school boy can tell you the longest word in the English dictionary, yet it is one which few English-speaking people have heard of, let alone used. Again, at the Seminary where we have taught, the students must of course learn Hebrew and Greek, as well as have a good knowledge of English since almost all their text books are in English. But in addition, courses have been offered in Latin, and also French and German Bible at various times. Since most of them come from non-Christian homes, and their knowledge of the Bible is usually very limited on entering the Seminary, we wonder if it would not be more profitable to spend greater time on the contents of the Bible and its implications in daily life.

My former sociology professor from the University of London was invited to Japan for a series of lectures a year or two ago, and since there was quite a large number of pre-war Japanese graduates from there living in the Tokyo area they invited me

[1] *Five Gentlemen of Japan.*

to an alumni tea to meet him. He told me he had discovered that the works of Hobhouse the economist, and of the poet T. S. Eliot, seemed to be better known in Japan than they were in Britain! I have since read that a publisher's opinion of the comparatively successful sale of Eliot's work in England is to some extent due to his "snob" value, and realized at once that that is probably why he is so popular in Japan. For the same reason Aldous Huxley is also well known, and most high school students have to study some of his writings because teachers like to be known as those who are able to lecture on difficult and abstruse works.

Since many Europeans are guilty of the same intellectual snobbery we cannot point the finger at the Japanese, but we must realize it is a definite hindrance to the simple preaching of the Gospel, there and here. Fortunately the Japanese thirst for knowledge includes a desire to learn foreign languages and to know of the conditions in other countries, so it does provide a good opportunity to present the Gospel by means of English and German Bible classes, and of gaining an entrance for the missionary into some of the schools and colleges.

Sometimes the attraction seems to have been more on the entertainment level. From the earliest days missionaries have sought to use this bait of English Bible classes. Kanzo Uchimura was offered the following enticements by a schoolmate who invited him to "go to a certain place in the foreigners' quarter where we can hear pretty women sing, and a tall big man with a long beard shout and howl upon an elevated place, flinging his arms and twisting his body in all fantastic manners, to all which admission is entirely free". Now the novelty has largely worn off, but the desire for English remains strong.

As we have seen, most C.I.M. workers are in small fishing or country towns in the north and though some hold English Bible classes for middle and high school students the standard of English there is low and they sometimes find it better to have some simple English conversation followed by Japanese Bible study. In Tokyo and the larger cities, however, there have been classes for older people as well. Over twenty people have been converted through these, quite apart from the group at

Sapporo which was begun entirely through interpreted English classes, and which up to the present has been by far the most fruitful of any C.I.M. work.

Margrit Bähler, a Swiss C.I.M. missionary, who worked in co-operation with a Presbyterian church in one of the larger cities of Hokkaido, was asked to hold a German Bible class even in that remote area. At first only three Japanese doctors attended, all brothers, and one of them a Christian. Their purpose was to improve their German since Japanese medicine is largely based on German text books.

In his testimony this Christian doctor relates that he attended Sunday School for three years because the pastor's son was a friend of his in primary school. His next contact with Christianity was not until some years after his marriage. He was so busy with the special ceremonies for the thirteenth anniversary of his father's death that he did not realize his five-year-old daughter had suddenly become critically ill. In her delirium she began to sing songs she had learned in Sunday School, and weeping by the bedside the mother, who had been a student in a mission school, said, "I'm going to the church." She returned with a pastor and his wife, and after they had prayed for the child, the doctor's wife asked if he would agree to their daughter being baptized. He did, and so both mother and child were baptized just before the latter's death. Very few were present at the funeral since their relatives disliked the Christian Church, but when the doctor's thought turned towards heaven the unbearable grief of separation was taken away, and before the end of the year he too was baptized.

During the war this man was imprisoned for believing that Christ was greater than the Emperor, and would one day return to earth to rule. At one time he used to wrap his medicines in paper stamped with Gospel texts, but now he admits he is not as zealous as he used to be. He is an outstanding personality, a gifted poet, as well as being interested in fencing and butterfly collecting, and like many at home finds it hard to put himself completely at the Lord's disposal.

The other two brothers, each with a different surname since they were both adopted into their wives' families, wanted

German only, and were wary of Christian teaching, knowing what it had cost their brother. One especially is influenced by his wife whose aim is social success. The other gradually believed what he heard was the truth, and also had a wonderful answer to prayer. One day at the class they learned the verse "Call upon me in the day of trouble; I will deliver you and you shall glorify me". Soon after the doctor found himself in a day of trouble for he received a demand note for £400 ($1,000) income tax, and he did not even possess that much money. He called upon the Lord, and the next day the tax inspector came, examined his books, and said the amount was too much. The new amount was only one quarter of the former. The doctor glorified the Lord that day, saying it was a miracle and nothing like that had ever happened in Japan before. His brother wanted him to be baptized at once, but he said he wanted to read the Bible for a year in order to prepare himself. He still comes to the Bible class and frequently reads his English, German and Japanese Bibles, but does not go to church, or show any evidence of a changed life.

After a time another man joined the German class—very different from the other three. One dark evening there had been a knock at the missionaries' door and they saw a dis-hevelled looking farmer of about thirty, smoking a cigarette and smelling of *sake*, who announced, "I am not a Christian, but I want to speak German." Somewhat alarmed by his appearance and unusual request, the ladies were afraid to invite him further in than the entrance hall, but Margrit Bähler offered him some German Christian magazines and invited him to attend the German Bible class.

Later they learned he came from a high-class family which had lost all its property in the great earthquake which des-troyed Tokyo and 150,000 people in 1923. The father had tried various questionable ways of getting rich quick without success; and, after a number of years, the mother—an unusual woman of strong character—had moved up to Hokkaido with the three sons to start farming. This boy, the eldest, much preferred study to farming, but had dutifully followed his mother. When he met the missionaries he had not seen his father for eight years; and, though he is thirty, he cannot marry until he has helped his younger brothers through school.

He had studied German in school in Tokyo, and one day when visiting the city he passed the church and saw the word "kindergarten" on the notice board. He recognized it as a German word, and found the pastor and asked if there were anyone who spoke German in the church. So the pastor sent him to Margrit Bähler.

He lived in a village forty minutes by bicycle from the city, but he came regularly to the German Bible class, and at his third visit, when the message was on the Prodigal Son, he accepted Christ. He bought a New Testament and soon read it through. He would stay till eleven o'clock some Monday nights asking questions about the Bible. He remarked that a Christian reading the Bible was like a cow—it eats and eats and then has to stop and digest! He certainly shows signs of having digested some of its teaching, for each night he came to the Bible class he would bring a basket of vegetables. He was told there was no need to do this, but he replied the Bible taught us to give a tenth, but unfortunately a tenth of his farm produce was too heavy for his bicycle! He also said it kept going through his mind that he should stop smoking, but he felt this would be very difficult. Margrit Bähler told him God could enable him to do this, and he at once prayed, in German, for God to help him. When he had finished he announced that when the ladies returned from the missionary conference, to which they were going soon, he would have stopped smoking. True to his word, they found he had done so, and had also started giving out tracts. He hopes that when his younger brother can carry on the farm he may be able to go to Bible school; but he has not yet had the courage to tell his mother about this. She, though baptized in a Presbyterian church, is now a zealous follower of Tenrikyo since she was once very sick and the group tried to help her.

Now unfortunately the pastor has left that church, and it was decided to withdraw our missionaries as well, but we are praying that God will continue the good work begun in this young man. Margrit Bähler feels that the German Bible class was a very clear illustration of the four types of ground of the Parable of the Sower, the "good" ground being humanly speaking the most unpromising at first appearance.

Since this church had a pastor, our three women's contribution (while always continuing language study of course) was mainly the running of Bible classes, in addition to house-to-house and hospital visitation giving out tracts. As the pastor was kept busy running the church kindergarten he was glad of this help. Several people were converted through the English Bible class, one of the most influential perhaps being a high school teacher, head of the English department in his school. He had always attended regularly and listened intently until the visit of Dr. Donald Grey Barnhouse to Japan in the summer of 1956. Dr. Barnhouse preached in their church by interpretation, and spoke of three types of people: the bad, the average and the very good, who nevertheless all fell short of the perfection of God. The following week when this teacher came to the class he looked so troubled that as Desley Barber saw him out at the door she felt compelled to say that if he had any problems he would care to discuss, to feel free to come and see them at any time. He always had to leave the class early to catch the last train to his home, but on hearing this he at once arranged a day and time to come and see them.

When he arrived he told them that he felt he was one of the bad people Dr. Barnhouse had talked about, and he wanted to be right with God. They answered all his questions from the Bible, and he finally accepted Christ that afternoon. He came to the Bible class the following day with a really peaceful look on his face. His attitude quite changed the atmosphere of the class, for previously he often used to tell questionable jokes before it began. Recently he gave his testimony and mentioning Matthew 4: 4 said: "This far I have lived on bread alone, but now I believe in God, and I live by every word that proceeds from His mouth." He is already working on the second part of a Bible Correspondence Course with much zeal and joy.

One more example must suffice to show what a valuable place English can have in areas where the educational standards are high. Soon after the commencement of the English Bible class there, a girl began to attend, and later urged her elder sister to go to church with her. The latter liked the music but thought the sermons were terrible. However, soon after that an Indian "Youth for Christ" visitor spoke in English at the church and she was converted, and can now give a testimony full of power. She is not at all strong, and is awaiting an operation which, the doctors say, she has not yet strength to undergo. She read a book about a girl who was sick and could not do much for Christ except write letters, so she decided she too could do this. In addition she keeps a list of all the people and needs the church asks prayer for. Recently she asked for a map of the hospital and has begun to help in the visitation there.

All these people mentioned so far in this chapter have been converted during the last two years (as have almost all those resulting from our mission work in Japan) so they have not yet stood the test of time—an important factor in the experience of a Japanese Christian. However, I would like to give two more examples of Japanese who are now valuable Christian workers, and who were converted through attending English Bible classes.

The first is a young woman who lived in part of the same house as we were in for a year, and whose sweet consistent Christian character we heard about from many others and witnessed ourselves. She was converted seven years ago through attending an English Bible class held in Tokyo by Ray Oram of the Christian Literature Crusade. For the last five years she has been a staff worker for the High School Evangelism Fellowship, the work in Japan of the American organization "Hi-B.A." She is one of the few Japanese we have met who is really alert to do personal work. When we had been in the house only a month she led to the Lord the girl who was helping us with the housework.

This young worker who knows her own nation so well, warned us that we should continually stress the importance of regular attendance at meetings, for the Japanese seem to need this fellowship with others to keep them strong. She has found that if they just read their Bibles at home, most gradually give up Christianity. The last time I saw her was at the showing of the film *Martin Luther*, at one of the U.S. Army chapels. She is planning to write the Japanese script for the film. This may well be the means of inspiring many Japanese to greater courage to stand alone for their convictions, as did Martin Luther.

The second is a Mr. Kurumada who spoke at a meeting for missionaries. For our encouragement, he told us that fifty-three years ago he had been converted through an English Bible class led by Mr. Ernest Kilbourne of the Oriental Missionary Society. Just before the war the Japan Holiness Church, the firstfruit of that society's work, went through a time of great difficulty when it split over the extreme views of its leader, Bishop Nakada, on the Second Coming of Christ. After the war this original church split into six groups. One of these, however, reorganized the former church which, though self-governing, had maintained a close link with the missionaries of the O.M.S. They had churches for Japanese in Korea, Manchuria, Formosa, Brazil and the South Sea Islands. Mr. Kurumada was elected the general superintendent of this reorganized church, and later when the Bible School was reopened, also became its principal. This has now the largest enrolment of any Bible School in Japan.

In the meeting he spoke of his recent visit, as general superintendent, to the Japanese Holiness Churches in Brazil. The report of the churches there was generally encouraging, for the Japanese, he kept emphasizing, had gone "with the idea of being buried in Brazil", and therefore presumably are more free in their ways of thought. The most moving thing he told us was the account of his brother-in-law's conversion. This man had been a graduate of Sapporo University forty years before, then had left for Brazil and had become one of its leading men. Mr. Kurumada had been praying for his conversion for over thirty years and now at last had had the joy of leading him to the Lord. What a joy it is to know of at least one Japanese won to Christ through an English Bible class and still bearing fruit in old age in very important administrative work.

This chapter on the use of English in reaching Japanese for

Christ would not be complete without reference to the work done by personnel of the American Armed Forces. While unfortunately the majority stationed in Japan do not live lives which commend their so-called Christian country to the Japanese, there are among them some who are real Christians and desire to serve our Lord. A good number of the new missionaries served in the occupation forces after the war, and have now returned in a higher service. Among the present military forces we have had contact with many fine men through the Officers' Christian Union. Some have been converted while in Japan and it has been wonderful to watch their development and growing concern for the Japanese around them. Some of the wives have bought Japanese Bibles for their maids and try to read with them each day, answering questions by means of their own English Bibles. Billy Graham's *Peace with God* has been used in the same way.

Some have held weekly Bible classes either in English or by interpretation. We know a teacher in an army school who had a Bible class of seven who all finally became Christians. There was an Air Force officer too, who had three accept Christ in one day at his class taught through an interpreter.

His interpreter was herself the fruit of an Air Force chaplain's witness, and is one of the most remarkable Japanese Christians I have met, mainly because she is not typically Japanese. She was brought up in the comparative freedom of China until she was sixteen. She told us that her parents completely changed when they had to return to Japan's close-knit society. She felt out of place and hated the other Japanese students at school, who obviously despised her. She found some relief in concentrating on English (strangely enough some other students originally from Manchuria, at the Tokyo Women's Christian College where I taught for a short time, said the same thing), and eventually she got a very good job as an interpreter. It was in the course of this work that she met the chaplain and was converted. Then God had to change her dislike of her fellow Japanese, and she began to feel her responsibility to win them to Christ. She thought of going to Bible School, but when she mentioned this to her father he threw a rice bowl at her head in anger, and threatened to turn her out of the house if she did. She therefore gave up the idea; but a little later, at an Officers' Christian Union conference, after much inner conflict she stood up to yield her life to God. In the train going back to Tokyo she was full of joy, giving out tracts, singing hymns softly and even reading a passage from her Bible to the staid-looking business man beside her in the second-class coach.

She was turned out of her home then, and the father forbade the mother to go and see her in the room she rented. Her witnessing grew more powerful and her spiritual maturity was very marked. Her heart was truly set to do God's will in all things. My husband had the joy of baptizing her together with a few officers and wives who had been converted in Japan. She later joined the church of which one of our Seminary graduates is pastor, so we learned from him of her zeal and outspokenness in the church. She told us that one evening she was trying to pray for a girl who was a student in Bible School and who attended one of her Bible classes, but found she somehow could not pray, so she went to sleep. During the night, however, the Lord awoke her and reminded her of part of a message of Billy Graham's which she had heard nearly a year before. In it he had said that God is a Judge as well as a Saviour. Why was God reminding her of this? She searched her heart and then realized she had been jealous of this other girl. This involved her in a very painful and embarrassing confession to the whole Bible class, but she knew she had to do God's will.

Eventually the chaplain who had led her to Christ tried to persuade her to go to the United States for Bible training; but she did not feel sure it was God's will she should go, when the need is so great in Japan. She would have to provide her own passage money, and as she had enough on hand to pay for this she decided to give it all away to Christian work, so that if God really wanted her to go, He Himself would provide it. The money came, and she is now in California working among the Nisei (overseas Japanese) there while she studies in a Bible School.

On 17th February, 1957 the New Life Crusade was formed at Tokyo Chapel Centre. It is an organization composed of

Christian servicemen, a few missionaries, and Japanese pastors and interpreters whose purpose is to carry on evangelistic meetings at the week-ends. Dr. Fred Jarvis has been largely responsible for this and provides much of the equipment, while the servicemen provide cars for transportation, give messages and testimonies, and give out tracts.

One criticism of this movement is that it is taking Japanese evangelists sometimes from areas where they were already working. There are no "spare" Japanese Christian workers, and all have more work than they can properly care for. This is unfortunate, but at the same time it may be a much needed impetus to get the Japanese themselves out in aggressive and co-operative evangelistic work, for there is great comfort in numbers. Both they and the people realize that these military men are not professional Christian workers, and their testimony therefore usually carries considerable weight. Further reports of these teams speak of large audiences listening and many professing conversion. Perhaps the most encouraging result of all was that one pastor wrote saying that "the next Sunday they had three times as many children out to Sunday School, and many more adults had attended the services". If these teams can visit areas where there is the possibility of follow-up work, permanent good will result. We can only thank God for another provision of the "all means" by which the Gospel may be preached and those in darkness and bondage enabled to see the light of freedom in Christ.

Chapter XXIV

BRUISED REEDS

RUTH BENEDICT in *The Chrysanthemum and the Sword* tells us how puzzled the Japanese press and public were during the war to hear that an American admiral had been decorated for saving two damaged ships and their crews. The Japanese, like most non-Christian peoples, have little concern for "damaged goods", and very inadequate provision was made for their sick and wounded during the war. To be taken as a prisoner was considered a great disgrace, even if it occurred while a man was wounded and unconscious, and scorn rather than compassion was the general reaction. Even today the wounded war veterans appear to receive little sympathy from the general public. Although Buddhists have done a certain amount of social and medical work in Japan the motive behind it seems to have been more to gain personal merit than to bring comfort and relief to the sufferer.

In most mission fields medical work has been one of the most effective methods of breaking down fear or dislike of the strange foreigner, as well as being a wonderful opportunity to show Christian compassion and to provide an audience to whom the Gospel can be preached. In Japan, however, there has been little scope for this service by foreigners. The government decided to adopt modern Western medicine in place of the Chinese system at the time of the Meiji Restoration, and every small town now has medical service of some kind. By 1935 there were 4,625 hospitals with 158,059 beds. Japanese doctors on the whole naturally do not wish for competition from foreigners, especially missionaries who might charge less, and so divert patients from them for that reason.

There are two C.I.M. women doctors in Japan and they were among the last group of foreigners who were able to write in English the examination required to practise medicine. This same examination must now be written in Japanese, which makes it almost impossible for any new foreign doctors to work in Japan. One of the doctors has her time fully occupied treating many of the missionaries. The other, until her marriage, while giving most of her time to evangelistic work, did for a time help to operate a clinic, begun by a doctor of another society, in one of the northern cities of Japan. The red tape involved in operating this simple clinic seemed surprisingly complex, even for the orient, and the patients who came were relatively few. Those who did come were usually people who had been unsuccessful in their search for healing in other places. It is only natural that Japanese patients would prefer to see a doctor of their own nationality, just as would most of us. Of those who did come, one or two received Christ as Saviour.

What is the standard of Japanese medicine today? It was rather disturbing recently to read that at the time of Pearl Harbour there were 77,512 licensed physicians, only 26,842 of whom were university graduates, however. The remainder had only attended junior colleges. A law was passed in 1948 requiring all doctors to receive six years' training at university level, plus one year's residence in hospital, but as the number of doctors had gone up to 92,422 by the end of 1954, it seems likely that the less trained ones continue to be regarded as doctors. This may explain why some missionaries occasionally have rather unfortunate experiences with local doctors, while others obtain very skilled and satisfactory treatment.

In general it may be said that the Japanese are highly skilled at surgery and anything involving the use of the hands, and are distinguishing themselves at various branches of research, but as a rule are inclined to be weak at diagnosis. Sometimes a patient's condition is diagnosed as some very serious complaint, perhaps because if he recovers the doctor's reputation may soar, and if he does not recover, that is only what was expected! The psychological effect of such a diagnosis on the patient and relatives does not seem to be considered. For instance one missionary we know was told he had either cancer or tuberculosis of the liver, and that he should return home at once. Fortunately, he was able to get another check at a military hospital in Tokyo, and was told there was no sign of either disease. One of our missionaries too, was told he had a cataract and another serious eye condition, neither of which was present when he was seen by another doctor soon afterwards.

Although shortage of equipment, such as microscopes, during training, may partly account for weakness in diagnosis, one of the main reasons behind much of it is possibly that there is no ethical teaching along with medical instruction in the colleges. Here the words of a Japanese doctor can speak with more authority than mine. In Tokyo there is a large hospital, St. Luke's, started by an American Episcopal missionary doctor. This was requisitioned by the Army during the occupation, and was recently handed back in an impressive ceremony to the Japanese civilian staff who had taken it over when all foreigners had to leave in 1941. A whole supplement was devoted to this by one of the Japanese newspapers, and it was very interesting to learn from it something of the general medical situation in Japan today.

Dr. Hirotoshi Hashimoto, the director of the hospital, in outlining the plans for its future, said that he hoped to continue the spirit of service to humanity with which it had been founded and that they did not intend to "become a mere market for medical treatment as is the case of so many of its counterparts in this country". He added, "Japanese hospitals are all run on commercial lines . . . but our aim will be to serve mankind, not to sell medical treatment."

Most patients in Japan have to take their own bedding into hospital, and also must have relatives near at hand to provide food and attention, but St. Luke's Hospital does not require this. Also as we were taken on an inspection tour of the wards at the reopening we were shown with great pride the curtains which could be drawn round each bed in the public wards, a privacy unknown in most Japanese hospitals.

Another point in which St. Luke's has pioneered is the training of nurses. At first, nurses were regarded more as maids to the doctors or charwomen hired by the patients, and it was very difficult getting any student nurses. Finally, some missionary teachers in girls' schools managed to persuade a few of their students to enter and as the newspaper article puts it "through endless teaching in the Christian spirit and faith in Christ and human beings, the pioneers in this field built their foundations on solid rock, bringing about a revolution in the field of nursing". This revolution, however, has still only touched a small section of the population, possibly mainly through religious channels. Of the 600 or so graduating high school students I have taught, not one has even considered nursing as a possible career.

Although there has been little scope for missionary medical work, evangelistic work among the sick has proved a most encouraging and fruitful field. Most Japanese doctors run their own little private hospital, and many of these have welcomed Christian visitation work, and many government institutions allow services also.[1] Some of the Japanese doctors too, have become Christians, and there are now over 400 members of the National Christian Medical Association.

In an over-populated country there are always many who are eager to seize the place of those who are incapacitated, and human life is cheap. Neither Buddhism nor Shintoism, nor for that matter, modern materialism, have any message of comfort for the sick or deformed. Buddhist philosophy would suggest that these things are the result of their actions in a former life, while in Shinto they prevent one taking one's proper place, and completely fulfilling all the ordinary obligations to Emperor, community and family, and thus such a person has no real place in the "web society".

When I asked Pastor Noguchi what made him and his wife decide to become Christians he answered, "Because we had no hope. I was sick", and he pointed to his chest, "and my wife is lame as a result of a fall when she was a girl. We had no hope," he repeated.

It is only Christ who gives the assurance that the smoking flax will not be quenched, nor the bruised reed broken. No

[1] There are 240,000 beds reserved for T.B. patients who make a fruitful field for Christian witness—there are over 5 million T.B. patients at present in Japan.

one is worthless who yields their life to Him, and all are welcome who wish to come. So in Japan many come to Him because He is the first who has ever offered them a welcome. In almost every little Christian group I have visited there have been those who were deformed or physically handicapped in some way. Because they are already so to speak "rejects", and have no secure place in the "web society", they perhaps do not feel the stigma of becoming Christians quite so much. Or it may be that the kindlier among their relatives are glad to find there is something which interests and helps them, and so do not offer as much opposition to their becoming Christians as they would to a physically fit member of the family. At any rate, whatever the reason, these handicapped people are often the most zealous and whole-hearted Christians in the churches.

In one of the C.I.M. groups which I visited there was a young woman, born with only one arm and with some disfigurement on her face and body. Others in her family had congenital troubles of some sort also, the result of the father's former dissipated life, according to local gossip. This girl was the first person to believe and be baptized after our missionaries went there. Now after eighteen months of Christian life we hear how very "bright natured" she is, and that she is beginning to lead the Sunday School. What courage must be required for one so abnormal to stand in front of a group of children, who can be so cruel and thoughtless. One day she was tempted to watch a baseball game instead of going to Sunday School, but she prayed and then went to class, "and ever since has been even happier than her usual happy self. She got very excited the other day at the new thought that faith can grow."

Another case comes to mind of a young man who through wrong treatment being given by the family doctor when he was fourteen years old, became unable to stand or walk, and can only crawl along. His father died when he was a child, and his mother when he was twenty-four. In addition to a very small government pension which just paid for his rice he earned a little by baking sweet-bean cakes for children.

One day he heard that some members of the Japan Evan-gelistic Band were to conduct a meeting in his village. He determined to get there somehow, and asked some children to help him. The method he chose was to have them spread two thin straw mats on the road. When he had crawled on to the front mat, they took up the one behind and spread it in front and so on all the way to the meeting hall. As soon as he heard the Gospel he believed and began to tell others. He was eventually baptized, and the Lord prospered his little business so that he hoped to be able to buy a wheel chair. However, someone told the owner of the chair that the young man was so poor he would never be able to finish paying for it, so he refused to sell. God overruled in this, however, and the cripple was finally able to get a cheaper and better chair through the help of a missionary, and by its aid was able to witness further afield for Christ.

From another missionary of the Japan Evangelistic Band I learned of a midget girl who led a very hard life. Though her body was normal size her legs and arms were extremely short and undeveloped and her head therefore only reached other people's hips. Yet her mother, a geisha, insisted on her taking an office job which was offered her in a place some distance by electric train from her home, in order to supplement the family income. So great was the danger of her being crushed or suffocated in the dense crowds daily travelling on the train, that she was forced to stand by the doors, and step out at each station to allow others to get out, thereby making herself especially conspicuous. She was often greeted with mockery or even stones by thoughtless children. So wretched was her existence that she often contemplated suicide, but fortunately came in contact with the Gospel and believed. Since she had a good knowledge of English the missionaries were able to help her by asking her to translate an English devotional book. It is hoped that eventually she may be able to do this type of work full-time, thus avoiding much public appearance. She herself was so comforted by the message of the Gospel that she even suggested she might work as an interpreter for some new missionary, which of course would mean standing up in front of an audience.

At a church in Yokohama where one of the Tokyo Theological

Seminary graduates is now pastor, I myself have seen another dwarf radiant with joy in the Lord, won through the ministry of the Woman's Union Missionary Society in Yokohama. She is well proportioned, so is not so conspicuous as the other girl. She is only thirty-nine inches high and at a casual glance looks like a small child but is actually twenty-four years old. She is a college graduate and does private tutoring in English in her home, and also teaches English in a night school. She had many doubts at first when she began to study the Bible, but she finally prayed that if there were a true God He would enable her to know Him and believe. Soon she was believing and at once tried to introduce Christ to some of her students.

In that same church is a young man who is a very bad spastic. When he first attended he could not utter a coherent "good morning" and was constantly falling over. Since he has become a Christian there has been a noticeable improvement in his speech and movements. He is a most faithful attender at all the meetings, his face radiant with joy. One of the first things he did after accepting Christ was to buy a pulpit microphone and ear receiver for a deaf woman who was coming to that church, and she believed in Christ soon afterwards.

A number of blind people also attend this church. According to the latest Bible Society report there are 140,000 registered blind people in Japan, and 3,000 of these are Christians. Most of the leaders of the Blind Associations are Christians and are enthusiastic in spreading the Gospel and introducing the Braille Bible to their members.

While travelling recently with a Lutheran missionary, Miss Anna Gulick, I was interested to see her writing a letter in Braille. She told me a moving story of her visits to a blind school in her district. The students there all had some Christian instruction; but the brighter ones were taught by the local Japanese pastor, while Miss Gulick was left with the intellectual dregs. One of her girls especially had a terribly low place in class. She had spent two or three years in every grade in the school, and was now almost an adult, but was not wanted at home and seemed incapable of learning any method of earning her living. It seemed impossible to get this group to understand anything she tried to teach them, so Miss Gulick finally decided she would just get them to memorize Scripture verses. Miraculously something of this seemed to penetrate that older girl's mind and heart, and she finally declared herself a Christian. The last time she went home during the school holiday she had even gathered together some of the children of her neighbourhood into a Sunday School and tried to teach them what she knew.

In recent years a fruitful work amongst the deaf[1] has also been carried on in Japan by an elderly American woman, and her daughter who for many years had been deaf herself. Humanly speaking it sounds an impossible task to come out and begin such a work with no knowledge of Japanese. They began with the help of a man who was not deaf himself but who taught in a Deaf School and knew both the sign language and English. Latterly their only teacher was a deaf boy who knew no English. He sat with a Japanese-English dictionary in front of him while the missionaries had an English-Japanese one.

Knowing the difficulty of ordinary Japanese I questioned this lady particularly about Japanese sign language, and she admitted that they manage to make even that rather indefinite! The Japanese Deaf Association and Schools are trying to do away with the sign language and have only lip-reading. The Japanese speak in their throats, however, and I have often noticed when sitting in buses and trains that for many words the upper lip does not seem to move at all when they are speaking. With lip-reading also the speaker must be properly facing his audience, so cannot effectively address more than about ten people. Sign language therefore seems by far the best means of evangelism, and this missionary told me that from her own experience when deaf she knows that using sign language is a tremendous relief to a deaf person. It helps to release them from the frustrations and tensions which build up so easily within them and make them feel anti-social.

[1] There are 250,000 deaf in Japan, all registered in an Association for the handicapped, so it is comparatively easy to find them in any city.

In Japan, although in some ways they are technically far in advance of many other oriental countries, with registration and special schools for many of the physically handicapped, it nevertheless remains a disgrace to be deaf, especially if a person is born that way. Very few of these have experienced real love in their homes. Parents who have such a dependant at home get a reduction in income tax, so the girls especially are kept at home, and sometimes almost treated like slaves, many not being allowed even to attend meetings. Those who do get jobs are often taken advantage of, and made to work longer hours for less pay than normal workers.

The course of Bible training the ladies are giving is short but very strenuous. Their main purpose is to saturate the students with Scripture until it becomes part of them. They study from nine to twelve o'clock, and two to five o'clock. Then from seven to nine o'clock they are shown a number of coloured slides from a series of 2,000 they now have on the Old Testament, the Gospels and Acts. Each student has to practise telling these stories in sign language.

When students first come into training they are not very friendly, never having been used to having any friends. But by the end they really develop a love for each other. There are now eleven full-time trained workers. One, a former *tatami* mat maker, is willing to be thrown out of his home and have his name removed from his family register, in order to go as a missionary to the deaf in Okinawa. In Osaka there is now an independent deaf church supporting its own pastor.

One of the most outstanding cripples known to many of our workers is a Mr. Threebridges (Mitsuhashi) who was a teacher for a time in the language school at Aomori. When he was three years of age he was stricken with polio and lost the use of both legs and his right arm. He was, therefore, never able to attend school. When later his father died, and his mother not long after that, he was rather grudgingly cared for by his only sister. Life had no happiness for him, until one day a friend introduced him to the Gospel and he gladly believed.

As a result of his love for his new found Saviour he would sit at one of the busiest intersections in the city and distribute tracts with his one good hand. He found another outlet for his desire to witness at the local leprosarium a few miles outside the city. He was much welcomed as a preacher by the crippled inmates there who loved to see his radiant face above a body even more handicapped than most of theirs. At that time he was associated with one of the older churches of Japan; but word was eventually passed to him that only those who were properly ordained should preach for them. This was a bitter blow, but fortunately there was also a small group of Christians in the city who were the fruit of a Brethren missionary's work. So he joined them. He had a great desire to go to Bible School and train for the ministry; but none that he knew of would accept him because of his great physical disability.

He prayed that God, according to His promise to supply all our need, would miraculously provide him with a wife, and in His own wonderful way God did. There was a student nurse among that group of Christians who had been converted about eighteen months and as she prayed with them over Mr. Threebridges' need she felt the Lord would have her take on this work of caring for him. She was an attractive girl, however, and all the friends and relatives on both sides were against the marriage, so much so that no one would give them any wedding presents!

Soon after their marriage, arrangements were made for them both to become language teachers at the small C.I.M. language school which had just been transferred to that city. Mrs. Threebridges rode a bicycle and pulled the small wooden cart on two wheels which the Japanese often use to transport their aged or crippled relatives. These are usually just three-sided unpadded wooden boxes in which the occupant sits on the floor. At their destination his wife would stoop in front of Mr. Threebridges, pull his one good arm over her shoulder and carry him to the chair from which he would teach, or preach if it was a service.

One day a well-dressed young girl knocked at the language school door and with tears on her face asked, "Is this where the Christians live?"

Fortunately Mrs. Threebridges was there at the time and so

was able to find out what the trouble was. The girl had just had a big shock, for her father whom she had always idolized had recently taken to drink. Now she had discovered a letter from him in her mother's drawer saying he was living with another woman. Mrs. Threebridges was able to tell her that this experience was very similar to her own. Her father had also become a slave to drink, their house had been burned down twice, and her heart had been very sad and bitter until she had heard about the Lord. Then she had received Him as her Saviour and He had taken all the bitterness out of her heart and given her peace.

This girl had gone to Sunday School once or twice when she was a child, and that was why she knew enough to think that Christians might be able to help her in her trouble. As Mrs. Threebridges finished speaking to her she said, "Isn't it a good thing I came here today!" Very soon she had the assurance of salvation and when I last heard was bringing some of her friends to the services.

After being a blessing and help to our missionaries in work and witness as well as teaching, the way opened for Mr. and Mrs. Threebridges to attend the Bible School in Karuizawa. There he was able to pay his way partially by working in their printing department. While there the Lord gave them the unexpected joy of a child, though this meant a very difficult time for the little wife, carrying and caring for both of them. However, I met someone not long ago who had lived opposite them in the Bible School grounds for the past year. She told me of their radiant lives, and that as far as she knew everyone to whom Mr. Threebridges witnessed for any length of time about Christ had been converted. The most outstanding case recently was that of a wounded war veteran who had become a Buddhist priest and had already walked three times round the islands of Japan visiting famous shrines to try to find peace of heart. Now he too has entered the Bible School to learn more of this new faith to which Mr. Threebridges introduced him.

So here and there in many little groups throughout Japan we find those who, though still captive to the limitations of their physical disabilities, have given those weak bodies to Christ. They have proved that God is able to use the weak things of the world to show forth His power and glory. Like Paul some even glory in their infirmities because it was these which brought them the knowledge and freedom of Christ.

Chapter XXV

HOPE OF THE FUTURE

IN spite of the great hold of the traditions of the past on the minds of those who were educated before and during the war, there is little doubt that slowly but surely a change is coming in the thinking of the youth of Japan. Whether it will be for the better is not yet certain, for the educational system devoid of religion (and so of the moral teaching of loyalty and obedience) which was instituted by the Occupation, is not an unqualified success. Half understood democracy easily produces an absence of control rather than the liberty which we know based on Christian principles. The absence of such moral teaching in the schools should therefore be a challenge to the Christian Church to concentrate on the winning of youth to Christ in their early years.

The Municipal Educational Institute of Osaka last year held a poll among 1,072 sixteen-year-old high school students on "Whom do you respect the most?" The answers were very interesting, and I doubt if a poll in an American or British group would reveal such impartial judgment. The top ten on the boys' list were as follows: (1) Abraham Lincoln, (2) Dr. H. Noguchi (famous bacteriologist), (3) Thomas Edison, (4) Y. Fukuzawa[1] (pioneer of Japan's Westernization), (5) Sontoku Ninomiya (a great scholar), (6) "My father and mother", (7) Hideyoshi[2] (the "Napoleon of Japan"), (8) Premier Nehru, (9) Dr. H. Yukawa (Nobel prize winner), (10) George Washington.

For their top ten selections the girls had: (1) "My father and mother", (2) Abraham Lincoln, (3) Y. Fukuzawa, (4) Dr. H. Noguchi, (5) Ninomiya, (6) Florence Nightingale, (7) Marie Curie, (8) Helen Keller, (9) "My teacher", (10) Jesus Christ. These I think are a pretty accurate indication of the place and

[1] See Chapter IV, page 52.   [2] See Chapter I, page 16.

strength of Christianity in the mind of Japan. Most significant about the poll, or according to one newspaper editorial the "most shocking result", was that nearly forty per cent returned blank sheets. One just wrote, "We find no one we can worship". Incidentally this illustrates well the failure to distinguish between respect and worship, which are such different things to us; but what a challenge to the church of Christ to fill this void! What a harvest field may be found in the 18 million primary school children of Japan, and the 4 million high school students! In the C.I.M. some workers have not started Sunday School or children's meetings when opening up new areas, afraid it might give the impression that Christianity is "kid stuff". A few felt it should wait until adults had been converted and were willing to act as teachers. However, some did start these from the beginning, while most have them now, and Margaret Maass is working full-time at the Japan Sunday School Union which produces not only graded Sunday School lessons, used widely throughout the country, but also material for Daily Vacation Bible Schools. This last year they also ran a Teachers' Training Course. Two women students from a Bible School took the course before holding a D.V.B.S. in a place where there was no church or regular preacher and seventy decisions for Christ were recorded out of an attendance of 153.

Just recently I have read the inspiring account of how an eight-year-old girl led her father to a knowledge of Christ, in Charles W. Iglehart's book *Cross and Crisis in Japan*. A little church had just been built in the apple-growing district of north Japan, and at the opening, sitting modestly at the back was the contractor. He had visited the missionary the day before, however, and told the following story. "I am just a common builder. Our business is crooked, and my home life has been bad. Always enough money and far too much drink. But recently something happened in our home. My precious Emiko, eight years old, began going to the Christian Sunday School held in Mrs. Yoshioka's home. I asked her what she was learning, and she began to tell me about God's love and about how the Christian people longed to build a place in which to worship, but couldn't scrape together half enough to do it. So I decided I'd see they got the church. I bid within their range, and started construction, thinking I was very virtuous. But as the work went on, I felt more and more un-comfortable. I was building a house of God, but my hands were not clean. I could hardly sleep at night. I asked Emiko about it and she said they had been studying about Jesus who died on a Cross so that people might be released from their sins, and that we must bear the cross too. Now that was strange teaching, but somehow I felt that I knew what she meant. So I went up behind the shrine on the hill and there found God. I gave my heart to Him and lost my load of a bad past. I dressed and went to have my photograph taken. Yesterday, when the last touches were put on the building, I climbed my ladder, placed myself (the photo) on the upright and nailed over it the crosspiece. I am there, on the cross, for life. I have told you because I felt you would understand and by your prayers would help me to remain constant." Many months have passed since then. Mr. G—— remained constant, though it meant the loss of his business and desertion by his wife. As a common carpenter he is living a blameless Christian life.

Most of the older missions have stressed the importance of children's work. The Japan Evangelistic Band for instance had at least three full-time children's evangelists before the war. Most believe strongly in Christian kindergartens as these are welcomed by the community, and reach the parents as well. One elderly missionary told us her present church was almost wholly the fruit of kindergarten work in the past. Unfortu-nately many church kindergartens are run by the pastor as a help in his support, and he therefore does not have proper time for pastoral work. If they can be run by trained Christian teachers belonging to the church they will fulfil a real need and be an effective means of evangelism, since most Japanese children when small are very spoilt; and most parents would go to a meeting to please a small child, though objecting strongly if an older one is interested in Christianity.

The government has never favoured Christian primary schools; but there are still a good number of high schools of

Christian origin started by various foreign missions though now under Japanese control. About 75,000 students attend these, the majority girls, since Christianity pioneered in women's education, and there are about 50,000 in Christian-founded colleges. It is unfortunate that most of these have been weakened in their impact on students by liberal theology. In one Christian university, for instance, where I taught for a short time, only two out of my class of twenty-eight girls made any claim of being Christian. Some said they enjoyed the atmosphere but did not understand what Christianity was (after being there two years). Most said they came because the standard of English was high there. Many evangelicals, therefore, think these are a greater hindrance to real Christianity than a heathen school. One thing they do seem to do, however, is to teach students to think for themselves; and sometimes it is easier for those who have been brought up with some familiarity of Christian terms and ethics to accept Christ later. In our work in both Itayanagi and Sapporo a number of the converts have been to mission schools. At the Seminary also there were two men who were converted while at a liberal university, and they are among the best thinkers there.

At a junior and senior high school for girls in Yokohama, begun ninety years ago by the Woman's Union Missionary Society which I visited recently, one can see the tremendous influence of a sound Christian school. There are about 900 students, and they have classroom devotions daily, as well as chapel assembly with a spoken message, and every class has both a Japanese and English Bible period a week. Summer retreats are arranged by the school for the girls, where many have been converted; and there is also a monthly parents' meeting where some have found the Lord. Out of the 129 girls in the senior-year classes taught by one missionary forty-five clearly professed belief in Christ, and only eleven stated flatly they did not believe. It is obvious therefore, how much good can result from such schools; but I do not know if it is even possible to establish any new ones. Certainly no evangelicals seem to be considering such a step.

After the war the need for sound Bible Schools seemed the

most urgent, and more than thirty have been opened, mostly with a small enrolment of from twelve to twenty students. This unfortunate duplication is due to a number of causes. Many new groups wanted to be sure of the doctrinal soundness of those who would carry on their work; some were duty-bound to reproduce all the characteristics of the home church which sent them out; sometimes the cause was incompatibility of Japanese leaders. In Japan there is a sharp cleavage between evangelicals of the Arminian and Calvinistic schools of thought which I had never met before. Of the prewar institutions the one begun by the Japan Evangelistic Band at Kobe, and that begun by the Oriental Missionary Society in Tokyo, have the largest enrolment with about sixty and 105 students respectively. I believe they both help finance the training of their students with gifts from abroad; but these are no rice-Christians getting a free education. Recently the girl students at Kobe bought the land themselves for a new dormitory, one girl giving her life savings of about $600. The O.M.S. School in Tokyo does not allow its students to go out doing part-time work for their support. In most of the newer schools, in accordance with both American and Japanese practice in universities, and the accepted indigenous policy, students are expected to pay their way, and this must be done by part-time work (or *arubaito* as the Japanese name it—after the German), since most students come from non-Christian homes and few parents are willing or even able to help financially. Having ourselves worked in a Japanese-run institution where foreign funds were scarce and *arubaito* was the rule, involving tiring journeys across crowded Tokyo, we saw that these and a heavy church responsibility at the weekends, often involving more travel, did not leave the student the necessary energy to do his academic work properly. At present, therefore, we have to choose between either undermining their spirit of independence or undermining their health in many cases. The solution will be when churches to which students belong can undertake their financial support.

The policy of the C.I.M. is to co-operate with others "of like faith" if this is possible, rather than start independent work of our own, so my husband and others have had the privilege of a teaching ministry in several Bible Schools. He has given several intensive two-week courses at the Lutheran Brethren school in one of the needy northern prefectures where this evangelical post-war group has begun a very well-planned work on indigenous lines. Mr. Leonard Street, C.I.M. Superintendent in Japan, has since helped there too.

Miss Mori, the girl who with her brother are the only remaining fruit from the tent campaign in the village where Arthur and Joy Reynolds afterwards worked, has now begun training in the Kyoritsu Bible School in Yokohama, the first training school for Christian women in Japan, founded in 1900 by the Woman's Union Missionary Society. They have students from Okinawa and Korea as well as Japan, and the present students' testimonies speak of a real experience of Christ. The thing which struck me most about them is the great concern of all for their parents' salvation, and some have already had the joy of leading theirs to a knowledge of Christ. Another girl mentioned that when she first went into training she felt a Bible School student could not be expected to tithe, when she might not even have enough to pay her expenses, but she had no peace until she finally began to tithe; and then the Lord really "poured out blessing" upon her. They have many opportunities of practical training in that large city, including prison work and contact with would-be suicides. Some of the Seminary teachers have been giving help down there.

Most of the Bible Schools are located in the big cities of Japan, where it is both easier for the students to support themselves, and also get experience in practical work, but one recently started by Pastors Ando and Hatori, with some help from the Central Japan Pioneer Mission, is in a rural area of Fukushima. It is situated on farm land belonging to Pastor Ando, a man with a wide Christian ministry before the war, and the students work the land to provide their food supply. The emphasis is on rural evangelism, although Pastor Hatori is responsible for the major evangelical radio programme messages heard throughout Japan, and does much literature work as well. In addition to the regular three-year course they have recently started a three-month Layman's Course, held in the long vacations at New Year and summer. Fifteen attended the whole course this last summer though there were thirty present part-time. Other evangelical missions and Japanese have helped with the teaching, and this is meeting a real need in the Central Japan area. One of the Christians from Kanagi, the boy who worked such long hours in the bookstore, is now in his second year at this school, and is doing well.

Another much smaller rural Bible School is that in Karuizawa where Mr. and Mrs. Threebridges are in training. This school also grows much of its own produce; does some printing and publishing, and holds a number of Christian conferences. Several of our missionaries have helped here.

With the strong liberal influences in the pre-war Union Seminaries a need was felt for an evangelical interdenominational institution of high scholastic level, for training university graduates in the historic doctrines of Christianity, particularly the infallibility of the Scriptures. The only one in the south which I know of maintaining this stand is the Kobe Reformed Theological Seminary where Dr. McIlwaine is principal. This at present has nineteen men in training. In Tokyo the Revs. J. M. L. Young and P. Foxwell have gradually built up the Japan Christian Theological Seminary which, though under the auspices of the Independent Board of Presbyterian Foreign Missions, is interdenominational in character. It began with a strong, well-qualified missionary staff, and now is beginning to include some of its own graduates. The Rev. R. S. Hasegawa at first worked with them, but, in 1951, continued on independently in his own home under the name of the Tokyo Theological Seminary. It is rather typical of the country that in the Japanese controlled school the curriculum is almost an exact replica of that at an American Seminary, while at the other, judging by its syllabus, an attempt is made in the classroom to train the students to meet the difficulties of their cultural background. This of course may be done more easily by the Japanese in ordinary social contact in the school. It has been found best to make it compulsory for students in training for Christian work in Japan to be in residence for at least part of their course. Being brought up in non-Christian homes, there are so many things they need to learn about Christian living which cannot always be demonstrated in a classroom lecture.

My husband and Arthur Reynolds became visiting lecturers at the Tokyo Theological Seminary just in time to teach the first group of graduating students. Later, we as a family were accommodated on the third floor of that unusual Japanese home, and for almost two years happily shared in the life there. Nine graduates are now pastors of churches, as well as giving help in seminary or Bible college; and one has already written two small books. Another was an assistant pastor, and secretary-treasurer at the Seminary, but is now on the faculty of the Japan Christian College. Two are in full-time literary production work. Three now form the staff of the Japan Inter-Varsity Christian Fellowship, and have considerably promoted that work. Although there are not yet many official groups on campuses they had representatives of thirty-five universities at a recent summer conference. They are also translating some of the British I.V.F. literature. We thank God for the way He is using these graduates, and look for increasing fruitfulness in the years to come. Others have taken their places in the classrooms, and at present there are about a dozen students, one of whom is Shenada San, a young man whom Miss Glass led to Christ in her living-room four years ago at Mori. He is not a university graduate, so has had to take a correspondence course at one of the Tokyo universities and spend all the hot summers down there in order to make up for this lack. He is bravely going through the full five-year course.

One of the most interesting things my husband did there was to prepare radio programmes with the students for transmission by the Far East Broadcasting Company from Manila and now from Okinawa.

While only three women have graduated so far, several others attended shorter courses and these, with two of the graduates, are now married to pastors and sharing fully in their work. We rejoice over these Christian homes being established. We often take the character of a Christian home for granted; but it is such a new and attractive idea to the average Japanese that the students at the seminary actually requested a course on this subject as part of their studies. Kanzo Uchimura tells us that there is no suitable Japanese equivalent for the word "home"; and accordingly they have adopted the English word, *ho-mu* being the nearest they can get to the sound. Recently the Board of the Tokyo Theological Seminary decided to amalgamate with the newly formed Japan Bible Seminary under the chairmanship of Mr. A. Hatori.

One of the newest ventures in Christian training is the Japan Christian College. This is a type of institution which is becoming increasingly popular in America where humanistic teaching is perhaps more dogmatic even than in British universities. Shortage of qualified Japanese staff has made it impossible to offer as wide a range of subjects as was at first envisaged for a liberal arts course, but two courses are offered, a four-year college course with a Bible and Theology major, and a three-year Bible School diploma course. There are at present twenty Japanese and eight foreigners teaching there. There are 150 students, one of whom is the young man from Samani who turned down a much coveted entrance to a Japanese secular college in order to have some Christian training.

The college is an inter-mission project, though the men whose vision and persistence made it a reality sooner than seemed possible were Donald Hoke and John Reid, both of The Evangelical Alliance Mission. The financial needs of the College are not underwritten by any agency, but the needs are made known to friends at home and in Japan as they arise. Joining in the faith and prayer put forth for needed supplies has been an important spiritual exercise for the students too. Recently more land had to be bought for a new dormitory building which cost $15,000. A down payment was made in October, and the remainder was due on 21st December, but when the school closed on the 20th $1,666 was still lacking. A cable next morning told of $900 in gifts, but they were still $700 short. However, the owner of the land came along during the morning to say the paper work for the transaction was not complete and there would have to be a delay in the payment for five days. The following day a gift was received which more than covered the remaining need.

One of the most interesting results of this was that it made one of the students realize she could ask the Lord's help for her own financial needs. Before she had thought these were just her own responsibility. When she heard how wonderfully God had met the needs of the college that day she suddenly realized she could pray about her own outstanding expenses at the college. So she did, and that very evening received a letter containing more than half the amount of money she was needing. So many things which are obvious to us are quite unknown to the Japanese Christian until quite late in their Christian life, as in the case of the one-armed girl I mentioned who had not realized that faith could grow.

One of the students at the Tokyo Seminary was once turned out of her home with practically nothing because she refused a non-Christian marriage. A small room was emptied for her at the Seminary, and she immediately became very sick —the sickness incidentally which her mother's rabid sect claims will attack a child who disobeys its parents! The following day I received a sum of money from one of the C.I.M. family in London, to be used for anyone in need at the Seminary, the first and only time such a thing has happened. I passed it to one of the Japanese teachers who said it could go into the scholarship fund, and later the sick girl could work for it. It seemed to me, however, that here was a time to break the letter of the law of indigenous policy. This was not a foreigner giving an embarrassing gift to a Japanese, but a loving heavenly Father who six weeks before had been able to speak to one of His obedient children so that another of His children should be provided for at the exact time of her need, both physical and emotional, with the assurance that "when my father and my mother forsake me, then the Lord will take me up". This seemed to be a new idea even to the teacher, and I do not know if it was passed on to the girl or not. But I feel one of the most needed contributions of the missionary is to communicate something of the *size* of God to the Japanese, the depth and the fullness of His love and grace and power. Their gods have been so small, their teaching has been of "the humanness of gods and the divineness of men", for after all their gods are for the most part only their human relatives and military heroes. Self effort too, has been so emphatically taught that it is hard for some of them to realize the need, or even the possibility of a real dependence on God. It was only after Kanzo Uchimura had been a Christian for six years and in the United States for a few months that, while reading a book by Phillip Brooks, he made what seems to us to be a very ordinary discovery. In his diary is the entry that he had made the "great discovery that I am God's *son*, not His brother or His equal. Why strive to compete with Him. . . . Presumptuous little god of the world. Know thyself and things will be well with thee."

Entrance at the Japan Christian College is limited to those who are truly Christian and whose lives are dedicated to some form of Christian service. About eighty per cent of those in training are already committed to their future sphere, and it is surprising to learn that more than a dozen feel called to foreign mission work. Our first reaction is apt to be that with so much need at home what is the point of going abroad? God's field is the world, however, and the man who was instrumental in founding in 1956 the Japanese Evangelical Overseas Mission with which some of these hope to work, was for twenty years a business man in China (out of the "web society"). In writing of this new undertaking in the *Japan Harvest* he says, "How are the expenses met? The Lord is our supplier. We draw from the Heavenly Bank as Hudson Taylor and others did. We stand on the simple belief that whatsoever we shall ask in His name He will give, as long as we put His righteousness first."

When this man began business over again in Japan, he was concerned about tithing, and questioned several pastors, but was told it was only a system of the Old Testament time and not applicable today. Under the present tax system it was impossible for Japanese. "I said to myself that if the truths of the Bible were not practicable in the business world, but only applied to the life which was apart from daily reality, I'd rather not be a Christian. I made up my mind to begin tithing and based my hopes on the promise of Malachi 3: 10, 'Bring ye all the tithes into the storehouse . . . and prove Me now herewith, saith the Lord of hosts, if I will not open you the windows of heaven, and pour you out a blessing, that there shall not be room enough to receive it.' Just at that time an unknown American sent me a small notebook for tithers called *An Account between God and Me*. It helped me a great deal to start tithing." He found that his tithe increased consistently month after month, and he no longer had any doubts about Malachi 3: 10. He has now published a Japanese tither's notebook, and challenges his fellow Japanese "to receive the immeasurable amount of heavenly blessings by becoming a tither. Then you also will be revived. And we shall even be able to send missionaries to foreign fields from our own small Japanese churches."

That the work at home will not be weakened by this we can be assured from two recent examples given in *Japan Harvest*. A young seminary graduate, after working four months with a missionary evangelist, said, "If God can send Americans to Japan to learn my language and preach the Gospel to my people, the same Lord can take me up and send me to another country where I can learn the language and preach to them. By God's grace I endeavour to go to Indonesia . . . but I don't want Americans to support me. We Japanese must do that." So he went back and started a church near his home, with two members. There are now twenty-two members who support him and his wife and child. and are praying about sending him as their missionary. Another young church in Kyushu which sent one of its Bible School graduate members as a missionary to Okinawa found that their church offerings had tripled as a result, and their missionary vision had enlarged as well.

Sometimes, as we have seen the Japanese extreme love of learning and erudition, we have wondered if God may not use some fisherman like Peter, or farmer like Amos, or shop-assistant like Moody to confound the wise, and bring a great turning to God in Japan. But we remember too, that God has also used great minds with orthodox training like Paul, Luther, Calvin, Wesley to turn thousands to Himself. So as far as we

can judge, these young men and women of the Bible schools
and seminaries are the hope of the future. They have burned
their bridges behind them, and given their allegiance to a new
Master. They have counted the cost, and for many, especially
the university graduates, this is very high. Their families have
usually sacrificed a great deal to send them there and even the
few parents who are Christians do not want their sons to be
pastors, for these are very underpaid compared with other
professional workers and can offer little security to their
parents in their old age. How they must face this cost is told by
one of our students at the seminary who will graduate next
spring.

"The harvest truly is great but the labourers few. Therefore
I prayed 'Send me forth into the harvest'. Last autumn this
prayer was answered. A desire—no, something stronger than a
desire—was created in my heart to become an evangelist for
the witness of the Lord.

"Then it was I began thinking of the sorrow I would cause
my parents who, after helping me through college, were
looking forward to my getting a good job. I thought of all the
unpleasantness I would have to go through, and so I began to
regret the step I had taken. The Lord was displeased with my
unbelief. Days of worry and confusion followed. I would
think of the pain my parents would feel, the Lord would rebuke
such unbelief: Satan would whisper that my thinking of being
called to be an evangelist was not of the Lord, but from my
human desires and ambition. However, as time went by the
voice of the Holy Spirit was not only not diminished but
became stronger. I knew no rest until, realizing that I could
not escape from the hands of God, and that my thinking had
really been self-centred, I surrendered everything to God."

Those who have put their hand to the plough of full-time
service do not usually give up their faith as do so many lay
Christians. They may, however, become very discouraged, or
bitter or critical of their fellow workers, and in the past have
often followed Western theological fashions blindly. Our hope
is that in these training schools of today these young men and
women may go out with the truths of the Bible firmly implanted

as the standard of truth, and with a deep experimental knowledge of the greatness and power and love of God in their hearts, so that they may effectively evangelize and shepherd their own people—steadfast, unmovable, always abounding in the work of the Lord.

As I travelled along the Hidaka coast and saw the stretches of smooth water broken here and there by lonely black rocks I was reminded of a few of the Christians I had met standing alone against every attempt of their communities to wear away their resistance to the symmetry of their age-long customs. On the small beaches the dark grey sand revealed the process by which other rocks had been relentlessly ground out of the way by constant pressure. So it has been with many professing Christians. Even some of those I have mentioned in earlier chapters, such as Narumi San, Mr. Greatheart and the man with the saw business, have gone under for a time; but Mr. Greatheart is now back at church, I understand. Perhaps an over optimistic impression has been given by the mention of Christians in every chapter, but remember these fifty or sixty mentioned are only a part of a population of 90 million. Last year however there were 1,312 students in evangelical Bible Schools and colleges preparing to serve the Lord. Let us pray that they may go forth fully prepared to fight the Lord's battles, clad in His armour, their loins girt with truth, so that they may be able to stand against all the wiles of the devil; and not only able to stand, but with their lips quick to proclaim clearly the Gospel of release for the captives, so that Satan may experience a defeat from which he can never recover in this land which he has held in his power so long.

GLOSSARY

Shogun, a kind of generalissimo, the military and political ruler for some centuries before the Meiji Restoration of the Emperor as head of the state.

Daimyo, feudal lord.

Samurai, warrior retainers of the feudal lord.

Eta, a pariah caste allowed only to slaughter and work in leather in pre-Meiji times.

Kyodan, short for *Nihon Kirisuto Kyodan*, Church of Christ in Japan; a government enforced amalgamation of all churches during the war which has continued since under the same name, often called the United Church; though many have since withdrawn from membership, it contains just over half the Protestant membership in Japan.

Yamato damashii, spirit or soul of Japan.

Bushido, Way of the Warrior, or Retainer's Code of Honour.

Hara-kiri, ceremonial suicide by disembowelment.

Seppuku, more elegant term for *hara-kiri*.

Soodan, discussion.

Mondai, problem.

Ronin, masterless samurai.

Kami, god, or anything awsome.

Uji, settlement, community.

Ujigami, god of the community.

Ujiko, people (children) of the community.

Kamidana, god shelf.

Butsudan, Buddha shelf.

Tokonoma, special alcove in all Japanese living or guest rooms in which a flower arrangement and ornamental scroll are placed.

Tatami, straw mats with which all Japanese rooms are covered. They measure six feet by three feet, and are made of hard pressed straw two inches thick, and covered with a thin woven rush mat, the two long sides bordered with strips of black or brown linen.

Sake, a native rice wine.

Obento (the "O"=honourable), a cold lunch carried to work, school, or a picnic.

Futon, the thick cotton-wadded quilts on which the Japanese sleep on the *tatami*.

Arubaito, part-time work engaged in by students to pay their school expenses.

Muga, expertness, or the elimination of the observer-self in Zen training.

Koan, problems with no rational answer, used in Zen training.

On, incurred obligations.

Gimu, and *giri*, types of Japanese obligations.

Chu, duty to the Emperor or feudal lord.

Ko, duty to one's parents and ancestors.

Nimmu, duty to one's work.

Haji, shame.

Muzukashii, difficult.

O-harai, the great purification.

Geisha, a highly trained courtesan, or female entertainer at a restaurant.

BIBLIOGRAPHY

Japanese history and culture

The Chrysanthemum and the Sword, by Ruth Benedict, Houghton, Mifflin Co., Boston.

Five Gentlemen of Japan, by Frank Gibney, Farrar, Straus, and Cudahy Inc., New York.

A Case History of Japan, by F. J. Horner, Sheed.

Land and Life of Japan, by K. Shepherd.

The Japanese Nation, by John F. Embree, Farrar and Rinehart Inc., New York.

Japan: an Attempt at Interpretation, by Lafcadio Hearn, Mac-Millan Co., New York.

The Religions of Japan, by W. C. Griffis, Charles Scribners, New York.

The National Faith of Japan, by Daniel C. Holton, E. P. Dutton & Co., New York.

Studies in Japanese Buddhism, by A. K. Reischauer, MacMillan Co., New York.

Sacred Scriptures of the Japanese, by Post Wheeler, George Allen & Unwin, Ltd.

Windows for the Crown Prince, by Elizabeth G. Vining, J. B. Lippicott Co.

Japanese Sense of Humour, by Hollington K. Tong.

Christianity in Japan

Spirit of Japan, by G. H. Moule, 1913.

Historical Stories of Christianity in Japan, by Junichi Natori, Hokuseido Press, 1957.

Life of Gracia Tama Hosokawa, by Junichi Natori, Hokuseido Press, 1957.

Japan Speaks for Herself, published by Student Christian Movement, 1928.

From Buddha to Christ, by Taisei Michihata, Church Publishing Soc.

Cross and Crisis in Japan, by Charles W. Iglehart, Friendship Press, New York, 1957.

Missions at Work, published by Mission Workshop, Committee of Tokyo Council of Church Women, 1956.

In the Grey Rain, by Hazel Severson McCartney, Harper Bros., New York.

Darkness of the Sun, by R. T. Baker, Abingdon-Cokesbury Press, New York.

Night Came to Japan, by Eric Gosden, Marshall Morgan & Scott.

The Reward of Faith, by Godfrey Buxton, Lutterworth Press.

Letters from Japan, by Amy Carmichael.

Forty Years in Japan, by Gurney Binford.

Charles Cowman, Missionary: Warrior, by Lettie B. Cowman, Oriental Missionary Soc.

Japan Harvest, quarterly periodical of The Evangelical Missionary Association of Japan, Overseas Subscription offices: P.O. Box 757, Elyria, Ohio, U.S.A.; England, c/o 19 John Street, London, W.C.1.

Japan Christian Quarterly, Christian Literature Society of Japan, Tokyo.

Japan Christian Year Book, Christian Lit. Soc., Kyo Bun Kuan, 2 Ginza 4-chome, Tokyo.

Diary and English magazine articles by Kanzo Uchimura.

Books about Japan by Japanese writers

The Japanese Are Like That, by Ichiro Kawasaki, Charles E. Tuttle Co., Rutland, Vermont.

Bushido, by I. Nitobe.

Homecoming, by Jiro Osaragi, Alfred A. Knopf Inc., New York.

My Narrow Isle, by Sumie Mishima, John Day Co.

The Broader Way, by Sumie Mishima, John Day Co.

Daughter of the Samurai, by Etsu Sugimoto, Doubleday and Co., New York.

Daughter of the Pacific, by Yoko Matsuoka.

Japan in a Nutshell, by Atsuharu Sakai.

Kokoro, by Natsume Soseki.

Japanese newspapers, *Nippon Times, Mainichi, Asahi Evening News*.

Meijiro Tatler, English newspaper of the Japan Women's University.

Map of Japan